Giant Country

Giant Country

Essays

on

Texas

Don Graham

TCU Press / *Fort Worth*

For Mimi and Fred Berry

Library of Congress Cataloging-in-Publication Data

Graham, Don, 1940-
  Giant country: essays on Texas / Don Graham.
    p. cm.
  ISBN 0-87565-182-8 (alk. paper).—ISBN 0-87565-183-6 (pbk.:
alk. paper)
    1. American literature—Texas—History and criticism. 2. Graham,
Don. 1940- —Homes and haunts—Texas. 3. Texas in motion pictures.
4. Texas—In literature. 5. Texas—Civililization.
I. Title.
PS266.T4G67 1998
810.9'32764—dc21
                                                    97-27684
                                                    CIP

Design by Barbara Whitehead
Cover photo by Kevin Cruff

. . . and kids,
When their imagination bids,
Hitch-hike a thousand miles to find
The Hesperides that's on their mind,
Some Texas where real cowboys seem
Lost in a movie-cowboy's dream.

W .H. Auden, "New Year's Letter" (*January 1, 1940*)

....

"In Russia they got it mapped out, so that everyone
pulls for everyone else. That's the theory, anyway.
But what I know about is Texas, and down here
you're on your own."

Joel and Ethan Coen, *Blood Simple*

Contents

Pictures

With Thanks . . . .

I owe so many debts stretching back nearly twenty years in the making of the essays that comprise this book that it would be impossible to thank or even recall everybody who offered a suggestion, a hint, a lead, a bit of encouragement. But before that, to my parents, Willie and Joyce Graham, now both deceased, I owe an incalculable debt: they each supported with love and without condition my lifelong interest in literature and writing.

I also want to thank a handful of people from whom I sought advice during the putting together of this collection. These are longtime friends Jim Lee, Tom Pilkington, Mark Busby, and Clay Reynolds. A special thanks to Mark for some cogent last-minute suggestions. Thanks also to a new friend, historian John Leffler, who ran down a quotation that I couldn't locate and who likewise offered some good insights.

Many thanks also to Judy Alter, director of TCU Press, who has enthusiastically supported this project from the beginning. My connections with TCU go all the way back to my freshman year in college when I was lucky enough to take Honors English from Professor Mabel Major. To the University of Texas I am grateful for a faculty research assignment which provided time for me to finish this project.

The reader will note that my wife, Betsy Berry, appears as a co-conspirator in a number of the essays, and I greatly value her unerring editorial sense. But most of all, I'd like to thank her for being Betsy Berry.

Greed, Creed, and Me: The Author Interviews Himself by Way of an Introduction

Don caught up with himself poolside at the Allen Park Inn, Houston, Texas. He looked tanned and fit.

Q: Thanks for the piña colada, Don. Now that you've finished *Giant Country* and are resting, catching some rays, mind if I ask the author a few questions?

A: Not at all. Fire away.

Q: What made you choose Houston over other places as your vacation spot?

A: I'm temporarily light. I couldn't afford where I really wanted to go—which is northern Italy, Venice.

I've always found Houston to be the best that Texas has to offer in the way of cities. I know a lot of people wouldn't agree, but once you get inside the freeways, it's great. It has what I look for in a city: good restaurants, good shopping, good bars. A cosmopolitan edge. And, of course, it's not Austin. People in Houston wear shoes, unlike in Austin, the Birkenstock capital of the free world, and another thing, here in Houston there aren't that many VW vans with Save the Whales bumper stickers. So it's a relief from the Austin scene.

Q: And Houston's museums, of course.

A: [*orders another drink*] That's what they say. I'm not really into museums.

Q: Why this particular motel, Don? I mean, it's nice, but it's not the Four Seasons.

A: A couple of reasons. One, my wife and I always meet interesting people here. Not stars, but the relatives of stars. Remember John Riggins, the great Redskins running back? We met his cousin here one night, round 2 a.m., out here by the pool. Great guy. Another time, not Sissy Spacek, but her sister. It's that kind of place. Second, they serve red-eye gravy with the biscuits for breakfast, and outside of Mississippi, there's hardly any place left that serves red-eye gravy.

Q: Turning to your book, how did that come about, Don?

A: Well, the further we got into the nineties, the more I realized that a certain preoccupation with Texas on my part—and perhaps on the part of others—might be cresting. Or ending.

Q: What do you mean?

A: I found that in the eighties I'd written a good deal about Texas, and it seemed about time to sort out what I thought was the best of that work and then . . . move on . . . new pastures, new venues.

See, the eighties, which Bill and Hillary like to brand as the decade of greed, was for academics a pretty darn good decade. For me the eighties were boom years. Universities had money for raises, and they had money for conferences and talks. In the Sesquicentennial year alone, 1986, I gave twenty-three talks—from Beaumont to Amarillo. This is how great it was: I remember once at a museum in San Antonio I talked for five minutes, introduced a classic Texas film, collected a check on site for five hundred bucks, went back out to the car where Betsy was waiting with the motor idling, and we were out of there. "Saks," she said. "Saks is open."

Q: And what happened to the glory years?

A: Beats me. All I know is it all came tumbling down. The decade of creed took over.

Q: The decade of creed?

A: Ideology, political correctness, neo-puritanism, you name it. Now, in the nineties, everything in Texas is sort of becalmed—

literarily speaking. At least it seems that way to me. Everybody's writing crime novels or film scripts. I should know; I've just written a film script myself. Maybe I'm wrong, I hope I am, but I don't see much going on in the way of serious writing.

Q: Does this book represent for you, then, the end of an era of Texas culture?

A: Hard to say, but certainly some things are over. I doubt seriously if we're going to see another urban cowboy phase. Which is probably a good thing.

Let's just say that I thought, in looking back over the past fifteen years, there was a certain historicity to it. *Giant Country*, for me, was a summing up.

Q: You pointed out that these essays go back a few years. Did you print them exactly as they were published, or what?

A: No, I found that I couldn't leave them alone. I changed some titles—many titles, actually—and I did other things: in some cases writing new introductions to reposition the essays for the nineties.

Q: I notice that nearly all of these essays were published regionally, in Texas, several of them in *Texas Monthly* and *The Texas Observer*. Care to comment?

A: Sure, it seems natural. Most of the pieces deal with Texas, obviously. And, besides, it's frustrating sending stuff out to big-name magazines. I mean they actually manage to lose your stuff.

Q: What do you mean?

A: I'll tell you. Last year I sent an essay on Texans and guns to *The New Republic;* the tie-in was deer season. Months passed, many months, and so I thought I'd better make an inquiry about the status of the manuscript. I received an embarrassed reply and phone call: they'd lost the manuscript. During the same six-month period the *New Yorker* had done exactly the same thing; they'd lost a short story I'd sent them.

Q: Why did you write these essays in the first place?

A: The subject interested me, or some editor asked me to write on the subject.

Q: Was money ever a motive?

A: That, and audiences. In the early eighties, I decided that I wanted to write for a larger audience than the usual academic crew. It was a simple ambition: I wanted to be read on airplanes.

Q: What do you mean?

A: Well, you know, you're on an airplane, they haven't brought the drink yet, you haven't ordered the drink yet, the drink may never come, and you look around for something to read. There it is: an in-flight magazine.

Q: Did you ever write for an in-flight magazine?

A: Yeah.

Q: Yeah?

A: One time this editor calls me out of the blue and says we want you to write a fifteen-hundred-word piece on any subject you like. And I said, terrific. Can I write on why I hate the movie *Paris, Texas?*

Q: How did it turn out?

A: Great. The pay was good and in the next issue, in the letters to the editor, a woman wrote in. She took offense at everything I had said. I love it when people write in.

Q: Can you give me an example of one of the pieces that you wrote simply because you wanted to, or because the subject demanded it?

A: Yes. The one about my father's funeral. I felt I had to write that. It brought together the personal and the literary, which, for me, is one of the things that makes literature important. Well over half the essays are like that: attempts, in the root form of *essayer*, to find out something, tease it out, see what I think.

Q: Any regrets about any of the writing you've done over this period?

A: Well, I'd have probably been better off if I'd never reviewed a book by a living writer. Meaning especially friends and acquaintances. It's a no-win situation. You can't like a book enough, and if you don't say it's the best thing since Tolstoy they take it kinda personal. Also, I learned that you shouldn't make lists of "best" books because authors who aren't on it never forget, and they treat you badly at parties.

Q: You're kidding.

A. No, I'm not. A couple of years ago I did a piece for *Texas Monthly*, which they asked me to do, in which I listed the twenty best Texas books since 1980. Well, an Austin writer came up to me at a literary gathering right after the piece appeared and said, and I am quoting exactly what she said: "How does it feel to know—to absolutely know—that you have only nineteen friends in the whole state, since one of your twenty is already dead?"

Q: What did you say?

A: What could I say? I probably mumbled something incoherent.

Q: Does the fact you don't use footnotes in these essays make some kind of statement?

A: Not really. Originally, about half the essays in the collection had extensive documentation and anybody interested in that can go back to the originals. But I like a clean text myself. It's more reader-friendly.

Q: Care to comment on the organization of *Giant Country*?

A. I think it's pretty straightforward. It's a series of Ps. The first section is "Places" and those pieces, mostly narrative and somewhat autobiographical, are set in various places including, let's see, Oklahoma City, Philadelphia, Texas in 1940, England, Marfa, and Collin County. The second section, "Pages," explores certain major figures in Texas literature, namely George Sessions Perry, Katherine Anne Porter, William Humphrey, J. Frank Dobie, Walter P. Webb, Roy Bedichek, Billy Lee Brammer, and Larry McMurtry. "Polemics" brings together several shorter pieces that take a sometimes irreverent view of subjects ranging from the Texas literary scene to Larry McMurtry, the film *Paris, Texas*, and the *Bridges of Madison County* guy, I can't think of his name, oh yeah, Robert James Waller. There's also a parodic homage to my current favorite "Texas" writer, Cormac McCarthy. Finally, the last batch, "Pictures," offers a sampling of writing I've done about Texas in the movies, including a personal survey of the best Texas-based films on video.

Q: How do you see your book as we approach the millennium?

A. As a rule, I don't take questions on the millennium, but I think it's fair to say that with this book I'm trying to build a bridge to the twenty-first century.

Q: What kind of bridge?

A. A bridge of understanding. A way to connect our recent past, this century, with the next. And so on like that.

Q: So how would you define this book's objectives?

A. I think it provides a picture of a transitional period in Texas history, from a rural way of life to an urban one. Which is where we are now, obviously. Since 1940, Texas has flip-flopped its population from country to city. We're now eighty-two percent urban. Many of the essays touch upon a vanishing Texas. There is also in this book an evaluation of what our mythology tells us about our past and what our actual experience tells us. I'm interested in the gap between mythology and experience. It's where I live, in Irony Gap. And there are other objectives, other themes, but those are for readers to find for themselves.

Q: Do you see any tendencies in your writing now, compared to when you started out?

A: Yes, I think there's an increased emphasis on narrative. My biography of Audie Murphy followed a narrative line, and several of the travel pieces quite naturally do as well. The "Harry and Jamie" story in this collection is just one of a number of fictionalized travel pieces I've done recently.

Q: So is travel important to you?

A: Yes, travel is very important. And I've learned a lot from travel—particularly from repeated trips to Australia and Australian writers like Michael Wilding. It's a definite influence on my work.

Q: Is it fair to say that you no longer find Texas and its culture endlessly fascinating?

A: Not endlessly fascinating, no. I never did. But I think the demographics predicted for the state in about 2020 promise a very interesting future. A truly multicultural population. It will be interesting to see what survives of the past and of the mythology. In any event I'm a Texan, and this state is part of me. I know certain things about Texas in my blood and bones. But Texas ain't the whole world, not by a long shot.

Q: So you're moving on?

A: Absolutely. I'm movin' on.

Q: Word has it that your latest project, a novel, is top secret. Could you at least give us an idea of what it's about?

A: Ummm . . . Texas.

Q: On a personal note, are the rumors true that your wife, Betsy Berry, urges you to make obscene amounts of money so that she may pursue exotic beauty regimens in European capitals?

A: Yes.

Q: Tell me, Don, why you consented to this interview instead of writing a more conventional introduction to your book.

A. First, I thought a standard sort of introductory essay would be boring, and second, I thought this short-hand kind of q. & a. might be something different.

Q: Do you think some readers will find it coyly post-modern?

A. Oh, now don't take that tone with me. Actually, I think until now you've asked some probing questions. I think we've touched all the bases, laid down the groundwork, set up some parameters; in short, I think you can stick a fork in this interview, it's done.

Q. Hey, thanks, big guy. Listen, we appreciate the time you've taken from your busy vacation, and, as always, it's been fun. Say, could I have another one of those coladas?

Places

Filadelphia Story

In 1971 I moved from a ranch outside Buda, Texas (population 498) to Philadelphia (population 1,949,996) to take a teaching job at the University of Pennsylvania. It was a big step for me, and like every step in my pursuit of what I had trouble thinking of as a "career," it was happenstance from the word go.

At the time I had almost no conception of the University of Pennsylvania, nor of its actual location. I knew it was somewhere on or near the East Coast. Many of my friends in Texas never did get it straight. They always confused Penn with Penn State. They believed that I taught at Penn State for five years, and occasionally, years later, one would ask me what I thought of Joe Paterno—the absolute extent of their interest in the whole idea of Pennsylvania. I told them that, overall, he seemed like a nice guy, despite the swarthy ethnic look and the incredibly ugly uniforms his team wore (which they still do). I tried once to tell my friends about a game at Penn, but they couldn't conceive of what I was talking about—the lazy afternoon, the smell of pot wafting through the stands, and down on the field, the Quakers playing like a bunch of hippies throwing Frisbees at a Sunday picnic.

I got the Penn job by the usual route, through interviewing at the Modern Language Association. Academicians remember their interviews the way combat veterans recall firefights. Two heavyweights from Cal-Davis, both of whose names I recognized from having read their publications, gave me a very hard time of it, and I felt like a piece of meat from *Rocky* when I staggered into the Hilton hallway afterwards. But the Penn interview was nice, even pleasant. Of the four interviewers on the Penn team, two were southerners, and that helped relieve my nervousness a bit.

What helped most was the tone set by the chairman, R. M. Lumiansky, a famous medievalist and a no-nonsense sort of fellow. He began by asking me to "tell us about that dentist in San Francisco." (He meant the title character of *McTeague*, a novel by Frank Norris.) It was very refreshing to hear a question about my dissertation on Norris posed in English because I was trying to write the dissertation in English instead of some special lit crit twilight-zone academese.

After gnawing on *McTeague* for a while, we moved on to a book I'd recently reviewed, a study of Ezra Pound by a scholar with a Chinese name. The other southerner made a crack about the name's sounding like what they'd had for supper last night. I really liked the joke—it was exactly the kind of humor that would get me in trouble more than once in the years ahead. The interview sped along, and I emerged with no serious hemorrhaging.

Back in Buda, early in January, the call came. Lumiansky was direct as always: "We've got a job—do you want it?" I said I had to check a couple of possibilities, and he said okay. Actually I didn't have anything else going except some state university in upstate

New York where the chairman said he could see cows from his office window. Outside my window in Buda I could see a horse trying to bite the orange Plymouth sitting in the driveway. In time the horse managed to ripple the hood with his teeth.

I waited a decent interval and called Lumiansky back and said yes. Months passed and then it was U-Haul time. In San Marcos where I rented the U-Haul, the man named Daryl—he had it stitched on his shirt in order not to forget—looked up Philadelphia in the U-Haul Book to see if there was a drop-off station there. Of course there had to be, but Daryl said,

"Nope, this truck don't go there."

"You've got to be kidding," I said.

"Lookee here, you don't see it, do you," he said with no small amount of pride in his competence.

"Why don't we try the Ps, Daryl?" He was looking it up in the Fs.

Arriving in Filadelphia in late August was a bit overwhelming. At ninety degrees, the heat surpasses Texas's 100-plus temperatures in sweat, odors, and discomfort. But unlike Texas, Philadelphia heat didn't hang on through October, and by early September, with the semester cranking up, I was thrilled by the crisp days and ready to begin what I assumed would be a gradual development of a new, urban, eastern self. It didn't turn out that way.

The week before classes started, my grandfather died, so I flew back to Texas for his funeral. He was a wonderful man, 6'4", a farmer, generous and kind and interested in all sorts of things. He loved to talk politics with me and never understood why I hadn't run for governor. But now he was gone, and in the small country cemetery in Allen, a tiny community north of Dallas, he was laid to rest. Being there with my kin, then flying back to Philadelphia, made me feel my rural southern roots intensely.

But then, nearly everything that happened in Philadelphia threw me back upon my southern origins. On my first day of class, I wore a pin-striped suit. After all, this was the Ivy League, wasn't it?—even if *Esquire* erred that year and left Penn off its list of Ivy League schools. (The campus newspaper worried about this slight the whole year.

People were paying a ton of money and by god, Penn was a full-fledged member of the Ivy League!) But the suit didn't hide anything. One sentence out of my mouth and I was revealed for what I was, a Texan, a southerner. That first day set the tone for the next five years. Being from Texas made a difference. I began to understand Lyndon Johnson in a way I never had before. And Norman Mailer. I was why we were in Vietnam.

There were times when I liked the separateness and times when I didn't. In classes, with most students, the accent was an advantage—foreign but appealing. Also useful. I knew how Faulkner sounded, and they didn't.

And on the streets of Philadelphia the accent offered a certain advantage. Upon hearing it, people usually viewed me as simple-minded and would slowly explain, as to an idiot, where the bus stop was.

Sometimes the accent could lead to real misunderstandings, though. One night at a party in a gay district downtown, another Texan and I were sent to fetch some ice, and when Michael said to a couple of guys on the street, "Do you know where I can get some aaise?" it sounded like something else altogether. My habit of saying "ma'am" to women didn't work too well, either, so I stopped.

The thing is, Philadelphia was ethnic country, and Texas wasn't. Or hadn't been in all my years there. Now Texas is more like the rest of the nation; identity politics and ethnic consciousness have become much more pronounced in the last twenty-five years. In Philadelphia, I discovered that you had to declare yourself; people insisted upon it. Everybody was something: Italian, African-American, Jewish, Polish, Catholic, something. And what was I? An American, I thought. But what I really was, up there, was a Texan. I belonged to an ethnic minority whether I liked it or not.

I was also a cowboy. Because that's the other side of the Texas legacy. First, you're a southerner, and if you can prove you have renounced your membership in the KKK and are capable of reading something more challenging than the labels of Wolf Brand Chili, then you are a cowboy. At Penn I could not escape the western tag, the frontier baggage that every Texan carries round with him. Afternoons when the light filtered dimly through the high windows of the English building at 34th & Walnut, I'd sometimes find myself walking down an empty hallway when suddenly there would appear at the other end a man dressed in black leather pants who would, invariably, go into a gunfighter's crouch and mimic drawing his mythic pistol in an imaginary recreation of a thousand showdowns in a thousand western movies. I felt like an idiot (idjit we say in Texas), but I usually complied, giving my best impression of a slow-motion draw, the balletic figure of Gary Cooper flickering across my mind's eye. The man in the leather pants was a very hot ticket at the time, a young, hip, fast-track African-American who hated stereo-typing based on race and ethnicity. He wrote about it all the time. His idea of The Texan seemed a bit stereotypical to me, but I suppose it was simply a pop cult icon and therefore fair game.

Being a cowboy had certain advantages, I'll admit. It meant that long-distance drinking, barroom hijinks, a fondness for the lyrics of George Jones, and a general rowdiness were permissible, even expected.

The oddest thing about the cowboy label, personally, was its complete irrelevance to the Texas I'd grown up in. My background was rural, all right, but my parents were farmers, not ranchers, and the Texas I knew as a child, in Collin County, twenty miles northeast of Dallas, was closer to William Faulkner than to Zane Grey. It was southern in manners, mores, and economics. Having lived on a ranch near Buda didn't mean I was a cowboy, either. I didn't own a pair of boots, a pickup, or a deer rifle, and I didn't ride horses. Never have liked horses and wouldn't ride one today on a bet. The more I said about my lack of qualifications to be a true gun-toting, murderous soul-of-the-American-killer-type Texan, the more I was disbelieved. Nobody paid any attention. Nor do they today. I can wear all of the Italian clothes I want to, and everybody mythically sees me in boots and jeans. A few years ago I finally gave in and bought a pair of cow-boy boots, I got so tired of everybody expecting me to have some, but then I left them in a closet in an apartment in Montpellier in southern France where they had mildewed for six months and weren't fit to wear, which I hadn't been doing anyway. Now I own a pair of boots my late uncle left me. He always thought I needed a good pair of boots. As for the other accoutrements of the manly style in Texas wear, I possess neither a Stetson nor a big belt buckle with my name on it, and since there's nobody in my family left to will me the same, and since I don't intend to run for public office, the prospects for these tokens of Textosterone look slim.

At Penn the cowboy brand received a kind of official imprimatur in 1973 when the department, then under the chairmanship of Joel Conarroe, instituted two new courses in film: one in the detective film, the other in westerns. As the resident cowboy, I was the obvious choice for the westerns. Though I went into the course with some misgivings, never having thought of myself as a "film person," it turned out to be a bridge to many things that have made my career, such as it is, produce a small cactus rose or two. Forty students signed up for the first run of "Western Movies," and the next year, the enrollment went to one hundred. In an impressive, large old room in the administration building we saw many of the classics, including *Stagecoach, She Wore a Yellow Ribbon, High Noon,* and *The Wild Bunch.*

Publicly, I taught the movie course and did my committee work and began to publish articles on Frank Norris, Theodore Dreiser, and other mainline American lit writers. But by 1974-1975 the appeal of the western movies class was pulling me inexorably into a new field, popular culture, and an old area of reading, western and southwestern fiction. Owen Wister, Larry McMurtry, all that. I wrote an essay on *The Great Northfield Minnesota Raid,* one of the films we studied in class, and I began to see that more and more, the western movie connection was a rich and personally rewarding vein to explore. It was my tradition, I discovered.

Privately, the lure was even stronger. One of the films that came to Philadelphia in 1971-1972 was *The Last Picture Show.* Larry McMurtry's vision of terminal bleakness in a small Texas town won critical plaudits and popular acclaim, but it just made me homesick for the high, wide, and empty spaces of Texas. The drab grays of that film seemed much preferable to the actual grays of Philadelphia. Imbedded in *The Last Picture Show* is, of course, a scene from *Red River*. Seeing *Red River*, a film out of my childhood, then teaching it as a "text" in class, I began to recover my entire past, a Texas past that I thought would be erased with the passage of time in the East.

There was also a wild trip to Waco that reawakened all my Texas longings. A friend invited me to give a paper at the annual meeting of the Texas State Historical Association, held in Waco that year, and I worked feverishly on an essay eventually titled "Is Dallas Burning? Notes on Recent Texas Fiction." Landing in Waco at a small airport that gave upon a cow pasture, with the huge blue dome of the sky arching above, I felt keenly the sense of space I'd been missing. Then began the drinking. We started in the afternoon, in a bar downtown. At some point a large rat walked through the front door. We were sitting in a booth and saw the whole thing. This rat walked in, like he intended to get a drink or something, and it just happened that at the same time a large man wearing a beer distributor's suit with Lone Star emblazoned on it, walked in, saw the rat, and promptly dropped a case of beer on Mr. Rat. The bartender, without missing a beat, said, "We don't serve rats in here." This story never played in Philadelphia. Nobody ever believed it, when I tried to tell them.

In the mid-1970s, two other cowboy associations coalesced in Philadelphia, both from out of my past, both curiously memorable to someone undergoing the kind of imaginary journey that the combination of Philadelphia and western movies had set me off on. Roy Rogers came to town for the grand opening of the Roy Rogers Chuck Wagon—or some such thing—a fast-food venue on Walnut Street, around 38th or 39th, as I recall. Anyway, what Roy was selling was phony barbeque, something you could slip past easterners as barbeque—a dab of thin meat, a fall-apart bun, and a thin, tasteless sauce. Local TV covered the festivities, and there Roy was on the tiny silver screen, the first time I'd seen him in twenty years. He looked exactly the same, lean and kind of oriental. There beside him, in delicious parody, was the Cowboy, a local West Philadelphia character who frequented the streets around the university. (Those streets were full of wacked-out people. One of them, Duck Woman, quacked nonstop. She quacked on the street and she quacked on the bus—a pathetic but maddening figure.) The Cowboy wore cheap, ill-fitting duds and always walked ten paces in front of a woman following dutifully in his wake. Seeing Roy and his serendipitous sidekick was a highlight of my Philadelphia years.

The second real-life movie memory was even stranger. Tex Ritter died on his way to Philadelphia in 1974. His name was on the marquee at a local theater, but Tex never made it to town for that performance. Although Tex was never in the same box-office class with Gene or Roy, he made a lot of B movies that I saw and liked as a kid, and he always had the most authentic Texas voice of them all, a voice my students and I had heard recently at its mournful best, singing "Do not forsake me, oh my darlin'," in *High Noon*. When Tex talked in the movies, you knew you were hearing the real thing. He sounded like all the people I'd grown up with.

When I left Penn in 1976, all the old associations with the South and with Texas were coming to the fore. On the southern front, Jimmy Carter was making his run for the presidency. Up there, he looked pretty good to me, and I spent much of my last semester at Penn trying to explain to skeptical Yankee friends that Carter was not a variant spelling of Cretin and might even make a good president. I'm thankful I wasn't in Philadelphia later on, when the Carter presidency began to unravel. The point is, while I was in Philadelphia, I felt I had to be loyal to Carter. He talked funny and came from the sticks, two reasons why my friends distrusted him. But hadn't they ever seen the *Waltons*, the television drama that made Carter viable in the first place? Back in Texas, I could take a critical view of Carter without worrying about feeling disloyal to Dixie.

On the Texas front, things began to move about the time I arrived in Austin to teach at the University of Texas. The department wanted me to develop a western movie course and to teach J. Frank Dobie's famous course, "Life and Literature of the Southwest." No turn of events could have surprised me more, because I had taken my Ph.D. at Texas and had never thought of returning. But being at

Penn had detoxified my too local credentials, and *voila*, here I was, back in Texas. And Texas, as I say, was on the move, culturally speaking. In 1975 *Atlantic Monthly* devoted an entire issue to Texas, and *Texas Monthly*, founded in 1974, was beginning to attract attention nation-wide. The Austin progressive country music scene, especially Willie Nelson, was exploding, and *The Best Little Whorehouse in Texas*, *Dallas*, and *Urban Cowboy* were just around the corner.

Back in Texas on my home range as it were, I experienced some new ironies. Among many of my colleagues in the English department, I was a cowboy. Of course, the overwhelming number of those colleagues were from other places and couldn't be expected to know anything. Statewide, the westernization of Texas was obvious everywhere. Collin County, where I'd started out, was becoming thoroughly westernized. A century of southern agrarian life, cotton farming, gave way to the Ewing ranch, fabled Southfork, where the Ewing clan hung their various hats and rested their lusty libidos. The big white-columned house became a major shrine located just three country miles from where, in a slightly smaller house, I was born. Same county, different myth.

Into the early eighties, in the afterglow of Texas chic, as people were unloading their urban cowboy duds in garage sales, I was just warming up. The burst of Texiness in the late seventies would take at least a decade to sort out, and I thought that I was in a nice, ironical situation to do some of the sorting. As it turned out, I spent much of the eighties writing and lecturing about Texas film and literature. Made some money, too, but I spent it all. Another Texas tradition.

The
Ground Sense
Necessary

It seems highly probable that the most satisfactory funeral service for the average family is one in which the cost has necessitated some degree of sacrifice. This permits the survivors to atone for any real or fancied neglect of the deceased prior to his death.

National Funeral Service Journal, 1961

When I was an undergraduate at North Texas State University in the early 1960s I read Jessica Mitford's new book, *The American Way of Death*, with a good deal of excitement. What Mitford had to say about American burial practices struck a deeply responsive chord, and I remember the wave of denunciation that arose from the highest councils of the funeral industry. On the local front, in my hometown of Carrollton, the book drew a hearty condemnation from the leading mortician. He declared the author a communist, and that was that. In Dallas in those days, anything critical of the American way of life, or death, was considered suspicious if not treasonous.

Already at odds with many of the values trumpeted daily in the *Dallas Morning News* editorials of that pre-assassination era, I believed that Mitford was right on target. She had the goods on funeral homes. She was especially adept at exposing absurd euphemisms. Somewhere in this vast and amusing land she had found an undertaker who styled himself a grief therapist, a delicious phrase that has stuck with me to this day. Her muckraking attack left no coffin unopened, no unctuous undertaker unscathed.

Mitford's critique tallied beautifully with ideas I was gaining from reading and with my own, thankfully, limited experience with funerals. Great literature seemed preoccupied with two subjects, love and death. Poetry particularly spoke to the second. Emily Dickinson: "Because I could not stop for Death—He kindly stopped for me—"; Wallace Stevens: "Death is the mother of beauty"; Andrew Marvell: "The grave's a fine and private place/But none, I think, do there embrace." In great poetry death made for compelling, unforgettable lines, just as, in bad poetry, it made for the mawkish, the sentimental. As an English major trained to scorn the sentimental and as a youth disposed to the hardboiled, the laconic tone, the weary resignation, whether in a Hemingway novel or a western movie in which the hero takes a lonely walk down the godforsaken streets of Tombstone, I felt naturally at home with lean rhetoric and leaner rituals. The fulsome never pleased. That's how I came to love one of the most moving funeral poems in American literature: William Carlos Williams' "Tract." Williams strips the cant and phony rhetoric away from the event of death, of burial, forcing us to look at the dignity and beauty of the bare coffin, unadorned, solitary, as pure as an imagist poem, and as spare: "On this the coffin lies / of its own weight" and "I will teach you my townspeople/how to perform a funeral," Williams wrote, and I believed him.

Closer to home, in Texas literature, the most memorable treatment of death for me was in a bright new novel published by another North Texas State English major who had graduated a couple of years before my time. That was Larry McMurtry, and the novel was *Horseman, Pass By*. The scene was the burial of the old cattleman, Homer Bannon. McMurtry, I learned later, started with this scene when he conceived the novel. Told from the young grandson's point of view, the burial scene is a thorough-going critique of the Protestant way of death; Jessica Mitford couldn't have done it better herself. The service is dishonest, materialistic, and nauseating. The only emotional power generated in the service comes from such old hymns as "Shall We Gather at the River."

Many years and several funerals later, I find, upon glancing through Mitford's book, how accurate her view was and how little things have changed. The funeral industry marches on, secure in its faith in Christian capitalism. McMurtry's perspective, though, I feel a bit differently about. Oh, he is right; the service he describes is bloody awful; and it is a service familiar to anyone who has attended a Protestant funeral in Texas. But the point of view is that of a very young man. In my recent experiences with death and funerals, I have come to appreciate the need for rituals, for the ceremony, where once I simply felt impatience, even disgust, at the whole procedure. It is hard, though, hard to make a meaningful ceremony out of death in America in our time. Certainly the funeral industry isn't interested in authenticity; it's interested in efficiency, profit, and assembly-line repetition. Most Protestant funerals in Texas have all the individuality of a fast-food chain or a mall.

My father's funeral in July 1983 is the only funeral I have attended that seemed meaningful. I dreaded the prospect, just as I had dreaded the imminent death of my father. His health had failed long ago. In fact, crowning irony, his health was permanently impaired in a wreck in 1948, when he worked for the very same funeral home where, thirty-five years later, he lay at rest. He was a great automobile driver, and if he had been driving the ambulance that night long ago, I doubt the wreck would have happened. But he wasn't. They were doing eighty-miles-an-hour down a dark country road when they hit a mule. The mule's dead weight smashed into the passenger's side where Dad was riding shotgun, and then, as he liked to put it, it was "Katy bar the door."

The wreck also ended his career with the funeral home. It was a job he liked, and I think now, in retrospect, I know why. It gave him a sense of community service. It also must have satisfied a thirst for excitement, for the out-of-the-ordinary. Driving an ambulance on round-the-clock call broke day and night into unpredictable segments. Suddenly a call would come in, and he was off to a distant place, Amarillo or Ardmore, to retrieve a body, bringing it home to Collin County for burial. He dealt with the living, too. He liked to recall one trip he made to take a sick man to an Oral Roberts sermon—this was another long trip, before interstates, to Tulsa.

He was a man who had seen thousands of funerals and who had performed the various professional roles of attendant, consoler, and efficient dispatcher of the dead. Then, at seventy-two, after a ruptured spleen and nearly forty-eight hours of acute suffering, he joined the long procession.

The first decision the living had to make was to select the place where he was to be buried. Years ago my parents had purchased burial plots in a North Dallas cemetery, one with a restful and phony name. All the connotations were wrong. My father had nothing to do with North Dallas. Collin County was his true home, old Collin County, before Southfork, before Plano's real estate boom. He belonged in Collin County. That decision was easy: the plots in North Dallas would be sold and new ones purchased at the funeral home southwest of McKinney.

Now one ran square up against the funeral industry's method of marketing. First, one had to drive through the cemetery. The automobile signifies several things: status, comfort, security. You are driving, and the dead aren't. It would be unseemly to walk, though the cemetery is not large. It would be shabby; it would look bad to anybody driving by. The memorial park (their name for cemetery) has the feel of a suburb, with its grids of roads and geometrically imposed design upon the random prairie. It also has the feel of a golf course: the careful manicuring, the closely cropped grass, the decorous order of the graves. In the plush automobile, a Caddy, we were taken to the most expensive sites. These were patches of prairie conceptualized under allegorical motifs: Salvation Park, Gethsemane Way, and so on. Twelve-foot high statuary, Christ in robes, suffering little children to come unto him, that sort of thing, marked each motif. These sites were held in great esteem by the man conducting us on the tour. The statue seemed to confer certitude: here, one knew, the dead were safe in heaven's bosom.

Concrete has enormous significance in memorial parks. Concrete is a means of distancing us from the natural, and the purpose of memorial parks is to remove us entirely from the condition of nature. Grave sites close to the road are valued, that is, they cost more; and concrete walkways have a commensurate value. The message is consistent: the living must be comfortable in their dealings with the dead; the living must be kept aloof from the circumstances of nature—death, mud, unkempt graves. Like all memorial parks, this one promises perpetual care. There is a memorial park somewhere on I-35 between Austin and Waco that advertises: Perpetual Care Until the End of Time. After Judgment Day, one supposes, it is Under New Management.

As we drove through the cemetery, I asked about a site the driver hadn't mentioned. It wasn't near a concrete walkway and it wasn't blessed with any allegorical sculptures. But it was pretty, and there were two shade trees and a small sapling. The man seemed a little embarrassed. Yes, there were some unclaimed plots there, and yes, they cost less than those in the Garden of Gethesmane Way. My mother liked the spot, too, and that's what we chose. Some Collin County prairie and some good shade trees were as close as we could come, in that cemetery, to the real.

I won't go into the selection of the coffin. It's a no-win situation, and the undertakers reap heavy profits in this transaction. Not once but twice, because every funeral I've been to involved two purchases: a coffin and a vault. Again the purpose is to preserve the illusion that nature has no hold over us.

Until then, my experiences at funerals had been confined to observing the ceremony. This time I would have something to say about the structure and content of that ceremony. I wasn't hopeful about the prospects. The "chapel" was one I knew well, having attended in recent years three or four funerals there. The chapel, of course, is part of the funeral home, a prime example of the all-purpose industrial organization of the operation. The chapel's best feature, unintentional I'm sure, is a stark brick wall behind the pulpit. Neither flowers ("floral tributes") nor the displayed coffin (always open in Collin County services) conceals the blankness of that wall. The wall speaks more eloquently than it is meant to, of oblivion.

In the best of funerals, from the funeral "director's" point of view, the family goes along for the ride. The ride is smooth, fast, and unruffled by variation or departure from the script. The funeral home has a plan, and they reveal it to you by stages. One stage is the selection of music. They've got that covered. They have a piped-in system of taped music. It's unbelievably bad: worse than Wayne Newton, worse than Lawrence Welk. We wanted none of that prefab mellomuck elevator music. Reliable singers (human singers) could not be found on such short notice, but we were able to round up passable tapes of appropriate hymns, ones that Dad liked, "Amazing Grace," "The Old Rugged Cross." The funeral home thespians told us this was only the second time in memory that the "family" had requested its own music.

The most depressing prospect of all was the preacher. Was there a decent Protestant preacher in Texas? I hadn't the faintest idea. I only knew that in all my years as a desultory attender of church services (mostly weddings and funerals), I had never heard a preacher I cared to hear again. Mother had an inspired idea. She remembered a preacher from the early 1930s when, recently married, she and Dad had lived on the farm in Lucas and had made friends with a young seminary student assigned to preach the gospel. She called this man, now retired and living in Fort Worth, and, as old as my parents now, he came and gave the only good Protestant funeral sermon I've ever heard. He began by reading a short biography of my father that he had asked me to write—after all, it had been over fifty years since he had known Dad. Then he transformed that barren brick and lacquered wood chapel into a sacred place. He made a perfunctory act into a moving ceremony. He quoted from the Bible, from Alfred North Whitehead, and from James M. Barrie. Two of these texts, I dare say, were new to this chapel. The ceremony ended with "Amazing Grace"—our version.

We were lucky. Without the saving wisdom and dignity of the preacher, the ceremony would not have been complete. It was a traditional funeral, but the tradition was older than the impersonal, ersatz, plasticized K-Mart style of funeral home traditions. For us, the ceremony invoked a sense of my father's past, of his ties with the land, the music, and the simple verities of a Protestant funeral reduced to its essentials.

I know a very bright man, a long-time acquaintance, who insists that when he dies he wants to be thrown into a ditch. He hates ceremonies and wants no part of them. I can't agree. The ceremony is for the living and the dead, and even in our time it's possible to treat death, the final act in humanity's drama, with some measure of serious attention.

Texas in 1940:
The WPA
Guide

Nineteen-forty, another time. The speed limit in Texas was forty-five miles per hour; Lyndon Johnson was serving his first term in the U.S. House of Representatives; Audie Murphy, sixteen years old, was living hand to mouth with his disintegrating sharecropper family in Hunt County; Howard Hughes, a leading Hollywood film producer and holder of international airplane racing titles, was only a few years away from the cantilevered bra and his plunge into terminal weirdness; the future famous author Larry McMurtry was four years old; J. Frank Dobie had recently converted from ranch conservatism to New Deal liberalism; and the University of Texas had an enrollment of 10,969 students. Another place, Texas in 1940.

Sixty percent of the population lived in rural areas; cotton was king in the black waxy belt stretching from north of Dallas to east of Austin; babies were still sometimes born at home; and country doctors made house calls. It all sounds a bit like a Merle Haggard song about the way things used to be. One thing is certain: Texas in 1940 was a bigger place than it is now. It took a lot longer to get somewhere. The highway from Dallas to Houston was a narrow two-lane blacktop with bad shoulders or none. Travel by auto was still an exhilarating adventure, and going across the barren wastes of West Texas meant you needed a canvas bag of water slung over the radiator for the inevitable boil-over.

Culturally things were quieter then. No MTV, no Information Superhighway, no World Wide Websites—just radio programs and the movies. In 1940 everybody went to the movies, families to the general releases and kids to the Saturday matinees. Every town had its Dixie or Texas or Ritz theater and usually a smaller theater off the square where westerns and serials were shown. Country people spent all day Saturday in town and returned to homes lit by coal-oil lamps and serviced by outdoor toilets. Rural electrification was still a very big deal in 1940. Hit less hard than some states by the Depression, Texas was still hit hard enough, and in 1940 the Depression hung on. It would take the events set in motion on December 7, 1941, to put the economy in high gear and launch the nation on a course of industrial expansion unparalleled in modern history. Texas in 1940 was a bit like America before World War I: a hungry, provincial, isolated empire waiting to play a larger role on a larger stage.

Today, over fifty years later, in sunny Sunbelt Texas where centers are centres and banks are bancs, it requires an act of the imagination to conceive of what Texas was like just four and a half decades ago. *Texas: A Guide to the Lone Star State* invites us to return to those quiet days of yesteryear, to that remote era before the world was convulsed by the second great war of the century and the atomic age made apocalypse as familiar as be-bop. *Texas: A Guide*, issued in 1940, was one of forty-eight state guides produced under the auspices of the Federal Writers' Project, one of the programs created by the Works Project Administration. To understand the achievement of *Texas: A Guide*, it's necessary to recall the big picture. The Works Project Administration (WPA) was a unique and ambitious attempt on the part of the Roosevelt administration to put America to work. The most original part of the program was its provisions for what one proponent called "white collar relief." Artists, painters, sculptors, and writers were hired by the federal government to use their brains and talent to produce culturally valuable pieces of work. The Writers' Project, funded in 1935 at $27,000,000, lasted for seven-and-a-half years. It survived a number of internal and external threats and overcame many adversities. It produced some 1,000 publications, ranging from small pamphlets to the centerpiece of its original intentions, the creation of a complete series of guidebooks to these United States. Long ago Emerson had declared that America was a great poem, and it was the cardinal principle of the guide series to inventory the poem of twentieth-century American life.

The sheer scope of the project was staggering. Operating from a central office in Washington, the Writers' Project hired over 6,000 writers and thousands of support personnel. One wag in the central office wore a funny couplet about the size of the undertaking:

> There's no way out but suicide,
> For only God can end the Guide.

Nothing in the way of an American guidebook series had ever been attempted on this scale before. The only guidebook prior to the Writers' Project multi-volume series was a Baedeker's dating from 1893 and revised in 1909. Barely coming into the horseless carriage era, it was clearly outdated and inadequate. The American guides would change all that. Such an obvious and laudable aim met with criticism, however, from both the right and the left. The anti-New Dealers attacked the plan as another Roosevelt boondoggle and feared that a lot of discontented radicals would be put on the public payrolls. On the left, the more radical elements mistrusted the plan as well. One fire-eater called it "mass bribery" and said, "We're all taking hush money."

The writers hired to work on the series ranged from no-talent hacks to young authors of great promise. Among those who contributed to the New York guide, for example, were future luminaries such as John Cheever, Richard Wright, Willard Motley, and Ralph

Ellison. Many other significant writers of the thirties worked on projects in other states, including Jack Conroy (Illinois), Nelson Algren (Illinois), Saul Bellow (Illinois), Kenneth Rexroth (California), Conrad Aiken (Massachusetts), and Vardis Fisher (Idaho).

The publication of the guides beginning with *Idaho* in 1937 silenced most criticism. Intelligent readers and reviewers recognized the outstanding merits of the series. Texas congressman Maury Maverick wittily disposed of WPA critics: "There are those who believe that the WPA should be confined to hard, dirty work; that anything clean, cultured or beautiful is a Sin. The guidebook of the Capital, by that token, is a book of sin, because it is a clean, cultured, thoughtful work." The eminent British journalist Alistair Cooke wrote the director of the Project, Henry A. Alsberg, that he hoped to "buy, beg, steal, annex, or 'protect' a complete library of the guides before I die."

In 1938 the guidebook series suffered its most serious assault from the right, in the form of hostile hearings of the Congressional Committee on Un-American Activities, headed by representative Martin Dies of Jefferson County, Texas. Dies' simple-minded brand of Americanism obliged him to focus on what he saw as left-wing propaganda emanating from guides written by known Communists or Communist sympathizers. The spark that set off this firestorm of reaction was the fact that the Massachusetts guide contained nine lines on the Boston Tea Party and forty-one on the Sacco-Vanzetti case.

The Dies committee hearings had a dampening effect on the Writers' Project, but other, larger factors were at work, too. The New Deal began to lose force in 1939, and by 1940-1941 the momentum of national self-interest began to shift towards the upcoming war in Europe and the South Pacific. The Writers Project ended in 1942, a casualty of World War II. But an enormous amount of solid work had been accomplished, and critics such as Lewis Mumford were probably correct in calling the guide series "the finest contribution made to American patriotism" in his lifetime. Years later, in 1961, John Steinbeck, who knew a thing or two about the U.S. himself, wrote in *Travels with Charley* that "the complete set comprises the most comprehensive account of the United States ever got together and nothing since has approached it."

Texas: A Guide came out in 1940 after several delays and did not receive the kind of widespread attention earned by earlier or more politically controversial volumes. Still the *Dallas Morning News* praised the book as a work of "real merit . . . . one of the better of the state guidebook series issued to date," and a "monumental contribution to Texas cultural development." The person most responsible for the Texas guide was state director J. Frank Davis, a man whom history had largely overlooked. A novelist, Davis authored three forgotten novels, *Almanzar* (1918), a racially sympathetic study of a Negro servant; *The Chinese Label* (1920), an off-beat detective novel set in San Antonio; and *The Road to San Jacinto*, an historical novel published in the centennial year, 1936. In a curious historical irony, Davis suffered a fatal heart attack in 1942 on the day the Federal Writers' Project officially ended. But what happened later, in a reprint of *Texas: A Guide* in 1969, was nearly as bad; Davis' contribution was simply erased. Possibly because Davis parted his name on the side as did a more famous Texas writer, J. Frank Dobie, the 1969 Hastings House edition bore a preface that credited directorship of the Project to Dobie, and poor J. Frank Davis' name appeared neither on the title page or anywhere else. The Hastings House reprint should be approached with caution for other reasons as well. Its updated bibliography contains such howlers as these: Willi[e] Morris, *North to [Toward] Home;* William A. Owens, *[This] Stubborn Soil;* and J. Frank Dobie, *Guide to Life and Literature of Texas [Southwest].*

Davis had plenty of help in putting the *Guide* together. His own preface for the 1940 edition mentions a small army of 2,914 local consultants and volunteers, many of whom traveled thousands of miles of backroads measuring mileage and gathering facts for the tour section of the book, a standard and invaluable feature of all the guides. For the historical essays, Davis drew upon such recognized authorities as Carlos E. Casteñeda and J. Frank Dobie for literature and folklore.

The book that finally emerged from this massive collective effort was 718 pages long and filled with facts drawn from the present and past and, in some cases, interpretative points of considerable interest both then and now. Most of the guides were praised for their forthright, vigorous, and unpretentious style, and *Texas: A Guide* exemplifies these traits admirably. In all the tons of verbiage written about the Alamo, for example, the terse description of the meaning of this event in *Texas: A Guide* ranks well above most accounts: "The heroism of the men of the Alamo needs no garnishing. They were there of their own choice. They remained, when they could have fled. They died."

In a lean expository style *Texas: A Guide* conveys an astonishing array of concrete information. On one page of the essay on education, for example, we learn the following: the Masonic Order was important in fostering public education in early Texas; Andrew Female College (defunct) once offered a degree bearing the imposing title of Mistress of Polite Literature; and the first municipal high school was established in Brenham in 1875. Nor is such pithy and interesting information confined to the essay sections. Individual treatments of fifteen key cities in Texas are chockfull of similar data, and the thirty-three tours that make up nearly half of the book are studded with fascinating details. For the traveler who found himself near Boraches Spring, in the vicinity of Dog Creek and Dog Canyon in the remote Big Bend, there is this consoling information. The name Boraches is a corruption of "huaraches" (sandals), and, best of all, the Glasscock Filling Station, just a few miles from Boraches Springs, sells "gas, oil, liquor, lunch, and cold beer."

There is no Texan, then or now, who cannot learn a great deal about the state from nearly every page of the *Guide*. The section on literature, about which I presume some competency, cites several works completely new to me and which are not found in any other source. Perhaps the most astonishing thing about the wealth of information in the *Guide* is that new facts are likely to appear anywhere! Thus the section on Dallas ends with a list of writers currently living in Dallas and mentions the following tantalizing literary note: "Dallas was the locale of some of the Earthworm Tractor stories of William Hazlitt Upson, once a machinery salesman in the city." What are these stories? Who is Upson? The *Guide* is like that; it sends one to the library.

Texas: A Guide is also valuable as a repository of social history. There are pictorial vignettes drawn from close observation of phases of Texas life that have passed from the scene. In this respect *Texas: A Guide* shares with the more illustrious earlier volumes of the series a passion for recording the here-and-now of American life. A thumbnail sketch of a black district in Houston catches the externals of black community life with the documentary skill one finds in photography or good fiction: "Signs on business establishments include 'Mammy's Washiteria,' the 'Welcome Home Shine Parlor,' and the 'Harlem Grill.'" Wherever possible, the prose is enlivened with authentic American speech and research into primary documents such as newspapers and deeds. Rice farmers in southeast Texas are quoted to the effect that a local varmint, rice rats, "raise rice on the shares." And from the tour section, in a brief account of the history of Lufkin, we learn that for the first deed in Angelina County the land transaction involved payment of "one white shirt, eight brass bracelets, one handful of vermilion, one fathom of ribbon, one gun, and other items of value."

In a book so crammed with specific information and drawing upon so many contributions from diverse hands, there are bound to be errors. But they are surprisingly few. One that the *Dallas Morning News* review noted has to do with a remark on that touchiest of Texas topics, the weather. Under the heading of "norther," the *Guide* observes that the temperature has been known to drop 50 percent in thirty-six hours. The *News* amends that to thirty-six minutes, attributing the error "possibly to some incredulous Yankee proofreader" who changed minutes to hours.

Not surprisingly, *Texas: A Guide* steered clear of the kind of social criticism that marked some of the more controversial guides. The "feudal" condition of Mexican citizens in south Texas is mentioned in passing, and Negro life in Texas is presented in generally progressive terms. There is nothing like the pointed social criticism that appeared in the Washington, D.C. guide: "In this border city, southern in so many aspects, there is a denial of democracy, at times hypocritical and at times flagrant." Instead *Texas: A Guide* developed broad interpretational themes without regard to questions of social justice. Two points are particularly salient in this regard. One is the emphasis upon Texas as a "Southwestern empire," an argument voiced early and often in the volume. The second is the perception that Texas was truly a transitional state partaking of both southern and western qualities. The *Guide* was certain that this was the case and said so in these terms: "More Southern than Western is the State's approach to most political and social questions: more Western than Southern are the manners of most of its people."

Always in search of the enlivening detail, *Texas: A Guide* affords us amusement on more than one occasion. In a patent attempt to translate the western aspects of the state into colorful anecdote, Texas' lenient view of homicide provides ample fare. Thus a Texas jurist is quoted with regard to a murder case: "In Texas the first question to be decided by a jury in any homicide case is, 'Should the deceased have departed?'" And with the memory of Bonnie and Clyde still green in 1940, the *Guide* notes that "Texas bankers are authorized to carry arms and to 'shoot it out' with bandits if they care to." This is a Texas drawn in the lurid colors of the wild and woolly West.

Texas: A Guide, like all the others in the American Guide Series, suffered an ironic fate. Written for the masses, the series meant more to enlightened critics and European travelers than it did to common folk in the Depression and World War II era. The reason lay in the very fact of those lean years: many Americans could not afford to take automobile tours to see these United States or explore the ample dimensions of this southwestern empire. Then the war intervened and the guides were forgotten, or at least they never replaced the Sears catalogues as the second most important book in American households. In 1951 that tireless cataloguer of countries, John Gunther, felt obliged to conclude at the end of his *Inside U.S.A.* that America remained an "enormously provincial nation." Said Gunther: "I do not know any country that is so ignorant about itself." True or not, it was not the fault of the great American Guide Series. There, in forty-eight volumes, Texas among them, sprawled all of America.

Doing
England

....

"England is a garden."—R. W. Emerson

"Oh, I say, it's the Americans! The Americans are here!" The little, ruddy-faced guy named Jerry opened the door of the Thistledown, a B & B on a side street in Windermere, and swooshed us in.

"I've been expecting you. James, from down the street, said you were coming and here you are." He takes a breath.

"When he called, I just said to the Japs, I said, 'Go on, now; go on; there's no room for you here; I have Americans coming.'

"See them? They're just down the street there. The Japs, you know, are impossible. They poke under the mattresses, they look at everything, they haggle about the prices. Give me Americans any day."

In the tiny living room Elvis was playing on the record player, and there was a boy, Jerry's friend, lounging languidly on the sofa. Betsy gave me a look that said, "Does this guy remind you of L.A. or what?"

At breakfast the next morning—an English breakfast with scrambled eggs unredeemable by any measure of salt, some stewed tomatoes (beloved of all Englishmen and good for Vitamin C), and a pink, meat-like substance said to be bacon, curling with fat—Elvis was still playing—the late, gross years of "I Did It My Way"—and Jerry, who made a point of serving the men first, was still on the subject of the Japs, which led us, the girl from Liverpool who sounded just like John Lennon, and the English woman with her family, to talk about stereotypes. We asked them what they thought of when they thought of Americans, and the girl who sounded like John Lennon didn't really know, but the very stereotypical English woman with the family replied,

"Well, you know, we say that Americans come to a car park, get out of the bus, spend forty-five minutes at the castle, gather up all the brochures and pile them on their coffee tables when they get back to America.

"They 'do' England," she concluded.

Guilty as charged. We had been doing England for a couple of weeks now, and we'd trooped around the Tower of London, we'd been to the Roman baths at Bath, we'd seen our share of abbeys, ruins, and memorial gardens, and we were absolutely daft about England.

But Windermere was a little disappointing. Too much traffic, too many tourists. Wordsworth had seen it coming long ago, at midpoint of the previous century. He'd deplored the advent of the railroad to Windermere in 1847 and fought, successfully, to keep the trains from reaching his cherished Grasmere, eight miles away. Wordsworth, who by then had become very conservative (he lived nearly forever) worried that if workers were able to leave their humble cottages and go on sight-seeing trips they would disrupt the pastoral quietude of his native country and ruin their own morals to boot. He was right about the first, anyway, and he might have been right about the second.

At the pubs in Windermere we wondered how Wordsworth would have felt about the state of yeomanry a century and a half later. The Queens menu was pretty typical: "pizza marguerita" suggested a new if uncertain eclecticism. (Most pubs now serve lasagna, and most have something they call "chili con carne," which is served with rice.) The Queens had a small pool table. Pool tables, like plumbing, are something that the British haven't mastered. The tables have the thinnest of felt surfaces, the balls are tiny, the openings to the pockets minuscule. One game can last a whole afternoon. On the wall above the table, a series of framed photographs of dogs shooting pool looked down upon the players. On another wall, a calendar from a lorry firm showed a young woman displaying the full glory of her abundant chest. In all of England we saw such art only in the Lake District.

The lake at Windermere was disappointing too. It looked like a tourist-developed lake anywhere; it could have been in the Poconos. Lots of carny-type hustle, signs for boat tours, lots of ducks, and very little quiet. The English are crazy about the Lake District. "It's the most beautiful part of England," they kept telling us. A fascination with lakes must be the explanation because there are scores of places—Lyme Regis, the moors north of York, Whitby on the eastern coast—that easily offer just as much beauty.

Grasmere was better, smaller, less traffic-ridden, closer to the Wordsworth bone. The poet is buried here, in the graveyard of the parish church alongside assorted kin, including his sister Dorothy. A stream ripples close by, and on all sides rise inviting mountains, very tame mountains made for hiking and wine-and-cheese picnics. Closer at hand are shops that feature woven shawls and sweaters and the like, all the rich handicraft of a region whose chief pastoral economy for hundreds of years has been the raising of sheep. Dove Cottage, where the poet and his sister lived, is a short walk from the graveyard. During the visit to Grasmere, one have-to is the ginger-

bread, based on a recipe dating from the 1850s. Tangy, spicy, dense-
ly textured, it's a perfect expression of the British genius for sweets
and an item you won't find at any airport. Such pleasures make
Grasmere a place where, unlike Windermere, something of the sense
of a village still remains.

The thing to do at Grasmere is walk; the hills invite you as they
did the Wordsworths and Beatrix Potter, another author who lived in
the Lake District, at nearby Sawrey. For us, Grasmere was a place to
come back to because, true Americans, we didn't have time on this
trip; we had to get the Hertz back on the road; we were going east
now, across to Whitby, about which we knew nothing (a sea coast
town is all we knew and we wanted to see some ocean); and there
was work to be done back in Oxford on Monday where we were living and I was teaching a summer course, "American Writers in
England," part of a University of Texas summer program abroad. So
we hit the road. Betsy drove. She drove most of the time. English
roads made me nervous. Shifting with the left hand was okay, the
roundabouts were okay (roundabouts are a circular system for rout-
ing traffic that the British prefer over stop lights; whirlabouts would
be a better name), and even driving on the wrong side of the road
was okay, but what kept bothering me, on narrow two-lane roads,
was how one kept shaving the left side, barely missing hedgerows
and, scarier, bicyclists. Betsy, fearless, drove.

Nearing Whitby, we topped a rolling hillside covered in heather,
and there lay the ocean shimmering in the late-afternoon sun of the
warmest day we'd experienced yet (low eighties). But more striking
even than the sweep of the ocean was the abbey poised at the crown
of a high hill overlooking the town, the harbor, and the sea beyond.
Whitby was a sensation, a town we'd never heard of.

Alone among the seacoast towns, it offered a sense of the epic.
No wonder, then, to learn that it was from here that Captain Cook
set sail on his doomed journey to the South Seas. Nor that the first
English author, Caedmon, composed his "Hymn of Creation" here at
Streaneshalch monastery. Like the Algarve in southern Portugal
where Prince Henry and Vasco De Gama dreamed and brought into

being conceptions of a wider world, Whitby looked exactly like the sort of harbor where the imagination reached outward, not inward. The town itself, much changed for the worse now by increased tourism we were told, seemed splendid to us. We wandered off onto a side street and into a pub that had rarely seen any tourists, let alone Americans. It had a nautical look, and the barman moved between two rooms behind a bar that gave the illusion of a captain's deck. Ahab could have recruited the crew of the *Pequod* here. The accents of both the barman and the old salt who sat peering out from behind eyes as scaly as a serpent's were utterly strange, different from anything we'd heard in England. Ordering a "black and tan" was a major feat of communication.

Dropping down to York, we were back in packaged England. Not packaged too badly, mind you, but it felt wrapped up and ready to be presented to the legions of well-dressed tourists that thronged the streets on Sunday morning. Take Shambles Street, for example. Billed as one of the oldest extant medieval streets in England, Shambles Street in its heyday was a place where butchers displayed their bloody wares on benches called "shamels" from which the modern meaning of "shambles" derives. The street was so narrow that second-story buildings nearly touched at the top, forming a kind of rickety uneven archway the length of the street. The overhanging upper stories helped to keep the meat cool and shaded. And, like any self-respecting old English street, Shambles had its religious martyr, in this case Margaret Clithero, who was canonized in 1970. A butcher's wife, she was found guilty in 1585 of harboring Catholic priests. For this crime against the Queen's conception of the state, she was put to death by the gradual piling of heavy stones on her body. Each year on Whit Monday Catholics come to her dwelling place at Number 35 Shambles Street to pay homage. In modern Shambles Street the buildings still lean towards each other in one place, but otherwise it's hard to conjure a medieval atmosphere amidst the present-day arts and crafts shops.

By contrast, uncelebrated Brasenose Lane in Oxford positively reeks of medieval smells and dankness. Most mornings there's a puddle of vomit not yet licked up by dogs and the buildings loom up on either side and a giant tree sprawls its leafy shade over one end. Oxford was our first and last and most sustained look at England because that's where we lived and worked for five weeks. How to describe Oxford?

Hawthorne tried and couldn't do it. In *Our Old Home*, a book of English travel sketches, he remarks, "And now I take leave of Oxford without even an attempt to describe it,—there being no literary faculty, attainable or conceivable by me, which can avail to put it adequately, or even tolerably, upon paper."

Henry James couldn't do it. In his early story, "A Passionate Pilgrim" (1875), his American hero who dotes on everything English. moves to Oxford in order to die in the most English of all sites. James writes, "Of Oxford I feel small vocation to speak in detail . . . . The impression it produces, the emotions it stirs, in an American mind, are too large and various to be compressed by words." Then there is the testimony of Jan Morris, a superb contemporary travel writer who devotes a whole book to encompassing Oxford. For her, Oxford is the place where "you may see it all—century by century, or face by face. She is an England in miniature: an essence of England, drawn from the wood."

Hawthorne, James, and Morris are right, and one naturally turns to the expression "My Oxford," the personal view, as the only way to express one's sense of an ultimate and fatally charming town-and-gown city. Like most of England, it is bloody ground, too. Plaques remind us of martyrs like Archbishop Thomas Cranmer, a Protestant who was burned to death on Broad Street in 1556, two blocks from where we were living. And there are fictive sufferings like those of Evelyn Waugh's Anthony Blaine, who leaned out from a window on the Bridge of Sighs, a covered crosswalk between two Oxford buildings, and threw up into the window of a fellow student. Waugh's hero, given a second life by the Masterpiece Theater production of *Brideshead Revisited*, is a favorite of the tour guide and the video generation aboard the double-decker buses. On a stone wall in Christ Church Meadow a marker commemorates the flight of an English

balloonist in the late eighteenth century. Markers and memorials are
everywhere.

Such prolonged human habitation, so much history! And nature
is never far away. Flowers grow in profusion—in window boxes, in
formal and not-so-formal gardens, on the scantiest plot in an idle
corner of a pub's grounds. Within the university itself, at Magdalene
College, are nearly a hundred deer, descendants of the herd that T.
E. Lawrence and Robert Graves planned to steal and relocate inside
their own college's walls. The Thames, or the Isis as local tradition
names it, rambles through the town touching at one point, at the
Head of the River Pub, the outer grounds of Christ Church Meadow.
Magpies—huge black and white birds that one had imagined only
lived in books—thrive along the canals and on the riverbank.

Euroteens thrive in Oxford too. There were 3.4 million of them
in the United Kingdom that summer, mostly from Italy, teenagers
with money and credit cards spending the summer in England studying English at places like Oxford, a city of schools. They all dress
exactly alike—oversize sweaters and tops, pants two sizes too big, in
mostly earth-tones that go well with their tanned and sometimes
stunning good looks. They hang out in multiples of six and they have
a great deal of time on their hands. One sees them everywhere, in
packs at Blenheim talking against the grain of the docent's monologue, at Westminster Abbey in London "mugging" among the
tombs (mugging means making out, a bit of new teen lingo the summer offered us), but one sees them most at McDonald's on
Cornmarket Street in Oxford, a main artery of the city. There, from
morning to midnight they gather, pullulating to the beat of puberty.
No one knows where they spend the balance of the night once
Mickey Dee's closes.

Every day except Sunday the streets of Oxford were jammed
with a gaudy array of ordinary folk, punks with spikes and tattoos,
students, old people, a few sad drunks, and tourists snapping photos
of the turrets, spires, towers, and gargoyles that can be found almost
anywhere in the university and the surrounding streets of a city
nearly ten centuries old. In the narrow alley leading off Cornmarket

Street to Frewin Hall where we lived in a flat inside a fenced-in, pro-
tected island of quiet amidst the din of the city, the two Oxfords
were nicely juxtaposed. First one walked past the Dolly, a punk
venue in the cellar of a pub where after hours kids with spiked hair,
ear and nose rings, and deathly pale pancake makeup gathered to
dance to the latest in heavy metal rock. Just a few doors farther on
was the entrance gate to the Oxford Union Society, where since its
founding in 1823 Oxfordians have gathered to debate the burning
issues of the day. In 1824, for example, the topic was whether the
United States had derived any benefits at all from its separation from
the mother country. There were arguments to be made on both
sides, and our trip made me wonder about the question anew as one
saw the mother country up close and firsthand at the same time one
read about the claims and counter-claims of American vs. English
culture in Emerson, Hawthorne, Artemus Ward, Twain, and, above
all, Henry James. There was no single or simple answer, but the six
weeks' experience threw off hints, glimmerings, awakenings.

Everything about Oxford was stimulating, including the worka-
day world of the Covered Market. To get from Frewin Hall to
Brasenose, where our students resided, you had to walk past the
Covered Market, inside which were newspaper stands, vegetable and
fruit markets, sandwich shops, a pet store, and an amazing number of
"high class" butcher shops. The Covered Market offered ready
instances of the raw and the cooked. Down the narrow street
between Cornmarket and Turl Lane, which runs adjacent to the walls
of Brasenose and other colleges on one side of the university, six days
a week lorry drivers contort themselves squeezing in and out of tight
spots. Mostly, it seems, they are delivering meat. England is simply
obsessed with meat, and the Covered Market is a kind of temple of
meat. Huge plucked geese are arrayed in great heaps outside the
shops, then hung up for sale, and inside each shop a small army of
butchers hack and saw away at mounds of meat, pork, beef, fowl, and
fish of every description from sturgeon to John Dory. There's certainly nothing new about the British preoccupation with fleshy
foods. In the seventeenth century at lavish dinners for foreign visi-

tors, for example, the Brits sat at long banquet tables laden with everything that lived on land or sea: one dish might have two pheasants in it; another, twenty-four partridges; 144 larks in a third, some swans thrown in for good measure, a pair of pigs, and so through a cornucopia of plovers, knotts, sturgeons, snipe, teals, jugged hares—the whole gamut of the animal kingdom.

The British do a great many things to meat, few of them good. The kitchen at the site of Glastonbury Abbey, thought to be King Arthur's legendary home, suggests that the monks dumped great chunks of venison and whatever else was at hand, into huge pots and made a kind of hunter's stew. Things haven't improved much since then. What Brits like to do most is glue several different kinds of meat together—pork, chicken, duck, beef—anything really so long as the combination is numerous and various—with a gelatinous adhesive, then wrap the mess in dough, bake it, and drown it in a sauce. *Voila!*—meat pies and other coronary concoctions that the British dote on.

But the British on the whole are not fat and they are very much alive. The reason, one has to assume, is that they walk so much. If they didn't it's not hard to imagine the whole nation collapsing en masse in one vast cholesterol stoppage. Americans could learn from the British. Any K-Mart in America will yield a far higher percentage of grossly obese average citizens, their polyester waist bands near the snapping point, their blood-pressure zooming. The reason is that they never walk anywhere. They drive in their great smoking hulks to the K-Mart, padding across the pavement after parking as close as they can, and once done shopping, they return to the groaning Pontiacs and Buicks and glide away to a Whopper Burger, and then home to the couch. Americans of the same class as the leaner, fitter Brits don't walk and couldn't be paid to.

We, on the other hand, jogged, and the Brits looked at us as though we were Martians. Or Americans. We ran at Christ Church Meadow, a pasture with walking trails, past enclosures with grazing cattle and a canal along which amateur punters tried to steer their unwieldy crafts. (There's a service business in Oxford composed of enterprising university students who for a fee dive to retrieve lost jewelry, etc., in the canals and the Isis). Given the Brits' obvious distaste for runners, it's odd to realize that Roger Bannister, who still lives in Oxford, broke the four-minute mile barrier here in 1954. But he was running for sport and not, as Americans do, to stay in shape, and so the Brits applaud the one and are puzzled by the other. Walking, as I said, does the job for them.

Early on in our adventure with British cuisine (a French borrowing that can only be viewed as ironic in a British setting), we gave up on the heavier meats, and then we gave up on fish, too. Though England is an island surrounded by fish, in nearly fourteen hundred years they seem never to have learned anything about how to prepare fish. The pubs drown the finny tribe in batter and butter and sprinkle peas and parsley generously on top so that the first task is to locate the fish buried beneath the hillock of green. They do slightly better with prawns. According to pub practice the main course must always be covered with several layers of boiled vegetables and fresh parsley; it's the law. And chips: not a meal goes by without chips (French fries). In a small pub in Selby, beneath the shadow of eight giant smokestacks belching coal smoke into air currents that deposit acid rain in not-so-far-away Scandinavia, we saw a man order a chips sandwich. It consisted of a hamburger bun and a thick clot of fried potatoes—chips. And that's all. He ate it happily, a Brit and his pub food.

Some pub food, however, we grew to love. Bangers and beans, bangers and mash: bangers are sausages, mash is mashed potatoes. Bangers and beans were my favorite, based perhaps on my childhood familiarity with its distant and watered-down American version, Campbell's pork 'n beans. Food aside, the pubs are delightful for drinking. Beer and ale served usually at room temperature, with plenty of body and sediment, are what beer and ale should be, and explains why American beer, with its thin, horse-pissy taste, is palatable only near freezing point. In Oxford, we went most often to the Buttery, in the basement of one of the dormitories in Brasenose College. It's a minimalist pub reduced to the essentials: varieties of beer, ale, and liquor, and a dart board. Frequented almost entirely by students, it became a favorite hangout of American students from the University of Texas and Georgetown. Because the Buttery, like all British pubs, closed at eleven, a great deal more serious study was achieved than might otherwise have been the case. During those nights of mild hilarity the American students were following ancient and hallowed traditions. Read any memoir or history of Oxford life, and one will find that the tradition of carousing goes as far back in time as any Oxford custom. Closing time was the diciest hour. Students went reeling into the quad and home to their rooms or somebody's rooms. In a grand gesture one sorority girl that we became life-long friends with, pee'd in a large outdoor potted plant and got away with it; there were no reprisals; the plant flourished for weeks afterward.

English pubs are hard to resist. Somber Nathaniel Hawthorne seems to have let his New England hair down more than once during his years in England. In a catalogue of pleasures he experienced during a visit to Oxford, he enumerated "alcoved libraries," college halls, and kitchens with "cavernous cellars" replete with hogsheads of Archdeacon Ale, a local brew "with a richer flavor and a mightier spirit than you can find elsewhere in this weary world."

The Trout Inn is by far the most delightful pub in the area. One gets there by walking across Port Meadow, a large tract of grassland that has not been cultivated or "improved" upon for a thousand years. Or one can take the Nipper, a bright green local mini-bus that runs from the city out to Wolvercote near the inn. The bus has its own pleasures. The driver who took us out and brought us back each time had certain predictable peculiarities, so the citizens on the bus told us. He would be either cross, forgetful, or drunk. The first day he was forgetful; he said he didn't know where the Trout Inn was and asked some of his passengers to tell him. The second time he was cross, haranguing riders as they came aboard. The third time he was besotted, his speech slurred, his syntax garbled. But the little bus seemed to know the way and made the trip each time as though it ran on tracks.

Outside of Wolvercote, a small working-class residential suburb, where workers from the Covered Market, for example, live in tiny apartments, one walks across the Thames. Beyond Port Meadow, two or three miles away, the spires of Oxford gleam in the sunlight of early evening. Alongside the narrow roadbed are cottages bedecked in flowers and gardens of incredible richness. A slight mist begins to fall. Then, the Trout appears on the left. An ancient pub, it sits on the bank of the river. At the tables outside, hundreds of trout feed in the water below. A dozen peacocks patrol the grounds, insatiable for handouts but miserly in refusing to display their lacy splendor.

On this coolish summer evening with the temperature around sixty, there are few patrons. One is a flight steward from British Airways, and we learn from her where she's going to spend next summer—in Denton, Texas, with her sister. Denton! We warn her: it's going to be 108 in the shade. She has an idea about Denton; it'll be like Southfork: huge white plantation-style ranch houses and vast acres of grassy ranchland on which roam herds of cattle tended by colorful vaqueros. She is happy; Denton's in America. We haven't the heart to tell her the truth, and besides, she may actually like malls, concrete, suburban sprawl, and the air-conditioned lifestyle.

Across the river amidst dark green grass and trees, a large statue of a lion keeps watch. The statue, which looks ancient, is an import dating from about twenty-five years ago. Near the statue is a bomb shelter slightly older. Built during the blitz in the 1939-1945 war, it remains as a reminder of one of the two great wars Britain has endured in this century. Tradition has it that Hitler exempted Oxford from bombing during the war, but the Trout Inn was ready just in case. About a hundred yards beyond the line of trees sheltering the river stands Godstow nunnery, a ruin in which one is free to walk about. Henry II kept "Fair Rosamond" on ice here for a number of years, so it has its romantic as well as religious associations. Hawthorne stopped by the Godstow nunnery on his return from a visit to Blenheim Palace, about eight miles away. The Trout Inn stands as an emblem of England at its best: great beauty, great antiquity, great ale.

London, that "murky modern Babylon" as Henry James called it, is an hour bus-trip from Oxford. You disembark at Victoria Station and all of London is there before you. The city teems with life. James spent thirty years getting to know the city; others have spent lifetimes. We had only a few days. We made some usual tourist moves, oohed and aahed at Westminster Abbey; took the measure of Raphael's cartoons at the Victoria and Albert Museum (Twain was right; Raphael was a "bird"; he put three gigantic men in a tiny canoe and it stayed upright, but then Raphael was working in miracle country, illustrating stories from the Bible); walked in awe around the Albert Memorial, a monumentally bad piece of public statuary that stands in Kensington Park across from Albert Hall. For an American the kitsch factor is particularly touching in the tribute to the North American continent that marks one corner of the rectangular base: among a cluster of Native American types, the *pièce de résistance* is a giant shaggy buffalo ridden by a fetching bare-breasted American Indian maiden. The monument in its outsized scale combines phony classicism with Eastern and Oriental styles to create a crashing crescendo that literally is top-heavy. Experts wouldn't be surprised to see the whole three- or four-story thing collapse in upon itself at any time. Erected in the 1880s, the Albert Memorial has entertained Americans from Mark Twain to us.

There was Shakespeare at the Barbican, but there was also Soho, and Soho is where we went to prime ourselves for the plays. Soho was a kind of street play itself. Frith Street, no more than three blocks long, was our favorite. You came huffing up from a smelly tube exit on Charing Cross Street into a throng of humanity on the sidewalks and walked past the Sex Club where the punks queued up for tickets to see the heirs of Johnny Rotten, past a small park where old ladies sat huddled under newspapers to protect them from the intermittent showers, their talk going at a steady rate despite the rain, past a panhandler or two, one of whom made the only anti-American remark we heard our whole time in England—"fuckin' Yanks" is what he said when we didn't fork over the pound note he said he needed for tea—and onto Frith Street, which abounded with good restaurants and one Mexican restaurant that we didn't sample. Mexican food sounded like a dangerous proposition this far from the American Southwest, and the menu didn't allay any of our suspicions. It featured such dishes as "Mole Poblano de Guajolote," which translated into "roast turkey in a cocoa nut-based sauce." To our amazement, the menu announced that turkey was the "Mexican National Dish." José Luis Caballero provided the entertainment, singing "The Songs of Mexico." We concluded that the Soho Mexican experience would have to wait for another time.

What we ate instead was Indian food, and it never failed us either in London or Oxford. It was the solution to pub food, to English cuisine in general. We never got tired of it. From our window table in an immaculate brasserie on Frith, we could look across the street and see a surprising memorial, a plaque on the second floor above a Greek restaurant that announced that here, in 1926, the first television was demonstrated.

One evening at the brasserie, over rum and coke, we watched a street drama play out. A well-dressed derelict stashed his bottle in an alcove and after frequent snorts from his paper bag, he sallied forth to harass the passers-by. These were mostly women, but not always. The women in mini minis slapped him when he pinched them, and he laughed and hustled back to his bottle. Then he expanded his attack to include slow-moving automobiles and any likely looking prospect, male or female. After a while he moved on, having exhausted the possibilities of Frith Street, it seemed.

At the Gate of India, in Oxford, we ate two or three times a week. We always sat by the window, on the second floor, and watched the rain gusting against the panes or falling in a gentle mist. Because it was always raining when we were there. The rum and cokes were room temperature the way Brits like to serve drinks. In England ice cubes are rarer than rubies. Even in places where they have ice cubes, they like to conserve them, dispensing only one per rum and coke, and then only grudgingly. You sit there watching the tiny cube, already rounded from thawing, dissolving into the dark amber liquid.

We became favorites at the Gate of India because they were never very busy and because we liked the food as hot as they could make it. The waiters always warned us, but were always pleased when we plunged ahead and ate the spiciest dishes with obvious delight. One evening, before dark, there were only the two of us and one other man, an Indian who sat muttering out loud to himself. He was a regular, too, our waiter told us. Sotto voce, the waiter explained the problem. The lonely man soliloquizing over his prawn *vindaloo* suffered from too much education. A learned man, he had been ruined by his learning. Our waiter delivered the analysis with relish; he was never going to let himself be ruined by reading too many books, he said.

The six weeks ended far too quickly to absorb every lesson England tendered. One read English literature now with a local, regional sense, and one read American writers on England with a parallel sense of simultaneous discovery. And books, like flowers, meadows, and pubs, were everywhere: England was a paradise of book stores. In any size English town, no matter how small, you're apt to round a corner and come upon a quite good bookstore. Wales was the best, though. Hay-on-Wye, a charming little village on the Welsh border, has its own castle complete with peacocks, a monument listing the names of local soldiers killed in the Great War, narrow, winding streets, a reedy River Wye beyond which lie bright green and rich brown fields, a population of one thousand, and fourteen major book stores containing over a million second-hand books and prints. Indeed Hay-on-Wye bills itself as the Second-Hand Book Capital of the World. Unfortunately they take Visa. We sent back seven boxes of books to the states, mostly hardbacks at irresistible prices.

Here was where we bought the Bible, a Douay-Rheims copy dating from the Victorian era, of no value to a book collector but valuable to us, with embossed crosses on the heavy covers and metal clasps and lavish illustrations, a Bible any vicar would have been pleased to read from on some sleepy Sunday morning in the greening glory of a British day. Buying a Bible was the last thing I expected to do, and it set off false tremors back in Texas where my mom, when she heard about the purchase, hoped this unprecedented act might portend a latent spiritual influx at work. The stream of postcards that I had sent back extolling the beauties of English abbeys and especially of small village churches with graveyards under the yew trees and often, as in Oxford, people sitting serenely among the markers enjoying their lunches, such raptures were misleading. I simply liked the way English churches looked, liked how they felt. Even a spurious-gothic church built in the late nineteenth century had much more to offer than the brick Taco Bell-style of most Protestant churches in Texas. I liked too the plaques and tombs and memorials inside the churches and abbeys. Death in England seemed real and a vivid part of ongoing community life in a way that in abstract, antiseptic America with its "restland memorials" and "perpetual care memory gardens" it did not. The Bible we bought had more to do with memory than theology.

Reading, as I say, went on continuously; we read guide books and novels and history. In the course I was teaching, "Americans in England," we tracked the shifting responses of American literary figures who had made the English journey a century or more before us. There was Thomas Jefferson's cautionary letter, written in 1785, advising a young American not to study abroad. "If he goes to England," Jefferson wrote, "he learns drinking, horse racing, and boxing." (The continent was even worse, thought Jefferson, because there a young American might easily discover, among many vices, a "passion for whores.")

Then there was Washington Irving's *Sketch Book*, which taught several generations of Americans the proper emotions to feel when they stood in the presence of such shrines as Westminster Abbey and Shakespeare's grave. Later in the century, Mark Twain and Artemus Ward cast an ironic, sharp-edged Yankee eye on English history, exposing the cruelty of knighthood, the pathos of dungeons. Touring the Tower of London, Ward's American rube punctured the pretense of cultural myopia: "The Warder shows us some instrooments of tortur, such as thumbscrews, throat-collars, etc., statin that these was conkerd from the Spanish Armady, and addin what a crooil peple the Spaniards was in them days—which elissited from a bright-eyed little girl of about twelve summers the remark that she tho't it was rich to talk about the croolity of the Spaniards using thumb-screws, when we was in a Tower were so many poor peple's heads had been cut off. This made the Warder stammer and turn red."

It was Henry James, though, who traced the richest, most complex dialectics of like and dislike between the two cultures. "An International Episode" (1878) is typical. In this story a young, well-educated, and idealistic American girl proves herself superior in both learning and manners to Lord Lambeth, an amiable dunce ignorant of his nation's history and neglectful of any sense of responsibility to live up to the tradition of his inherited seat in Parliament. The American girl finds him very disappointing and refuses his offer of marriage.

Margaret Fuller, ardent feminist and contemporary of Emerson, believed there were three kinds of Americans who went abroad: the "servile" who traveled for the sole purpose of spending money, the "conceited" who bristled with national pride, and the "thinking American" who, she concluded, "can only become more American." Among our forty-eight students were all three types. Some came chiefly to spend money, it seemed, and they had plenty to spend. There were weekend jaunts by air to Paris, Amsterdam, Edinburgh, and Majorca. Harrod's in London was like the Galleria, only better. Indeed, all of England was a great open mall for the well-heeled. One student from Dallas, alas, had a limit of $10,000 on her Mastercard; Daddy had put his foot down. A few students returned to the U.S. untouched by England. One of these, a business major with a corporate job already lined up, said during the last week, "I want to go home to my middleclass family, watch my middleclass tv set, and sit in my middleclass jacuzzi." Whether spenders or chauvinists, most of the students, however much they liked England, came back "more

American," as Fuller put it. The fourth type, the kind Jefferson had warned about, were those who'd been hopelessly spoiled by England and were reluctant to leave. There were at least two of those, and their names were Don and Betsy.

But leave we had to, and back in Texas it was 104 in the shade, and we wilted thinking of England, of the coolest summer since 1936, of the wettest, too, because it had rained nearly every day, sometimes three or four times a day—delicious to us, upsetting to students who wanted a good tan. At the Chevron station on I-35, reality set in all too quickly. All that expanse of pavement, all those signs and billboards, all that ugliness. In most of England there are no billboards, nothing to disfigure the landscape. Wales is even purer in this regard. The sheer dowdiness of much of the New World struck us forcibly. Europe was supposed to be old, dirty, begrimed, and smelly, but nothing we saw there outdid the trashed-out H.E.B.'s and pawn shops and 7-11s and strip-shopping centers. To us now, Texas looked like a seedy, overdeveloped third world country with good roads.

Hurtling down I-35, we were back into the American mode, and we remembered the most American experience we'd had in England—in a rental on M5, a multilane carriageway (freeway). Headed toward the Lake District, we zipped past signs of castles, caught glimpses of hills, watched village roofs and steeples blur into the rearview mirror, unseen and unrealized. One could develop a theory of abstraction on M5 or I-35, about the loss of contact with place, land, village, community.

The tendencies toward systematizing experience away from place, history, and the local are always a threat in modern Britain. Shakespeare's Stratford is a grim example. Busloads of exhausted tourists arrive every five minutes; the banks of the Avon are cluttered with tourists. The most Americanized, i.e., automobilized of the tourist spots, Stratford is a lost cause. Shakespeare's house, which already had a phony feel to it in 1815 when Washington Irving stayed at the Red Horse Inn (recently demolished to make room for a Marks & Spencer department store), is even phonier now. This is one of those places where you don't believe any object is authentic. All the furniture—including the "chair Shakespeare sat in"—has a plasticized sheen. The tour of the "house" includes, true corruption, a viewing of the costumes that were worn in the BBC productions. These date from the mid-1980s and have about as much historical value as a box of Kleenex. On one of the placards the name of rare Ben Jonson is misspelled.

Resistance to such "development" is intermittent but encouraging. The *Times* carried a cheerful story on this note the week we left. It seems that plans to develop a vast theme-park, done in the American style, were foundering; the developers were having trouble coming up with enough capital to get something called WonderWorld built. The press had started calling it wonder-when. We left hoping it never gets built, that England resists the lure of theme-park simulation. And other lures: we wanted England to stay the way we saw it that summer, a green and misty garden.

American Narratives

································

There are only three or four Oklahoma narratives. There is the Boomer Sooner story, the opening of free land to anybody capable enough or lucky enough to grab it. There is the *Grapes of Wrath* story, the one all Oklahomans have been trying to live down since 1939. This is a story of being busted flat, of pulling up precarious stakes and heading farther West. John Steinbeck, the author who enshrined the word Okie in the American lexicon, is still a name that raises hackles in Oklahoma. Then there is the Oklahoma story according to Rogers and Hammerstein. This is the one where the wind comes sweeping down the plain and the corn is as high as an elephant's eye. Oklahomans love this story. And now, there is the story of the bombing of the Alfred P. Murrah Federal Building in downtown Oklahoma City. The chairman of the *Daily Oklahoman*, the top newspaper in the state, believes this may be Oklahoma's defining moment. He likens it to the assassination of President Kennedy in Dallas. After that tragedy, he says, Dallas came roaring back to become a boom town. This is the economic silver-lining thesis, very popular among Oklahoma optimists.

Months earlier I had made plans to be in the city on April 21, 1995, to attend the Seventh Annual Gathering of Cowboy Poets at the National Cowboy Hall of Fame. Then, on April 19, came the bomb that shook the nation as nothing since the Kennedy assassination. In spite of the disaster, the Cowboy Hall of Fame decided to go ahead with its two-day program. The analogy that again spurred them on was that weekend in November 1963 when the NFL had played its regular schedule the Sunday following the assassination, a decision which many later believed was the correct one. But after President Clinton declared Sunday a day of national mourning, the Cowboy Hall of Fame did indeed cancel the second day.

The Oklahoma City that I know bears little resemblance to the one that the national media describe as a typical city in America's Heartland. Where I stay, when I go there, is at a cheap chain motel. My booking this trip was way out north, on I-35, next stop, Wichita, Kansas, the same route by which Timothy McVeigh journeyed from Oklahoma City to Perry, ninety miles north. At the Holiday Inn next door to my motel that weekend, there was an NRA meeting, but the Star Trek convention had been canceled. The interstate is a no-man's land of temporary lodgings and chain eateries, where truckers and travelers pause on their flights across the flat lands of the southern Midwest. Oklahoma, however, does not picture itself as Midwest, preferring instead the romance and glamour of a western identity.

Coming out of the airport, I flicked on my lights in the bright afternoon sun. The freeways were alive with the lights of automobiles, in what seemed to be universal respect for the dead and the missing. Radio talk shows made much of this show of solidarity. They made much of everything. Oklahoma's insecurity complex was the subtext of a lot of the commentary from callers and talk-show hosts. And there was a great deal of talk of retribution, of crime and punishment. One caller, declaring himself no "offbeat redneck," proposed a public hanging—to show that such things can happen on the East Coast or the West Coast, but not here. (But of course it had.) A hanging would show the East Coast press that Oklahoma could take care of its problems and they could then just "leave us Okies alone." (By this time, late Friday afternoon, McVeigh was already in the hands of the authorities.) Another caller favored a public beheading so that citizens could have the satisfaction of seeing the criminal's head roll down the steps of the palace of justice.

But there were other callers who sounded a different note. Without condoning the act (nobody could brook the slaughter of the children), many callers agreed that the attack possessed a certain logic, an eye-for-an-eye retaliation against what they saw as the overweening power of the federal government. According to these callers, Waco and the Branch Davidian massacre were the driving force behind the assault on the Federal Building. Following this line of argument, David Koresh was a martyr: a man of the cloth (self-proclaimed, in the best Protestant tradition) who legally had the right to own as many firearms as he possessed the wherewithal to purchase. According to this view, the Justice Department, the ATF and, to personalize it, Janet Reno, were the arms of a repressive, invasive federal power out of control. Religion and guns are a volatile mix in the Heartland—among peace-loving folks, not just rabid fringe elements that may or may not belong to this or that militia. Although Koresh is dead and the federal government reigns supreme, the events in Waco will not go away. This view kept being aired again and again. Conspiracy theories sprang up instantaneously. A man claiming insider information (his brother works for a federal agency) called one station to point out that the government was focusing on the militia theory to divert attention from the Branch Davidian theory. Under the barrage of telephoners, the journalistic TV tag "Terror in the Heartland" began to lose its semantic precision.

And whose Heartland is it anyway? There are details that don't fit the prevailing narrative. Like the businesses on 63rd Street N.E. You turn off M.L. King Boulevard., past the Ralph Ellison Library on one corner and CashLand on the other, where the chief selling point is that you can cash post-dated checks (a very useful service indeed for the desperate, the down-and-out).

A street of pawn shops and family-owned businesses, some flourishing, some boarded-up, 63rd Street is Oklahoma City, too. The *Black Chronicle*, "The Paper That Tells The Truth," is located on this street, and so is the ALLAH-U-AKBAR, where "God is the Greatest" and where there is a *Juman* every Friday at 2 P.M. Next door is a small business, Mu'Min Oils. The Beauty of Holiness is just down the street, near Jamal's Fish Boat. Further on is Stell's Restaurant ("Fine Foods"), which serves delicious fried chicken and three vegetables for under $6 and whose patrons are predominately African Americans. The relief in this community that the perpetrators were white and not Muslim or black was palpable. The 63rd Street community was not represented on the stage at the Memorial Service on Sunday when the President and Mrs. Clinton and Billy Graham and other assorted dignitaries gathered to grieve officially on television. Actually, it was Billy Graham who received top billing in Oklahoma. As one radio host put it, "Billy Graham will be officiating and there will be many others there, including President and Hillary Clinton."

At the Cowboy Hall of Fame the narrative is a classical western story drawn straight from the lives of the participants. Or this is what they would have you believe. Everybody is quick to stress his or her ties to the land, his or her experience in corrals and feed lots and on horseback and in boots. Cowboy poetry, more than any verse I can think of, has its roots in actual work, in the traditions of ranching lore and life. The cowboy poets contrive not to look like working cowboys, however. Most of them are all decked out in the gaudy plumage of the drugstore cowboy. Hats are *de riguer*: The code of the cowboy begins with a hat. And boots, but here's the telltale sign of rampant cowboy dandyism: Most wear their jeans or ranch-style pants stuffed in their boots in order to highlight the loud, swirly designs of manly footwear. The effect is sometimes rather shocking, closer to the neon style of pimps and transvestites on Hollywood and Vine rather than actual cowboys and ranchers from gritty places like Guthrie, Oklahoma, or Buffalo Gap, Texas. Not shy in their dress (or dresses, though there is no cross-dressing), cowboy poets are not shy on stage either. Nor on their license plates. A pickup in the parking lot sported a plate reading "Cow Poet." The oral, declamatory nature of the poetry complements the amateur theatrical feel of many sessions. Some of the cowboy poets are actually more musicians than poets, and often the liveliest entertainers are men and women who can yodel like Jimmie Rodgers and sing like Gene and Roy. In this West all clocks are set to Standard Nostalgia Time.

Since sessions are staged concurrently, it is possible to drift in and out of simultaneous entertainments (drifting being an honored western tradition), and so I drifted, hearing a snatch of verse here, a scrap of song there, an entire session here, a fraction of one there. Six hours of wall-to-wall poetry can make a man restless. And it really doesn't matter much which session you're in because the tropes and themes are virtually identical, part of a continuously recycled threnody of observation, sentiment, rhyme, and gesture.

Cowboy poetry is a brand of performance poetry, a kind of folk art that has its own rules and conventions going back to the beginnings of cowboy poetry in the late nineteenth century and continuing to the present. Cowboy poetry is conservative in that it wants to preserve both a tradition and a way of life. It is almost entirely an outdoor poetry, and its values derive from living and working on the land. According to one of its best poets, Wallace McCrae, cowboy poetry "is not abstract or impressionistic; it's not religious preaching. It hinges on a cultural tradition: It's about a man and a horse following a cow." Everything about cowboy poetry sounds familiar; everything has been said a thousand times before. In his 1939 classic of range life, *We Pointed Them North*, Teddy Blue Abbot recalled how quickly "Bury Me Not on the Lone Prairie" wore out its welcome: "It was a saying on the range that even the horses nickered it and the coyotes howled it; it got so they'd throw you in the creek if you sang it. I first heard it along about '81 or '82, and by '85 it was prohibited."

It is entirely appropriate that cowboy poetry came to the forefront during the Reagan years. The first gathering of cowboy poets, at Elko, Nevada, in 1985, launched a movement so popular that ten years later there would be forty-eight cowboy poetry gatherings, ranging from predictable sites like Round Rock, Texas, to Pincher Creek, Alberta, and to a town named Capon Bridge, West Virginia, the eastern-most site. Reagan's favorite poet was Robert Service, the literary equivalent of Reagan's favorite president, Calvin Coolidge. A narrative poet, Service told in ringing rhythms stories of Alaskan mining camps and saloons. Reagan, it is reported, could give a mean rendition of such fare as "The Shooting of Dan McGrew": "A bunch of the boys were whooping it up in the Malamute saloon." Behind Service lay Rudyard Kipling, the manly poet of empire and barracks life. Kipling and Service are good poets, better than literary snobs who haven't read their work might think. To like them is to be a square, but Reagan didn't care (a line typical of Service's commitment to rhyme, by the way). Reagan was an unreconstructed square, still another reason he was so popular. Westerners are squares and proud of it (think of Orrin Hatch), and cowboy poetry is the squarest verse of all.

Of the types of performance poetry in our time, only cowboy poetry is work-specific, work-oriented. This is highly important in recognizing the populist basis of cowboy poetry. At the National Cowboy Hall of Fame you could always tell who the real cowboys and ranchers were because, offstage, they all talked about the same thing: whether the other had gotten any rain or not. Almost nobody had (though, ironically, it rained hard all that day in Oklahoma City, hampering the gruesome work going on just a few miles away).

J. B. Allen from Whiteface, Texas, was one of the few poets I heard at the Cowboy Hall of Fame who actually looked the part of a real cowboy. He wore jeans, a denim jacket, a western shirt, boots without the pants leg stuffed in them, and a hat creased just right and worn so low that his eyes were like slits beneath the brim. He recited only one poem (and that's another thing about cowboy poetry; hardly anybody reads from a text). Its title was "Saddlin' Up," and it spoke only of the pleasures of work. Cowboy poets constantly write about building fences, tending cattle, roping, and performing other pastoral duties. Many poems celebrate animals—a loyal dog, a skillful cutting horse, a favorite cow. One "lady cowboy poet," as she called herself, read a humorous poem, "Kamakazi Cow," about a mean bovine.

Cats don't get much play in cowboy poetry, but pigs, oddly enough, do. To a cowboy, there is apparently something inherently funny about putting the word pig in a poem. I heard several poems about pigs. One of them was about a pig who took to sucking a cow's teats. This led the poet, a woman, to use the word "tittie" with a slightly salacious titter, and it was one of the few blue notes that I heard at the gathering. Cowboy poetry is scrupulously decorous, except for the outright obscene, but that is another story, one already told in Guy Logsdon's *The Whorehouse Bells Were Ringing*. In such counter-tradition poems the Chisholm Trail becomes the "jism" trail, and so on.

A number of presenters, as they were called, referred to the tragedy, and a portion of the proceeds had been designated for relief funds. One poet, with an astounding number of volumes to his credit—138, the program said—was a medical doctor who came to the gathering for "therapy." A sheriff's car had driven him to the site from the morgue downtown where he had been on duty since the morning of the bombing, and when he concluded his recital of poetry he was scheduled to return to his grim task.

There is a star system among cowboy poets. The three brightest are Baxter Black, often heard on National Public Radio; Waddie Mitchell, famous for his sweeping handlebar mustache; and Wallace McCrae, author of the wildly popular and clever little classic, "Reincarnation." None of them were present at this gathering, but the man generally held to be number four and moving up fast, Red Steagall, from Azle, Texas, was there to headline the event. Guy Logsdon, who introduced Steagall, drew a connection between the disaster in Oklahoma City and the western spirit. "Oklahoma and other westerners do not give in to terrorism. We do not intimidate easily."

Steagall's performance summed up the meaning of cowboy poetry.

A professional country-western singer with Nashville-recorded hits to his credit, Steagall has the commanding stage presence of a veteran entertainer. He sang songs from his new album, accompanying himself on guitar, and wove in poems that sounded like stories and stories that sounded like poems. They were about the "values of family," a nice turn on the current bromide "family values." Many of them dealt with his recent role as grandfather, stories about the grit and pluck of his grandson, a born cowboy, it appears, who will follow in granddad's bootsteps. In an interlude in his quite enjoyable hour, Steagall remarked on issues dear to the heart of himself and other westerners. He mentioned the property rights issue, pointing out that "people in government can't take as good care of the land as its owners can." The audience applauded wildly. Then, in a personal aside which also drew much applause, he remarked, "I don't care to live in a socialistic society." He followed these remarks with a poem about successive generations "born to this land."

Oklahoma City, the National Cowboy Hall of Fame, and the cowboy poetry movement are a long way from Washington, D. C. The old-fashioned virtues celebrated in cowboy poetry offer clues to the rock-ribbed conservatism of this vast country that a lot of people in the White House still don't understand. And probably never will, not being born to the land and being, by education and by ideology, disinclined to listen to those who are.

Giant
Country

co-author Betsy Berry

"There's the Rio Grande, darling," said Jamie as they crossed over from Eagle Pass. Below them the river sort of crawled its way toward the Gulf.

"It don't look so grand here, does it, it don't look like it could hardly make it all the way to the ocean, does it, it looks like it might just curl up and die. It don't look a bit like it does in those mountains outside Pilar where it comes crashing out of that ravine and makes that turn towards Taos," said Harry.

"Is this gonna be one of those trips where you mix redneck vernacular with the occasional poetic phrase, striving for the sublime?" asked Jamie. "Cause if it is, I wanna be forewarned."

"Nope, I was just remarking," Harry said.

They had no interest in Mexico, not this trip. You had to get a little further into the country if you were seriously thinking about a real experience in Mexico. This was just the border, and all they were after, the reason they'd detoured down this way from their true destination farther to the north, was to get some drugs. Well, not drugs exactly but damned close. What they were looking for was some Percodan, and in Piedras Negras, they'd been told, you could buy it over the counter.

At the seventeenth *farmacia* in the first two blocks, Jamie told Harry to pull over.

"This looks like a good one."

While Harry sat outside humming off-key an old Marty Robbins tune ("I caught a good one/ It looked like it could run"), Jamie slipped inside to deal with the druggist. She was gone quite a while, and Harry could see her hands gesticulating above the boxes of feminine hygiene products that almost blocked the big plate glass window of the *farmacia*, but when she came out she wasn't carrying a package. The pharmacist had played dumb, he hadn't given in to Jamie's fast, idiomatic Spanish, and he didn't know *nada* about any over-the-counter Percodan.

"So much for the information source in Austin. So much for the Percodan."

"Right, but what bothers me is that guy over there. See him? The one in the baggy suit with some kind of half-assed badge on his chest? He's making me nervous."

The man Harry was sure was some sort of policeman continued to speak into a pay-phone receiver, glancing their way from time to time. Harry gunned the engine and drove a couple of blocks more away from the bridge, pulling up at the curb of a little green-and-red family restaurant where they ate the Number 7 Cabrito Plate and the Number 9 Enchilada Plate and washed them down with a couple of Carta Blancas apiece.

At the bridge going back into the states, the border guard in a brown uniform asked them what their business was in Mexico.

"Cabrito," Harry said. "We just crossed over to eat some good goat."

"Do you have anything to declare?"

"Yes, it was excellent. No, I mean nothing," kicking himself for not having thought to buy some little bauble. A bottle of tequila, a sombrero, anything.

"We're on our way to California. From Texas."

"Your occupations, please, señor," said the guard levelly. He must have personally taken the call from the cop in town, Harry reckoned.

"We're teachers. We're working on a book. That's why we're going to LA, Los Angeles. To do research." Harry trailed off.

The guard was unimpressed.

"Pull over to Bay 4 ahead," he told them.

"Calm down," Harry said to Jamie.

"You calm down," she hissed back. "That bastard's going to search the car."

Two hours later they finally got the car loaded again. The guards had gone through everything, opening bags, riffling through clothes, unscrewing bottles and sniffing Jamie's cosmetics, combing the carpet with a flashlight. Finally the customs officials were forced to let them go. Harry was relieved. He knew Jamie had a few reefers on her person, but they only searched the car.

As they drove away, he asked, "So where's the reefers?"

"Here they are, baby," pulling five joints from out of her bra.

Harry always called them reefers and she called them joints. Generational deal. Harry was from the Reefer Madness era; Jamie, from the Beatles. She bought dope on a monthly basis by mail from a nice, earth-mother hippie they'd met on the square in Santa Fe a road-trip or so ago. Harry didn't smoke, but he liked Percodan nearly as much as Jerry Lewis, and the occasional line of cocaine on trips to see a lawyer friend in Houston was not unpleasant either. But they could live without Percodan for a while. Had to, it appeared.

"I like Mexico, don't get me wrong," said Jamie. "Don't forget, I lived in Mexico City for two years. But Mexico never turns out the way you think it's going to. Never."

Harry hadn't forgotten. Jamie's years in Mexico City were one of those mysterious periods in her life that alternately intrigued and worried him. He didn't know what to think about those years and so, mostly, he tried not to think about them. He knew it was crazy to be jealous about the past, but sometimes he was.

Relieved, they drove north through the strange desert country beyond Del Rio. A huge lake had been built in that region, and it was disorienting to look on either side of the highway onto what had once been empty desert and see water. The weather had changed, too. Often it was cloudy and muggy-feeling, wet heat instead of dry desert air. Strange water birds flew back and forth among the little islands in the lake. The lake was fabled for its stock of huge bass, which was probably why it was built in the first place.

They planned to stop for a few days in Alpine and Marfa before heading on to California. This was a part of Texas that neither of them knew very well. They were excited about the big spaces, the great clarity of the upper Big Bend, the prospect of developing a story out of the events scheduled for that weekend, a tribute to the old movie classic *Giant*, which had been filmed in this country. Harry thought they might be able to sell it to *Texas Monthly* or one of the in-flight magazines, score a little extra cash for LA

Alpine looked promising. It was a clean little town from a distance, but up close it was littered with the kind of windy trash that blows against fences and swirls around back lots in every western town they had ever been in. There was a college in Alpine that sat on a hill. It looked like it might blow away any minute.

They found a motel and bought that bottle of tequila they should have bought in Piedras Negras and drank most of it and watched the sun burn itself out on the clear horizon outside their little motel room with the blood-red wallpaper, the overstuffed green divan, the yellow faux leather easy chair. They had Mexican food again that night and it went fine with the afternoon of tequilas and they made quite satisfactory love and slept the sleep of the expectantly just.

The next day they drove over to Marfa, twenty-six miles away. They ate at the old hotel downtown. In the lobby there were framed autographed pictures of Elizabeth Taylor, James Dean, Rock Hudson, Chill Wills, and other, lesser lights who had stopped there during the making of the movie in the summer of 1955. Mostly it was a roll call of the dead. There was a poster announcing a screening of the film, part of the weekend celebration. Harry thought it would be fun to see it on a big screen, like in the old days, but when he asked the girl at the desk about it, she said they weren't going to show it.

"It ain't never arrived," she said. "Besides, it don't really matter. You can rent it at the video store here anyways."

After lunch they drove out to the ranch where most of the location shooting had taken place. It was a huge spread with a low-slung rambling ranch house and several additional buildings, a house for the foreman, and a bunkhouse for the cowboys. Not far from the main house were the remains of the mansion constructed for the film. It was never a real structure, only a false-front for exteriors. A few years after the film was made, most of the boards were pulled down to build a barn.

No nostalgia for the movie then, but now things were different. The economy was depressed, local ranchers were hurting, and the present owner of the ranch, scion of the one back in the days when giants roamed the land, was as interested in turning a buck as any Hollywood player.

Now all that remained of Riata were huge poles, bigger than the ones used for telephone lines, lying in twisted heaps, oxidizing slowly into the desert. The wreckage looked like the skeleton of a ruined ship sailing a dust-colored sea, rather more like a melancholy copy of the *Bounty* than a cattle baron's Victorian Gothic mansion. Over the years the site had acquired the power of a minor shrine. Bill Brammer had laid the third part of his long roman à clef, *The Gay Place*, in that space between the plain and the mountains. In the seventies someone had written a rather bad, Carson McCullerish play about the lingering resonance of *Giant* called *Come Back to the Five & Dime, Jimmy Dean, Jimmy Dean*, which Robert Altman had eventually made into an appropriately tedious Robert Altman film. Finally, there was a likable little road film, *Fandango*, recently released, starring a promising young actor named Kevin Costner. It told the story of some University of Texas frat rats who make a soulful, tequila-sodden pilgrimage to the ranch. Now in the year of the Sesquicentennial

Harry and Jamie were there, tendering their respects. In modern Texas, with the economy in the tank, *Giant* was as close as you were going to get to the mythic old-time era of big money, big oil, big dreams.

The rancher, who had looked out his front window most of his life on the nails and sticks and bones of the movie-set relic, was vague about how to capitalize on an event that had happened thirty years ago. In fact he was sort of vague about everything. He was friendly enough in a Marlboro Man kind of way, living off the land and by its laws. Tight-lipped and mostly quiet like a lot of cowboys out this way, he looked like he took his cues from old western movies—Gary Cooper, Randolph Scott, men who'd spent their lives gazing into light real or artificial.

His wife, a pleasant behind-the-scenes kind of woman, fed them an early supper of beef and beans, potato salad and peppers, out in the bunkhouse with the cowboys, almost all of them Mexicans speaking rapid-fire border Spanish. Harry asked if many of the cowboys spoke English, a question that made his hosts visibly nervous.

"We don't like to talk much about that," the rancher said.

Harry didn't say anymore about it but made a mental note to find out why they didn't like to talk much about that.

In the cool of the evening they drove in to Marfa, passing by Clayton Williams' large spread on the way. Claytie was a big man in these parts; there were those who said he might be governor one of these days if he wanted it bad enough. West Texas needed a governor down in Austin. West Texas needed a lot of things. It needed rain, for example. That's what they talked about on the way to town, the need for rain. It hadn't rained in two months and probably wouldn't until the fall, if it did then. "If it was rain you was looking for, you come to the wrong place," was how the rancher wrapped it up.

About halfway to Alpine, they pulled off the road to a viewing spot marked by a sign and a couple of benches. "Marfa Lights" it said on the sign. It was a place of more than local interest. The Marfa

Chamber of Commerce urged visitors from everywhere to come to Marfa to see the strange, flickering lights on the horizon. Nobody had ever explained their origin or meaning. Science fiction aficionados trekked in from all over the world to see this authentic unsolved mystery.

"There they are. I see them," said Jamie, but the rancher thought not. "No, those are car lights," he said. "The Marfa lights jump around and look like they're alive."

"What color are they?" asked Harry.

"Oh, they're all different sorts of colors," said the rancher.

"Well, I'd sure like to see them," said Jamie, but they never did, not that night and not the next, and in the end they didn't know if they'd be back this way any time soon, so for Harry and Jamie the Marfa Lights remained only a possibility.

On a quiet, tree-lined street in town, they were taken to the home of another prominent rancher who split time between here and his ranch. He was a tall man with a graduate degree in Advanced Machismo. A small group of people were assembled in the living room, and Harry and Jamie were introduced by their new host.

"They's writers," he told everybody, and everybody returned to their drinks and conversation.

Jamie struck up a conversation with a nice woman who liked to read and wanted to talk about books, and they decided to exchange addresses. They might as well have been sharing recipes, but the host suddenly seemed very interested in their business. The folds deepening about his eyes, he turned sharply to Jamie.

"Whatcha writin' down there, little lady?"

"My address," answered Jamie. She couldn't ever recall having been addressed as little lady in her life. She still thought maybe she hadn't heard him right.

"Jack tells us you do quite a bit of writin', you and that fella over there." He stuck his thumb in back of him to indicate Harry without looking around at him.

"We. . . we teach. We teach English, and we write, yes."

"Well, oughta tell ya right now, we don't like writers round here. Never have. Me, I'd just as soon shoot one of 'em as look at 'em.

"We had a writer come through here oncet. Worked for that *Geographic* magazine, as I recall. Told nothin' about us but lies. Ever thang was lies. Asked us questions about our wetbacks. *Our* wetbacks. Then just last month, there was sumpin in the El Paso paper bout it. Well, none of their goddamned business, we all said. None of the government's neither." He paused to light a stub of a cigar.

"So my advice to you is, don't write nothin' while you're passin' through here. Just a little friendly advice. We just don't cotton to it. Don't think of ourselves as much to write about anyway. And nothin' personal intended, you understand."

The group laughed a little, to lighten the moment, and Jamie said, "Oh, you needn't worry about that. I write poems and nobody reads those. Harry writes about books. You don't have a thang to worry about," taking a chance he wouldn't notice the little dig.

He didn't. He turned away and went to another cluster of people to tell them what was what.

Then, moving over to Harry, she whispered: "Hey, couldn't you help me out on this?"

"Not me, darling. I'm kind of a chickenshit in the presence of hombres like that one, Mr. Wes' Texas. Want a little more bourbon & branch?"

"All right, cowboy, if that's the best you can do," and gave him an affectionate chuck on the chin.

Harry sidled up to the kitchen-qua-bar for a couple more vodkas with a trace of tonic.

That night they stayed at the rambling ranch house on the *Giant* property, and in the bright moonlight filtering into their room Harry tried to summon forth local lore in his mythy mind. But all he remembered was the story of Nelson Algren, who had done some writing on this range back in the thirties. Algren had been bumming around the country gathering impressions for the novel that would become *Somebody in Boots*, when he fetched up in Alpine. He strolled over to the empty college on the hill and found a proletarian writer's dream: a large room full of new, unused typewriters. The whole thing became for him a symbol of everything that was wrong with America in the Depression years: an allegory of plenty and poverty, machine and man. Eventually Algren had to return to Chicago, and so he decided to lift one of the typewriters and take it with him. It seemed a natural thing to do. There they sat in the empty room, he was a writer, he needed a machine to write on, so he took one on the lam. Of course someone with nothing better to do spotted him and notified the local sheriff. Miles out of town, clanging down the track, he was arrested and brought back to face the music. He was sentenced to several months in jail and served his time honorably and never, so far as Harry knew, ever returned to Alpine.

The next day the rancher took them on a guided pickup tour of his acreage. The property was huge. Jamie said it looked bigger than Drogheda, but the rancher, who had apparently not seen *The Thorn Birds*, gave no sign of recognition. There must have been two thousand gates setting off one bit of land from another, this one for grazing cattle, that one for running horses, and the like. The rancher asked Harry if he'd mind getting the gates, and at each one Harry had to fiddle anew with wire latches. Since no two were alike, the labor was tricky. And after the truck pulled through, Harry had to close the gate, knowing full well he'd be repeating the whole process on the way back. Couldn't have the horses mounting the cows, you know, or whatever the problem was, eating the wrong grass, mucking up the water tanks.

This was an old tradition in ranching country, number 453—"Humiliating the Tenderfoot"—in Stith Thompson's *Motif-Index of Folk Literature*. (Harry looked it up when he got back to civilization.) The rancher obviously enjoyed having Harry fumble with the gates. For lots of reasons. Mainly it gave him a chance to talk to Jamie while Harry was out opening and closing the bloody gates.

The rancher was melancholy and opened up to Jamie. He talked about the Big Issues—Life, Death, the Ranch, Where All the Flowers Had Gone. The flowers, it appeared, were veiled references to girls, women, love, romance—as they had always been in the lexicon of love. Jamie nodded and said uh-huh and looked out the pickup onto the sweeping expanses of desert and mesquite and cactus and low, gray mountains in the distance and kept up a kind of who-me banter as Harry bounced in and out of the truck.

The country was beautiful, empty and soulful, and the cattle were fat and lovely to look at. At the extreme edge of the ranch was a high bluff on which they paused to gaze down across a deep canyon through which snaked the Great River, the Rio Grande, still retaining some of its untrammeled majesty in this empty place. Beyond lay Mexico, from where all the ranch hands came. Because it was clear to Harry and Jamie by now that the ranches were stocked almost exclusively with wetback labor.

"Right here," the rancher told them, "is where Pancho Villa crossed over during the Mexican Revolution."

"When was that?" asked Jamie.

"Round 1913 or so."

Harry had already met two other ranchers who could point out the picturesque spot on their land where the legendary rebel leader had ridden his pony across into the United States. Villa was about the only Mexican they cared to talk about. He was long dead and mythical, like their own self-image as rugged individualists, lonesome cowboys, roamers through the bramble. These boys might be rugged enough, but as for individualism, they were all looking for federal handouts, tax breaks, bail-outs, lagniappe, just like everybody else in the Lone Star State of Self-Inflation. Harry didn't exempt himself. He'd as lief have a grant of free money as the next.

That noon, at lunch, they found themselves in the bunkhouse with the illegal aliens. The whole thing felt like the scene from *Giant* where the Mexican workers serve barbacoa and Elizabeth Taylor faints at the sight of steaming calf's brains. The rancher's wife served terrific down-home food again this day, chicken fried steak washed down with huge tumblers of iced tea.

Then they were taken down to the corrals and the large rodeo arena where the trainers worked the horses. Jamie was an excellent rider, and one of the ranch hands was happy to put her aboard a pert little roan. Jamie, the rancher, and the ranch hand loped prettily around the arena while Harry, who had grown up on a cotton farm and considered horses dangerous, cooled his Reeboks in the bleachers, enjoying the spectacle and nursing a beer. It was pleasant in the sun in late May. A cool breeze came off the low mountains in the distance. Very tranquil this idyllic ranch life so long as you weren't playing Walter Brennan to John Wayne in his pickup. "Yessir, Mr. Dunson, I'll get that gate."

Later, in the curtained dimness of the ranch house, with the cool tile floors and the light leeched out by the heavy drapes and the muted earth tones of the adobe and paneled walls, Harry and Jamie pored over a scrapbook of movie memorabilia, photos of Liz and Rock and Dennis Hopper and Mercedes McCambridge. Harry was amused. He had read McCambridge's autobiography. She was a crusty old dame who loved Jimmy Dean and hated the local dust, food, weather, and West Texas in general. There was also a working copy of the script, a gift from director George Stevens. It had the interest of most scripts, which is less than zero. Film lives or dies by what's on the screen, not what's on the page. But they regarded it with the proper awe.

Jamie was ready to rest a bit after such a long afternoon, and after they excused themselves they withdrew to the bedroom at the end of one wing of the house. They were tired of beings guests, of the strain of being pleasant, wide-eyed, appreciative, grateful. They should have stayed in a motel, they knew that now. But the rancher had insisted. Texas hospitality. Y'all come.

Jamie yawned and curled up like a kitten. Harry stretched out on the bed and sought to escape the stark clarity of West Texas for a while. He began to read *The Heart of the Matter*. He liked to read about colonial Africa: pye dogs, torrential rain on the tin roofs, the decanter of gin on the rickety wooden table. Then the inevitable discussions about God, which was what you always got around to in Greene. Harry didn't know whether Greene was a good Catholic or not, but he certainly liked the way Greene wrote about whiskey priests and lost souls in the tropics.

Soon he too drifted off to sleep, Jamie beside him.

At dusk the four of them, Harry and Jamie and the rancher and the rancher's wife, drove far out into the country. Their destination was an even more isolated ranch, on the northern rim of the Big Bend. The occasion was a child's birthday party at the ranch of some friends of their host, and the rancher's wife thought Harry and Jamie might enjoy tagging along.

The ranch was so remote it came complete with a landing strip, and Jamie stood on the long covered porch gazing out at a small plane parked there, its metallic propellers blinding against the hazy sunset, its wheels pegged down against the wind. Horses loped along a ridge in silhouette, like a memorable shot in a John Ford western.

All the ranchers at the party were dressed alike—formal attire according to the custom of that place—crisply starched dark blue jeans, expensive, exotic boots, starched white shirts, bolo ties, hand-tooled belts with heavy silver buckles, and cowboy hats, which several had removed and put rim-up on a table by the front door. Their brushed hair had hat creases above the temples. The ranchers lounged against a low adobe wall, long-necked beer bottles beaded with ice in hand, one foot against the wall, the other thrust out before them.

The women had their own dress code, too. They wore frilly, Sue Ellen-style skirts—probably imported from Santa Fe—long-sleeved shirts with ruffled collars, boots or sandals, Indian-crafted earrings and turquoise rings. But the women seldom lounged. For it was they who made the party go—for the adults and the kids. They poured the Kool-Aid, lit the candles, cut the cake; comforted their little ones when they took a tumble or suffered a slight, just as they did each other when husbands got out of line. They were all nice, friendly, and hospitable, infinitely patient. Unlike the ranchers, they were interested in Harry and Jamie, where they lived, what they did, where they were going. You got the feeling that they wouldn't have minded going somewhere themselves, glancing wistfully from their children to the little plane tied to its slab of runway, silent and still against the quiet country which stretched hundreds and hundreds of miles beyond, farther than the eye could see.

But the men, in all their laundered, creased finery, seemed sullenly content, one eye on Washington, the other on Mexico. They had figured everything out long ago: everything descended from and returned to a long line of tradition, everything fixed in its place. Again Harry and Jamie were struck by the clarity of the scene. Even the party games for the children, were telling. The little boys conducted a mock rodeo, circumscribing the yard on stick horses, their little legs kicking up dust, while the little girls in their miniature skirts, blouses, and boots, stood back and watched the action approvingly. There it was, a training session for survival, ways of living simplified and reduced to a party game for children, never too young to learn the ethos of the rancher—or the rancher's wife. Change their drink from strawberry Kool-Aid to Lone Star and Jack Daniels, and it stretched before you, the life to come, as unchanging as the dust that out here swirled around everyone like a fog.

The ride back to the ranch in the moonlight was long. Outside the window of the Suburban was the ragged, open, desolate-unless-it-was-yours country, and though there was such a severe drought that the rancher had lost several hundred head of cattle, the land is what he had, now and forever, amen. He thought he saw rain clouds to the north, lit up by heat lightning, but they probably weren't. With his wife there beside him, he didn't talk much.

Early the next morning Harry and Jamie were on their way, headed to new climes. Jamie took a last snapshot of the ancient pile crumbling into the desert, and Harry carried away a small, weathered scrap of wood with a rusted nail driven through it. That was what you did at shrines, and he wanted a piece of the true Riata.

As Harry drove, Jamie watched through the back window, the ranch house receding, the wife waving politely, the husband just a speck on the horizon as he neared the stables, ready to begin the day's round. The fast little Mitsubishi blasted through cooler, clearer country, past El Paso, a city so remote it hardly seemed to be part of

Texas, and into the blinding sparkle of New Mexico. In a fly-specked cafe on the main street of Lordsburg they bought a postcard of a Texas cowgirl lassoing a jackalope and wrote a nice thank-you to the rancher and his wife for their time and hospitality, and they both decided then, without saying a word about it, that the nostalgic piece on old Texas would go unwritten.

Pages

Cotton and Classicism: George Sessions Perry's Farm Novel

I t was not until long after my family had forsaken cotton fields and the labor thereof that I first read George Sessions Perry's novel of sharecropping life, *Hold Autumn in Your Hand*. It struck many resonant chords, though we were not sharecroppers, my father and mother and myself in that time of war so long ago, in the 1940s. My father raised cotton and corn on a piece of black-land soil his father owned that was about twice the size of Sam Tucker's sixty-eight acres in the novel, and he did it, until 1937, with horses. That year he traded in the animals, Togo and Stud, for a John Deere tractor.

Although the machine made the work a little easier, the eternal verities of cotton farming remained: low prices; exhausting stoop labor under a broiling sun; threats from rain or drought; insects, both those that killed cotton and those that tormented its tenders; long days; dreams and broken dreams; and Johnson grass: anyone who has worked on a cotton field in Texas is familiar with that most durable archenemy of man and cotton. The cotton sacks were longer than a limousine, I later believed, and bottomless, and the rows endless in the heat and sweat of mornings that crawled imperceptibly toward noon's brief halcyon. (Why is it that writing about cotton seems to induce Faulknerian languors of diction and syntax? Perhaps it is the latent aesthete's desire to escape the earth's immemorial retrograde, the downward tug of cotton.)

In 1948 we moved to town, and a few years later, to another town, just outside of Dallas. I was twelve and needed a summer job. There was a cotton farm close by (eventually the site, of course, of a strip mall, but that lay twenty years in the future), and Dad had heard that the farmer needed a hand. I was that hand, and a poorer one could probably not have been found. Because by then I had been hopelessly corrupted by easy town living. School out, one burning June day I resumed the work of my early childhood, hoeing cotton. The farmer was blessed with several strong, strapping sons who swung lustily up and down the rows at a back-breaking pace, while I struggled to keep up. By ten o'clock I was exhausted, but I hung on until noon, and then quit. I was too bushed to be humiliated. The next day I found a new job at a country club that had just opened a few miles from town, and so I became a caddy and said goodbye to cotton fields forever.

Now my relation to cotton is quite benign. I like to shop at the Cotton Club on West Gray in Houston where cotton shirts start at around $125. Made from Egyptian or Chinese cotton, the cloth is superior to American shirts because, in a nice irony, the cotton in those countries is picked by hand, while American cotton is picked entirely by machines. Instead of farming cotton, I farm literature—in the shade. The first third of my course, "Life and Literature of the Southwest," deals with the southern tradition in Texas writing: i.e., novels east of I-35. Novels such as Perry's are an act of repatriation, a restoration and reminder of the country of my childhood.

The prevailing myth in Texas culture, of course, is quite otherwise: it is western in origin and imagery. A couplet from a poem by Berta Hart Nance tidily sums up the popular conception: "Other states were carved or born/ Texas grew from hide and horn." The facts, however, say something different. The facts say that cotton, not cattle, was the dominant economic force in post-Civil War Texas. In *The Road to Spindletop* John Spratt points out that "cattle ran a distant second to cotton. In dollar value of the product, in number of persons employed, and in industrial activity generated, cotton stood alone—far in advance of all competitors." These facts lead Spratt to wonder why "the loneliest person on earth, the cowhand of the late nineteenth century [has] been clothed in heroic glamour, while the cotton farmer . . . has been dubbed an 'ignoramus.'"

The answer, in part, lies in the popularity and influence of the image of Texas set forth in the works of such cultural arbiters as J. Frank Dobie and Walter Prescott Webb. The Texas that Dobie and Webb valued was an economy and ethos on horseback, in arid country, dominated by cattle and cactus instead of cotton and calluses. In one of Dobie's autobiographical essays there is a paragraph that contains all that Dobie knew of cotton farming and all he thought he needed to know. In *Some Part of Myself* he writes of old-time trail boss Ab Blocker:

> He [Ab Blocker] cultivated a field out between Austin and Round Rock and planted it in cotton. While he was chopping cotton he saw Kansas-bound herds of longhorns stringing by on the unfenced prairies. He stayed with his cotton, raised a crop, helped pick it, sold it. Then, he used to tell in his crying voice: "I got down on my knees and promised God Almighty if I ever planted another seed of cotton I'd boil it three days first so it would be sure not to sprout." I was like Mr. Ab. All ranch work was congenial to me as I grew up, even doctoring wormy calves by day and skinning dead ones by lantern light, but the year we boys tried raising a bale of cotton remains a dark blot.

Dobie's pals Webb and Roy Bedichek held identical views. Said

Webb, "I never appreciated the nobility of farming. All I ever got out of it was sore fingers." And Bedichek had a cotton-field epiphany similar to mine. He wrote once, "I remember very well the place I was in the field when I came to the conclusion that I simply could not stand that kind of thing all my life. I decided that I was ready to branch out into something besides farm work. So I quit right in the middle of a row, chopping cotton." Bedichek then told his mother that he wanted to "get a job so that I can make my way through the University."

Escaping from cotton fields and cotton culture was a familiar motif in tenant farmer fiction. Ruth Cross, from northeast Texas, around Paris, wrote melodramatically of young farm-girl heroines fleeing from impoverished tenant farms on depleted land and going to exciting places like the University of Texas, in *The Golden Cocoon*, and Paris (France) in *The Big Road*. The UT novel contains an immortal line that must not be lost: Cross describes the UT faculty as a "backwash of incompetents whom life had rejected."

Edward Everett Davis' aptly titled novel, *The White Scourge*, which appeared in 1940, expressed the nadir of cotton-farming's status in Texas literary culture. Davis labeled the cotton field "the great open air slum of the South, a perennial Hades of poverty, ignorance, and social deformation."

"Cotton culture," he wrote, was "simple, an elemental means of subsistence for that portion of the South's rural proletariat composed of lowly blacks, peonized Mexicans, and moronic whites numbering into several millions."

Into this rural version of multiculturalism before multiculturalism was cool, I was born.

Hold Autumn in Your Hand appeared at the tail-end of the Depression, in 1941, though rural Texas was still mired in deep economic trouble. In 1940 the unemployment rate in Collin County, where my father farmed, was a whopping nineteen percent. In Milam County, where Perry's novel takes place, economic prospects were equally grim. Yet Perry chose neither to replicate the

Confederate ideology of southern apologists nor to launch a wholesale denunciation of tenancy. Instead he transformed the cotton-based novel into a celebration of labor, of planting and harvesting cotton as a creative act, thereby making a simple cotton farmer into a hero of modestly mythic proportions.

Hold Autumn in Your Hand seemed to happen at exactly the right moment. Behind it lay a deep if not distinguished tradition of Texas fiction, and ahead of it loomed economic and technological changes that would close off the entire topic for discussion, as tenant farming receded into the increasingly remote past. The sharecropping system would disappear within twenty years, and most of the cotton raising in Texas, in the U.S., would be accomplished by fewer people, riding in air-conditioned tractors and doing the work, by machine, that an entire people, black and white and brown, had once performed. And in Texas the cotton would be grown on huge irrigated farms in West Texas and on the South Plains around Lubbock, instead of on small farms in Collin or Milam or any one of scores of other East Texas counties.

At the national level Perry's novel came at the end of a decade of often brilliant writing about tenant farmers and rural poverty. Faulkner had kicked off the thirties with his dazzling modernist exploration of the consciousness of Mississippi hillbillies in *As I Lay Dying*, but faithful to the spirit and program of modernism, he hadn't cared a whit about socioeconomic causes. Faulkner's novel is more interested in the aesthetics of cubism than the price of cotton. Erskine Caldwell with his comic-gothic neo-naturalism in popular salacious novels such as *God's Little Acre* seemed as politically disengagé as Faulkner, although in photo-journalist texts like *You Have Seen Their Faces* he explored the real economic conditions of tenant-farming squalor. The most ambitious work devoted to the lives of sharecroppers, James Agee's *Let Us Now Praise Famous Men*, offered a richly detailed analysis of its subject. Agee, however, displayed his specimen families in such a lavishly wrought style that even abject poverty was aestheticized and acquired a luminous beauty—something that Agee worried about while being unable or unwilling to redirect his art back towards economic determinism.

Of more immediate relevance to Perry, of course, was the example of John Steinbeck, whose *The Grapes of Wrath* stands as the greatest achievement of thirties proletarian art. Echoes of Steinbeck are plentiful in Perry's novel, and one whole chapter is a kind of rewriting of the flight of the Joads west. A family named Clampett returns from California, and the Tucker family puts them up for a night and listens with interest to their tales of broken promises in the Promised Land. The son, Theo, who has dabbled in communism, stands as a kind of combined Jim Casey/Tom Joad, a prophet and preacher of working-stiff communitarinism. The Tuckers, by contrast, are stay-at-home Joads, and like Faulkner's Dilsey, they endure.

In another sense, too, Perry's novel resonated in a national context. Perry's hero is connected to the wilderness, to nature, placing him in a long line of American fictional heroes beginning with Natty Bumppo and including Huckleberry Finn, Nick Adams, Ike McCaslin, and Randall P. McMurphy. Sam Tucker loves to hunt and fish, and part of the appeal of the farm that he contracts to work during his "play-pretty" year is that it borders a small river full of fish, mystery, and wonder. Yet Sam Tucker's "wilderness" is quite tame and domesticated. Lead Pencil, the sixty-plus-pound catfish that Sam catches, is no whale or marlin out of Melville or Hemingway. The largest critter that Sam the hunter kills is a possum; there are no mythic bears or charging rhinos in this novel. Sam himself is a completely domesticated hero. Happily married and the father of two children, Sam cleaves to hearth and home—rare in a line of American fiction about wilderness heroes who exist, in Hemingway's title, as *Men Without Women*. The name of Perry's protagonist conveys this domestication. Sam is often "tuckered out" from the labor of the fields, of trying to keep food, "tucker," on the table. The name may also echo the old folk song "Old Dan Tucker": "Get out of the way for old Dan Tucker/He's too tired to eat his supper."

If Perry's novel gains from placing it in regional and national contexts, it also benefits from a previously unrecognized context, the deep affinity it shares with classical literature, specifically with the *Georgics* of Virgil. All regionalism seeks the imprimatur of universal themes, hoping thereby to avoid being dismissed as mere local color. Perry's novel finds its locus within the tradition of rural poetry best represented by Virgil's poetic meditations on country life. It is most important to realize that Perry's novel is a species of georgics, not pastoralism. Pastoralism also celebrates rural life, but in a much more artificial way. Pastoralism deals with leisure, love, and poetry. Georgics deal with agriculture, work, the rhythms of man cultivating the land. Pastoralism finds its natural equivalency in the western, which is a genre of herdsmanship, with cattle standing in for sheep. The cowboy, the rancher, a figure of idleness and repose, is much like a shepherd (including the singing of lullaby songs to the animals) and nothing like a farmer. Perry himself reflected this idealization of the rancher-cowboy figure in a notable passage from his informal history of the state, *Texas: A World in Itself*, published in 1942. Writes Perry:

> But to us Texans there is a quality of go and glamor about cow-men that farmers never attain. I don't know what makes it. Is it the fact that they ride horses? That probably has something to do with it. But I am led for some reason to believe that it is the cowman's mixture of pride and arrogance—plus his knowledge that he has casually put something over on the rest of us. For while the rancher goes through the violent motions of labor, he is actually having a wonderful time earning a living; doing something he would of spiritual necessity have had to do anyway for the good of his own soul, in order to live up to his own concepts of freedom and dignity. Perhaps that's it, that the ranchers are the last free men in a swiftly industrializing America, and that they become thereby a novel and enviable symbol of what so many of the rest of us have eternally lost.

This is an extremely telling passage in that the author of the best

Texas novel about farming implicitly repudiates his subject and hero while embracing the Dobie-Webb western hero, the cavalier on horseback. That Perry vastly admired Dobie—and devoted several paragraphs of his book to "the Texian who knows most about her [Texas] and loves her best"—may be part of the reason. The most curious thing about the passage, though, is how it elides the georgics of work into the pastoralism of leisure.

Whether Perry was familiar with it or not, Virgil's *Georgics* bears a number of striking parallels with motifs developed in *Hold Autumn in Your Hand*. Of the many translations of Virgil, one is particularly relevant to the case I am making, C. Day Lewis' *The Georgics of Virgil*. Published in 1940, it has a distinctly localized context and, thus, intriguing parallels with Perry's novel. The Second World War had already begun, in 1939, when Lewis published his translation. Not surprisingly, Lewis had one eye on classical Rome, the other on contemporary Europe. In "Dedicatory Stanzas" to Stephen Spender, which precede the translation, Lewis indicates that what draws him to Virgil is the Latin poet's testament to peace:

> . . . and for a vision
> That saw beyond an imperial day the hand
> Of man no longer armed against his fellow
> But all for vine and cattle, fruit and fallow,
> Subduing with love's positive force the land.

Later, in Book One, Lewis' translation reveals a striking historical analogy between Virgil's time and his own:

> Evil has so many faces, the plough so little
> Honour, the labourers are taken, the fields untended,
> And the curving sickle is beaten into the sword that
> yields not.
> There the East is in arms, here Germany marches:
> Neighbour cities, breaking their treaties attack each other:
> The wicked War-god runs amok through all the world.

Perry, whose book was written chiefly during 1939-1940, also alludes to the winds of war (one character remarks, "Folk acrost the waters is gettin organized by the sword"), just as Steinbeck does in *The Grapes of Wrath*. The time of the action in Perry's novel also connects it with events in far-off Europe. The time can be precisely dated, I believe, as 1940. The novel refers to the Twin Days as a propitious time for planting, and the Twin Days are February 28-29, i.e., a leap year. Nineteen forty was a leap year. Late in the novel, a cotton-picker speaks of "back in '36," which lends further credence to several years later, or, 1940. The reader, reading in 1941 and afterwards, following Perry's cues, has the war inevitably in the foreground.

Apart from the war atmosphere, Perry's novel reveals quite striking similarities with Virgil's poem. First, there is the rather amazing parallel between types of farmland. At the beginning of the novel Sam Tucker contracts to plant a crop of cotton and corn on a blackland farm. The thick black gumbo, enriched by recurrent flood waters, contrasts sharply with Sam's previous sandy-land farming, where although less effort is required, the result is punier, less bountiful crops. Here is Virgil on the distinctions between types of soil:

> As a rule, soil that is black and turns up right at the pressure
> Of the ploughshare, or crumbling soil (for this we reproduce
> By ploughing) is best for corn: no other plain will yield you
> So many wagonloads drawn home by the slow-gait oxen.
>
> In hill-country you'll get gravel, a hungry soil
> That gives the bees a bare subsistence of spurge and rosemary.

On Sam's blackland farm, his corn grows "like plants in a myth." Cotton, incidentally, is not a crop grown in Virgil's Italy, although there is one reference to cotton in his poem: "The soft cotton that glimmers in plantations of Ethiopia."

The Georgics is a kind of instruction manual and moral compendium of rural life. Indeed Virgil's poem contains enough practical information about agronomy to fulfill three credit hours in introductory farming at an agricultural and mechanical college. Virgil offers the best wisdom available on such topics as weather and soil conditions, the changing of the seasons, crop rotation, pruning, plowing, tools, planning, productive use of idle periods, and so on—all of which are elements of Sam Tucker's year-long cycle in the novel.

Aside from practical advice, the poem also offers ethical instruction aplenty. For as a man sows, so shall he reap—Biblical wisdom that could serve equally well as an epigraph for Virgil as for Perry. Virgil devotes more than one passage to a defense of labor; *The Georgics* is a poem about work, not the loaf-around pleasantries associated with the pastoral mode. According to Virgil,

> For the Father of agriculture
> Gave us a hard calling: he first decreed it an art
> To work the fields, sent worries to sharpen our mortal wits
> And would not allow his realm to grow listless from lethargy.

A few lines later, the poet sums up his theme of work: "Yes, unremitting labour/And harsh necessity's hand will master anything." Certainly Perry's novel is equally devoted to the appreciation and value of labor. Sam Tucker works so hard that my students have trouble understanding his concept of a "play pretty year." They look at his unremitting toil from dawn till dark, the stoop labor, the use of a mule, the sticky, stubborn soil, the harsh sun, the abysmal shack provided for him and his family, the lack of plumbing, water, or electricity, the absolute penury of his days, and they wonder what could be pleasant or appealing or attractive about such toil. Perry makes his case in Virgilian terms: Sam Tucker derives moral value, character value, from labor, from marshaling his intelligence and instincts and folk wisdom in an effort to deliver a marvelous crop from the good earth. And Perry makes it clear, through many references to an industrial order, that Sam Tucker could earn more money working in an auto assembly plant in Houston. But Sam has tried such work before and found it wanting: "The thing was that a man could not have the proper diet rubbing fenders. It took all that stuff out of you and didn't put anything back." Virgil is everywhere concerned to show the superiority of country living over residence in a city, an empire: "Oh, too lucky for words, if only he knew his luck,/Is the countryman who far from the clash of armaments/Lives, and rewarding earth is lavish of all he needs."

Virgil's list of nature's riches includes a number of parallels with events and episodes in the life of Sam Tucker. Virgil has a whole section devoted to bees and beekeeping ("the heavenly gift of honey"), and one of Sam's most savored treasures in the novel is his discovery of a beehive in a tree in the woods: "the very wildness and secret derivation of which placed it outside the realm of things which can be valued in money." Trees are also celebrated in Virgil's poem ("Nature is catholic in the propagation of trees"), and Sam finds much of value in trees, including a bumper pecan crop and various delicious varmints such as squirrels and possums hiding in their leafy bowers. The bounty of nature is a central theme in both works, including the very image of autumn itself caught in Perry's title and thus in Virgil: "Autumn drops her varied fruits at our feet . . . ."

Perhaps the dominant image most linking the two works is that of the man of peace. At one point Virgil imagines his farmer ploughing up "old spears eaten away with flaky rust" or "helmets"; thus he will "marvel at the heroic bones he has disinterred." Similarly Sam Tucker unearths arrowheads and pictures himself at one with Indians who once hunted on the land where he farms. The arts of peace are the center of both Virgil's and Perry's interest. Virgil movingly sums up the ethical nature of cultivation in Book Three:

> But still the farmer furrows the land with his curving plough:
> The land is his annual labor, it keeps his native country . . .
>
> And all the time he has dear children who dote on kisses,
> A house that preserves the tradition of chastity, cows that hang
> Their milky udders . . . .

The same may be said—and is—of Sam Tucker. Because Sam lives in a time of the disappearance of yeoman agriculture, the Jeffersonian ideal of the small farm is a diminishing if not impossible ideal. Because of national and regional economic conditions, Sam cannot keep his native country, a point which the novel's original ending made abundantly clear. In it, Perry has Sam come to the realization that his play-pretty year is over and that he must move himself and family to the industrial wasteland of Houston.

But in the novel, during the cycle of that year, Sam fulfills every one of Virgil's rural beatitudes. He upholds the land and himself with his curving plough, he dotes upon his two children, and his house is one of marital fidelity. He even has a cow, borrowed, that produces enough milk to nourish his children.

There is, finally, one further parallel between Virgil and Perry, and that, curiously, is Perry's "pagan" conception of religion. Though Sam Tucker and his family live in the heart of the Bible belt, Sam is more of a pre-Christian than anything. When confronting nature's whims and unknowns, he thinks more often of the "gods" than of God. In one lovely sentence, Perry connects the idea of place, locus, with gods in a classical sense. The occasion is a celebration of the river as a sacred site: "If you were ever to see the gods, say, see them coming down a leaning tree, wearing shiny orange robes, this would be the place." In sum, Perry's autochthonous imagination has an enormous number of parallels and precedents in Virgil's great poem. From a Texas cotton farm to the world of Virgil is how far his novel reaches.

Katherine
the Great

....

The third annual Texas Writers Month celebration in May 1997 featured William Sidney Porter (O. Henry) as its poster boy. Male writers had also been honored the two previous years, Horton Foote in 1995, John Graves in 1996. One could argue that the 1997 poster pictured the wrong Porter and that, indeed, if any Texas writer of the past deserved such homage it should be Katherine Anne Porter, the best writer the Lone Star State has produced. But being ignored in her native state is nothing new for Katherine Anne. Indeed, at the splashy first Texas Book Festival, held in November 1996, a panel of semi-distinguished commentators sang the praises of the familiar founding-fathers trinity of Texas letters, J. Frank Dobie, Walter P. Webb, and Roy Bedichek, but nary a word was proffered for Porter. Back in 1939, Porter's *Pale Horse, Pale Rider,* perhaps the greatest work of fiction produced by a Texas-born author, lost out in the Texas Institute of Letter's annual competition for best book of the year award to a collection of treasure-seeking tales by local culture hero Dobie titled *Apache Gold and Yaqui Silver*. Of course, Porter didn't write about cowboys, longhorns, rattlesnakes, mockingbirds, or buried bullion. And the fact that she had left Texas more or less for good when she was twenty-eight probably didn't help either.

Although Porter's 1962 novel, *Ship of Fools*, won the Texas Institute of Letters award for fiction, her standing in her home state remained shaky at best. As recently as 1981, a year after her death, Texas' leading novelist, Larry McMurtry, dissed her in an oft-quoted essay in the *Texas Observer*. In remarks that were hopelessly off-base, McMurtry wrote Porter off the Texas literary macho map, accusing her of being "genteel to the core," of having created too pure a style—of being, in short, all plumage. On the national scene Porter fared much better, winning both a Pulitzer and a National Book Award in 1966 for her *Collected Stories*. Today her stories are the only ones by a Texas author that are routinely included in anthologies of American literature.

In the nineties signs of a growing recognition of Porter's Texas roots have begun to appear, thanks to the efforts of academics exploring Porter's life and art and to a general reawakening of interest in Texas culture in the years following the sesquicentennial. There is, for example, a statue of Porter at San Antonio's Sea World, a somewhat surprising site, perhaps, until you realize that Harcourt-Brace, her publisher, used to own this aquatic amusement park. More significantly, her home-town of Kyle, a little one-exit-ramp burg on I-35, twenty miles south of Austin, now boasts both a historical marker summarizing Porter's life and a little museum located in the modest frame house where she lived from 1892 till 1901.

Callie Russell Porter was born on May 15, 1890, in a small frontier community named Indian Creek, Texas, near Brownwood, about 150 miles northwest of Austin. Her mother died when Callie was not quite two years old, and the father, Harrison Boone Porter, handsome, emotionally fragile, and utterly grief-stricken, moved back home with his four small children to his own mother's house at 508 W. Center Street in Kyle. Callie's grandfather Asbury D. Porter had died long before she was born. It was from her grandmother Catherine Ann Skaggs Porter, austere, loving, and authoritarian, that Porter eventually took her public name.

According to "Notes on the Texas I Remember," written for the *Atlantic Monthly* when she was eighty-five, the six-room house "of a style known as Queen Anne, who knows why?" was one with "no features at all except for two long galleries, front and back galleries—mind you, *not* porches or verandahs. . . ." These, she wrote, were covered with honeysuckle and roses and provided a wonderful venue for repose and conversation and iced tea and "tall frosted beakers of mint julep, for the gentlemen, of course." Gentlemen consuming mint julep on flower-embowered galleries is straight out of southern plantation mythology, and Porter, here and in her fiction about her family, ratchets up the social level several notches to attain a grander personal myth along the lines of Porter as the last of the southern belles.

A visitor to the little museum is likely to find the house's six rooms quite small and those "galleries" much less impressive than the ones in Porter's imagination. The museum occupies a small front living room and an even smaller adjoining dining room. Family photos, including some quite good ones of the young Callie Porter, as well as a smattering of books and magazine articles by and about Porter that lie open for perusal, are the chief objects on view. The front yard contains one remnant of cultural interest: an "upping" block, a small boulder about two feet high that was used to assist women in climbing aboard horses before the automobile era.

The Porter historical marker is located to the left of the Kyle City Hall. Installed in 1990, it imparts some of the basic information about Porter's life but contains one misleading statement:

"Following a brief failed marriage, she left Texas in 1915." Porter herself was particularly unreliable about that early marriage. Transacted when she was just a few days past her sixteenth birthday, it lasted nine years, seven of which she spent in residence with her husband, John Henry Koonst, who was from a prominent ranching family from Inez, Texas, near Victoria. Porter was married four times in all, had many lovers, sent nude photographs of herself to her family, and was once lifted and carried aloft like a trophy at a glittering literary gathering in New York by the famous Welsh poet Dylan Thomas. The Porter plaque makes no mention, of course, of any of this sort of history.

Another point of interest can be found in the Kyle Cemetery, about two miles south of town on Old Stagecoach Road. Here rest the remains of the grandmother and grandfather. A ten-foot-high granite sculpture marking their graves consists of two columns, one labeled "Mother," one "Father," with their names and dates of birth and death. Below, on the base, we read "Reunited." The two columns are crowned with an embellished arch. A student of mine who once visited this site for a class assignment wrote that the columns were those of the plantation the Porters never had in life.

Porter's grandmother figures in several of her stories set in and around Kyle. A powerful matriarch, she embodied the precepts of her generation, which Porter affectionately called the Old Order: the importance of religious instruction, family social standing, and traditional values. Porter both loved and feared her grandmother, and this woman's death, in 1901, was another crucial shock in her childhood, the loss of a second maternal figure before the little girl had reached puberty. Porter in fact witnessed her grandmother's death, an event that occurred during a trip the two made to Marfa in West Texas. Her grandmother suffered a stroke, and the eleven-year old Callie was permitted to wander in and out of the bedroom where the grandmother lay dying. This and other childhood incidents appear in Porter's fiction set in

Kyle, usually altered in some way but clearly discernible as being rooted in her experience.

It appears that Porter's early life was sufficiently fraught with both familial and cultural difficulties to make her feel it necessary to leave Texas for good. An early letter from her brother Paul, written on March 23, 1909, neatly sums up everything her family (its male members, at any rate) thought about women and their roles. The letter was apparently provoked by one Porter had written her brother complaining about some aspect of her marriage. By this time she was almost nineteen and had been married for nearly three years.

Early in the letter Paul tries to account for the "vehemence" of the letter she had written him. He speculates: "What was the trouble; had JK [John Koontz] asserted himself in contravention of the laws or rather, rights of woman. Poor old JK. He is probably an h.p. suffragist [i.e., henpecked] at home any way if merly [sic] for the sake of peace." The rest of the letter contains numerous arguments of the day against women's getting the ballot or doing anything except marrying, staying home, and having children. Near the end, Paul writes, "You say women are slaves; bound by routine and unappreciated labor. I should call them the White Mans [sic] Burden," using Rudyard Kipling's famous line about British imperialism. Paul wanted to keep women on a pedestal ("A man loves a woman on a pedestal"). At the end of the letter he waxes downright liturgical: "It matters little whether women vote or not, as man is boss now will he be then; finis."

Porter rebelled too against the strict Protestantism of her early upbringing, both in her later bohemian lifestyle and, earlier, in 1910, by converting to Catholicism, her first husband's faith and the bane of southern Protestants. She also resisted the rigidity and sometimes cruelty of racial stratification of that time and place. In an uncompleted short story of 1933-1934, tentatively titled "The Man in the Tree," Porter told of a lynching and how it affected the family of a little girl based upon herself. The child's reaction to the lynching is one of disgust and a desire to flee such a place where such a miscarriage of justice could occur: "I—I—I'm going to leave . . . get as far away as I—I can . . . I w-won't stay in this filthy country . . . . I won't s-stay here and—and—be murdered too!" In 1956 she stated in a letter that she had "left my native land to get away from . . . the Negro Question."

In 1914, when she was twenty-four, Porter made her first attempt to leave Texas. She spent several months in Chicago, where she landed a few bit parts in movies, but by 1915 was back in Texas. She spent some time in a sanitarium near San Angelo, recovering from a brush with tuberculosis, and in 1917 got a job writing society pieces and reviews for the *Fort Worth Critic*. The following year she took a job in Denver with the *Rocky Mountain News*. She came down with the virulent influenza that was sweeping the country and was so close to dying the newspaper prepared her obituary. In 1919 she moved to Greenwich Village, and the next year she made the first of numerous trips to Mexico, where she met a lot of famous people, including director Sergio Eisenstein, poet Hart Crane, and painter Frida Kahlo. As different from Kyle as it could possibly be, ancient, exotic, Catholic Mexico informed her earliest triumphs in fiction, stories such as "María Concepción" (1922) and "Flowering Judas" (1930). Through the rest of the twenties and thirties, Porter lived a nomadic existence, traveling to and sometimes staying for extended periods in the Northeast, Bermuda, Madrid, Paris, Berlin, and other locales.

After being away from Texas for nearly a decade, Porter began to rummage through her early life for material for fiction. In the late twenties she began an uncompleted novel titled "Many Redeemers," which dealt with family history and remembrance. Much of this material would find its way into stories published in the mid-thirties and on into the forties. It was necessary, it appears, for her to travel thousands of miles and live in faraway places before she could return, in her writing, to the landscape of her childhood. "My time in Mexico and Europe," she wrote in a

1954 essay, "served me in a way I had not dreamed of, even, besides its own charm and goodness: it gave me back my past and my own house and my own people—the native land of my heart."

Porter had always kept close ties with her family through letters, and in 1936 she returned to Texas for a visit. This was a time of both artistic maturity and personal reconciliation with her father, from whom she had been estranged since leaving her first marriage. The two of them journeyed to her mother's grave at Indian Creek, a moving experience for Porter and one that led to her decision to be buried there herself when the time came. On another visit to Texas about a year later, Porter and her father returned to the house in Kyle: "My father and I visited the dreary little place at Kyle, empty, full of dust, decayed, even smaller than I remembered it," she wrote to a childhood friend. The two also attended an Old Settlers' Reunion in San Marcos, where she was reminded powerfully of what the generation of the Old Order meant to her. In a letter to her friend Josephine Herbst, the novelist, Porter commented, "The world I was brought up in taught me nothing about the world I was to live in, but as I looked around me, I thought, these people are strong, and they are my people, and I have their toughness in me, and that is what I can rely upon."

The trips home complemented the creative journeys back to the past that Porter had been undertaking in her fiction. The results were the "Miranda stories," as they came to be called, some of which were written abroad, before the visits to Texas, and some afterward. "The Grave," for example, an American classic, appeared in 1935. In it Porter tells the story of two children, Miranda, a surrogate for herself, and her older brother, Paul. The children explore an empty graveyard and discover, through Paul's killing of a pregnant rabbit, profound truths about birth and death. The story is located solidly and unforgettably in the Kyle countryside of 1903. In all there are nine Miranda stories. Six of them, grouped under the heading "The Old Order," were collected in *The Leaning Tower and Other Stories* (1944). Another, "The Fig

Tree," though not published until 1960, was written much earlier. Finally, there are the two short novels, "Old Mortality" and *Pale Horse, Pale Rider*. Taken together, the nine works trace the education and maturing of a girl from age six or seven through her first marriage at seventeen and her near-death a few years later. They constitute a kind of shadow novel, among the best and most lasting of Porter's work, her own well wrought, unromanticized Old South of memory and desire.

Porter's personal and artistic reconciliation with Texas fared better than her public one. In the late fifties she had a keenly disappointing experience with the University of Texas. At the behest of Harry Ransom, then the vice president and provost of the university, Porter was invited to Austin in 1958 to deliver a lecture in the English department's "Program in Criticism." By this and other inducements—including a position as writer-in-residence—Ransom hope to secure her literary papers for a new library then under construction (now the Flawn Academic Center). Porter enjoyed the visit, renewed contacts with old friends from Kyle, and left with the conviction that the new library (or at the very least a room in that library) was going to be named after her. She held this conviction for over a year, writing to one friend that she thought having a library bearing her name would be a greater honor than winning the Nobel Prize; she even said that she envisioned being buried in the library. During this period the university continued negotiating with her for a position as visiting writer. Things got so far along that her schedule for the fall 1959 semester was set: "Short Story Workshop" at ten on Mondays, Wednesdays, and Fridays and "The Modern Short Story" at nine on Tuesdays, Thursdays, and Saturdays (a perfectly wretched schedule, by the way). Then everything unraveled, negotiations broke down in a fiasco of confusion and misunderstandings, and once again Porter felt estranged from her native state. The whole issue of her literary remains was settled in 1967, when the Katherine Anne Porter Room at the University of Maryland's McKeldin Library was established.

At long last, and quite late in her life, Porter received some measure of public approbation in Texas. In 1976 Howard Payne University in Brownwood, near the place of her birth, hosted a literary symposium in her honor, and Porter gratefully attended. Her future biographer, Joan Givner, wrote of Porter's reading at the symposium: "There was a feeling as she read that something had come full circle for Katherine Anne Porter on this day. A pattern had been completed, all loose ends gathered and tucked in, and nothing lost."

Before Porter's death in 1980 she had made arrangements for her final return to Texas. She had purchased a simple wooden coffin from an Arizona artisan, and, following cremation, her ashes were buried in the coffin beside her mother's grave in Indian Creek. The verse on the tombstone is from one of her favorite authors, T. S. Eliot, and was also the motto of Mary Queen of Scots, whom she admired: "In my end is my beginning."

William Humphrey:
Last of the Southern
Belle-Lettrists

F irst things first: his name was William Humphrey, not Humphries as I have heard absolutely hundreds of people say who should know better. There must be something in Texas linguistic patterns that makes people want to pluralize that name.

Second, and much more importantly, William Humphrey's death in 1997 at age seventy-three marks the end of a rich tradition in Texas writing, one whose like we shall not see again. The reasons are both historical and cultural. Humphrey, born in 1924 in Clarksville, Red River County, in the far northeastern corner of the state, grew up in a southern community almost indistinguishable from that of William Faulkner's Lafayette County in Mississippi. The main cash crop was cotton, and the hills and forests in the surrounding countryside afforded fine

venues for hunting. Humphrey's first novel, following an appren-
ticeship in short fiction capped by the publication, in 1953, of *The
Last Husband and Other Stories*, was *Home From the Hill*, published in
1958. Two years later it was made into a successful Hollywood
melodrama starring Robert Mitchum and Eleanor Parker. The
novel bore strong Faulknerian influences in its syntactical complexity and its fondness for yarn-spinning and hunting lore.

In 1965 Humphrey published what I think is his best novel,
The Ordways, which took the measure of the entire legendary matter of the Lone Star state. In this pan-Texas novel, Humphrey
begins with an epic account of the coming of the original
Ordway from the war-torn South to start anew in Texas, just over
the border from the Red River. Humphrey's description of the
perilous crossing of the river is one of the best sequences in all of
his fiction. This novel also contains the definitive rendering of
Decoration Day, an event of considerable importance in rural
Texas of the past, a day, usually in May, when families and neighbors gathered at the local cemetery to clean up the graveyard and
pay homage to both the past and the present. The highlight of
Decoration Day was dinner on the grounds, a feast of southern
cooking that left everybody grateful for having been born in the
South.

The main thrust of the novel, however, is the wanderings of
protagonist Sam Ordway, who undertakes a picaresque search to
recover his son who has been stolen by a family who lost their
only boy. Sam makes his way from safe, secure, tree embowered
East Texas to dangerous cities like Fort Worth and then to the
stark, empty, treeless prairies of cattle country out west, where, in
a hilarious send-up of cowboy lore, the cowpunchers turn out to
be gay caballeros. Sam eventually finds his long lost son, grown
up and living in a hacienda in the Valley, fully acculturated to
Hispanic Texas.

Other novels and collections of stories followed. *A Time and A
Place*, containing some of his best stories, came out in 1968. *Proud
Flesh*, a novel, appeared in 1973; *Hostages to Fortune*, 1984; and *No

Resting Place, 1989. His *Collected Stories* appeared in 1985. There were books about fishing: *The Spawning Run,* 1970, and *My Moby Dick,* 1978, made honorable additions to the anglers' bookshelf. His last book, *September Song,* published in 1992, was a collection of stories. In all there were thirteen books. He was not without honor in his home state, on three occasions receiving prizes from the Texas Institute of Letters for individual books; and in 1996, he won the Lon Tinkle Award for Lifetime Achievement, but he was too ill to attend the annual meeting.

Though Humphrey rarely returned to Texas, in the mid-1970s he revisited his home town, and the result was one of his best books, the memoir, *Farther Off from Heaven* (1977), which provides a definitive portrait, from a child's perspective, of Clarksville in the 1920s and 1930s. His father, a figure of considerable personality and physical charm, was a world-class auto mechanic at the beginning of the auto age. To diagnose what ailed a car, he would lie atop the hood, listening to the engine as the owner slowly drove through the streets of Clarksville. The changes in small-town life wrought by the advent of the automobile have rarely been depicted as thoroughly or as charmingly. The father also instructed his son in the rituals and joys of hunting game in the nearby woods. Added to the intimate portrait of a child's view of childhood and the mysterious adult behavior which he lacks the experience and even language to uncode, is Humphrey's retrospective look back at a lost world. In one dazzling passage, he defines the new East Texas against the old East Texas:

> Gone were the spreading cotton fields I remembered, though this was the season when they should have been beginning to whiten. The few patches that remained were small and sparse, like the patches of snow lingering on in sunless spots in New England in March and April. The prairie grass that had been there before the fields were broken for cotton had reclaimed them. The woods were gone—even Sulphur Bottom, that wilderness into which

my father had gone in pursuit of the fugitive gunman: grazing land now, nearly all of it. For in a move that reverses Texas history, a move totally opposite to what I knew in my childhood, one which all but turns the world upside down, which makes the sun set in the East, Red River County has ceased to be Old South and become Far West. I who for years had had to set my Northern friends straight by pointing out that I was a Southerner, not a Westerner, and that I had never seen a cowboy or for that matter a beef cow any more than they had, found myself now in that Texas of legend and the popular image which when I was a child had seemed more romantic to me than to a boy of New England precisely because it was closer to me than to him and yet still worlds away. Gone from the square were the bib overalls of my childhood when the farmers came to town on Saturday. Ranchers now, they came in high-heeled boots and rolled-brim hats, a costume that would have provoked as much surprise, and even more derision, there, in my time, as it would on Manhattan's Madison Avenue.

In this prescient analysis, Humphrey anticipated both the iconography of the TV show *Dallas* (1978) and the Urban Cowboy phenomenon of 1980.

The father's death in an auto accident, when the boy was thirteen, spelled the end of childhood. Humphrey moved with his mother to Dallas and attended Southern Methodist University and the University of Texas without graduating, and eventually ended up in New York state. Like many Texas writers of his generation, Humphrey lived far from his native state but continued to mine his early life there in his writing. He settled in Hudson, New York, and one of the pleasant ironies of that location was that one of his neighbors, with whom he would become friends, was another Texan, Williarn A. Owens, of tiny Pin Hook, Texas, a rural community near Paris, not all that far from Clarksville.

These two Williams, plus a third, William Goyen, created a significant body of Texas writing in the southern tradition. Their three chief books, Goyen's *The House of Breath* (1950), Owens' *This Stubborn Soil* (1966), and Humphrey's *The Ordwavs* (1965) are among the best works of the imagination produced in Texas. Their predecessors were Katherine Anne Porter and George Sessions Perry. Humphrey in particular recognized in Porter a pioneering literary artist. He told her in a letter that every time he sat down to write, he had open before him for inspiration such works of hers as "Old Mortality," "Noon Wine," "The Cracked Looking-Glass," and "The Old Order."

The works of this tradition of southern writers in Texas are deeply, permanently grounded in East Texas, not the West Texas of ranching and cowboy legend so celebrated by the better known trinity of Texas writing, J. Frank Dobie, Roy Bedichek, and Walter Prescott Webb. Porter, Perry, Goyen, and Owens are gone; now Humphrey has joined them. The world they wrote about, in large part, is gone too, and good riddance, many would say. It was the era of tenant farmers and segregation, of unbroken continuity with the Confederate South, of Civil War memories and agricultural poverty. It was a time when Greenville, Texas, had a banner, celebrated then, but later notorious, over one of its main streets that read:

Welcome to Greenville, Texas
The Blackest Land, The Whitest People.

All of these writers, of course, traveled far beyond, in both physical and intellectual distance, the prejudices and provincialisms of their rural East Texas heritage, but they never forgot that this homeland, whatever its shortcomings, also offered things of value, and not least among these was a pattern of remembering and ways of speech, both crucial for such artists as they would become. In the case of the modern and last of the southern writers in Texas, the three Williams, the East Texas that they grew up in changed rather remarkably during their lifetimes. The passage of civil rights legislation, the erosion of an agriculturally based economy, the shift of population in Texas from rural to urban areas, all of these changes and more meant the end of the way of life recorded in these writers' works.

Humphrey's oeuvre will remain an invaluable repository of language and lore, a record and testimony of ways of being in a Texas now mostly vanished.

Pen Pals:
Dobie, Bedichek
and Webb

I n front of the famed Barton Springs Swimming Pool in Zilker Park in Austin, there is something new under the sun: a statue honoring the memory of three men who were neither statesmen nor soldiers, the usual subjects of such public approbation. Passersby wonder out loud who these men are. Few recognize them, but invariably someone will ask, "Which one is LBJ?"

Although many of their books remain in print, to a large number of Texas' whopping 18.4 million population, the names of J. Frank Dobie, Roy Bedichek, and Walter Prescott Webb are either unknown or known in a blurred, confused manner. Among the current generation of students at the University of Texas, few have the faintest conception of these once-revered figures, and finding one who knows anything accurate is rarer than spotting a golden-cheeked warbler at a tractor pull. In a recent section of my "Life and Literature of the Southwest" class (which, by the way, Dobie invented in 1930) I polled my 165 students to see if they knew who Dobie, Webb, and Bedichek were. About ninety-five per cent said they hadn't the foggiest. The shrewder ones guessed that Dobie Mall, a high-rise shopping center that Dobie would have deplored, was named after him, and one student who had attended Bedichek Middle School in Austin recognized the name but did not know why the school bore it. The more detailed the identifications, the more erroneous. Said one student: "J. Frank Dobie—infamous businessman involved with UT who hated the UT Tower." Part of that is true. Dobie wasn't fond of the Tower. Trading on an old joke, he called it "[UT president] Battle's last erection," and said it ought to be laid on its side and a porch put around it, like a ranch house. Another student had another idea about the man who in his lifetime was called Mr. Texas: "J. Frank Dobie—the man after which Dobie Mall is named. He was, I think, a Texas Ranger with some authority. He was an outspoken Racist. I learned that in a class, The History of Mexican Americans in the U.S." The confusion of Dobie with Webb (who wrote a book called *The Texas Rangers*), the thorough mishmash of error, and the politically correct misinterpretation contained in this statement are sobering. Alexander Pope was right: A little learning is a dangerous thing.

The bronze old men belong to Old Texas, and as a recent governor was fond of saying, we live in New Texas. Designed by noted Santa Fe sculptor Glenna Goodacre and installed in the fall of 1994, the statue is an act of public commemoration—and an excellent starting point for newcomers to learn about Texas culture.

The statue is officially named Philosophers' Rock, after a limestone shelf of rock that once stood along the banks of the springs. In its day, the rock was also known as Conversation Rock or, more frequently, Bedichek's Rock or Bedi's Rock. Close friends of the three men always associated it with Bedichek. Wilson Hudson, a

University of Texas English professor and member of the Dobie-Bedichek-Webb inner circle, called it Bedichek's Rock and wrote a splendid couplet in his friend's honor: "Bedichek sat on Bedichek's rock/The water was cold, but Bedi was hot." In a 1967 tribute Hudson observed, "Let Bedichek's rock remain, unaltered in any way, unmarked by a bronze inscription." Nature took care of this sentiment some years later by sweeping the rock away in a flood, but what nature hath wrought, the sculpture hath corrected.

Situated in front of the entrance to the swimming hole, it is a large, looming presence. It depicts three old men engaged in a circle of voluble discourse. One (Bedichek) is holding an open book that contains a Latin inscription: *Amicitianon potest esse ni si in bonis.* Where I went to public school in North Texas they didn't teach Latin, but I have it on good authority that the translation, from Cicero, says: "Friendship is only possible among good people."

Bedichek and Dobie are wearing swimming trunks, and Webb, who did not swim, is standing alongside the rock with his trousers rolled up, like a resolute Prufrock ("I shall wear the bottoms of my trousers rolled"). Although there is no photographic evidence to indicate that it was ever a Webb site, it is appropriate for him to be included in the circle of sages at Barton Springs. Webb did not have to be there physically, and much of what transpired there was communicated to him by Bedi and Dobie, either in conversation or in letters.

The likenesses of the images are in the eyes of the beholder. To me, the statue's Dobie looks a bit like Babe Ruth, and Webb, with his large bald dome, like an alien from a *Star Trek* episode. Bedichek is closest to the mark, bearing some resemblance to an elderly John Mackovic, UT's head football coach. The enormous feet of all three are a problem, but then I think that feet in sculpture usually are. My favorite detail in the statue is a cigarette that Webb, an inveterate smoker, is holding in his right hand. It is surprising that the Austin City Council permitted this violation of the anti-smoking ordinance. It sets such a bad example for our youth. Perhaps it would have better if Webb, who dabbled in real estate, could have been given a cellular phone—emblem of the new Austin. Not far away from the statue is a playground called a "playscape." Children bored with the playscape like to come down and romp on the sculapturescape, though there is a sign prohibiting romping. The tactile quality of the sculpture proves irresistible to children, who climb into the laps of Bedichek and Dobie, kindly bronze grandfathers.

The triumvirate, as they are sometimes grandly called, were intellectuals and writers who asserted the values of the life of the mind at a time when other pursuits tended to dominate the energies of a still-close-to-the-frontier society: agriculture, oil, mercantilism, football. Dobie was the most famous of the three and the most prolific writer. Besides his many years of industrious labor on behalf of the Texas Folklore Society, he published, from 1929 until his death in 1964, a continuous flow of books. Many of them dealt with critters—there was one each on longhorns, mustangs, coyotes, and rattlesnakes—and there were books about the men who lived on the land—*A Vaquero of the Brush Country* and *Coronado's Children*—all looking back to the past. One of his most appealing books is the posthumously published *Some Part of Myself*, a collection of autobiographical essays. Webb, his longtime friend and colleague at the University of Texas, was the foremost western historian of his generation. His books include *The Great Plains*, *The Texas Rangers*, and *The Great Frontier*. Bedichek, the eldest of the three (Dobie and Webb were born the same year, 1888, Bedichek in 1878), was also connected with the University of Texas. For many years he headed the University Interscholastic League, which then, as now, oversaw all public school competitions, from essay writing contests to football games. Bedichek did not write his first book until he was sixty-eight, and he did so then because Dobie and Webb practically confined him to an upstairs room in the house at Webb's Friday Mountain Ranch, southwest of Austin, and told him he couldn't come out until he had written his book. There Bedichek composed *Adventures with a Texas Naturalist*, his best-known work. He went on to complete three more books before his death. With Dobie in the lead, they cornered the market on Texas literature. If they didn't invent Texas writing, and they didn't, they certainly left the impression that they did.

But Dobie, Bedichek, and Webb didn't become legends simply on the basis of their writings. It was their personalities, their roles in the public and the intellectual lives of their era, that clinched their fame. Especially Dobie, for he was the darling of the press and he courted publicity with the ardor of a man running for office. Webb was the quieter, more professorial sort, though, like Dobie, he also chafed at the rituals and duties of academic life. He once wrote Bedichek about what lay ahead on a particular day: "And now it's eight o'clock and I've got to read a goddamned Ph.D. thesis and go to town and hold a seminar and sit on a goddamned faculty club council. It makes me want to stretch sheet iron." Bedi, humorous, philosophical, and gentle, was the glue that cemented the threesome's life-long professional and private friendships.

In the public arena all three were outspoken in defense of civilized values. Dobie garnered headlines with his iconoclastic views and actions. Webb wrote of him, "Dobie is by nature a maverick, and has always been so." Bedichek called him "a sort of gadfly." It appears that Dobie delighted in living up to the labels. His mavericity ranged from grandstanding to serious fulminating against follies he observed in political and public life. Two examples of grandstanding: In 1936, local headlines proclaimed that J. Frank Dobie was going to jail rather than pay a parking ticket. This is Dobie cultivating the civil disobedience persona, sort of a southwestern Thoreau. The real story is a little less dramatic. He did refuse to pay a parking fine, and he wrote the police chief a letter explaining why: "I don't think I'm so high and mighty that I can overrun the law—a man would be a damn fool to try that—but I am protesting my right to park on a street where . . . my car was the only one parked for half a block." Instead of going to jail, he had to type an essay on traffic safety and give police officers a lecture on Texas history so they could explain historical stuff to all the tourists coming through celebrating the Texas Centennial. A second such episode seems more like a stunt than anything else. Late in his life, he wrote a check of $25 to Southwestern University in Georgetown, where he had earned his B.A. many years before. Nothing exceptional about that except he wrote it on a "shake," a wooden shingle, an idea he got from the old hunter Ben Lilly about whom he had written a book. He went with the woman from the University to the bank and when the nonplussed teller asked what she was to do with the shingle, Dobie said, "Cash it!" Dobie was what old-time Texans would call a "character."

He could also, and often did, take on very serious subjects. The board of regents drew many scornful observations from Dobie, the best known of which was a remark in a letter in 1956 defending the campus newspaper, *The Daily Texan*, from censorship. He said of the regents: "They are as much concerned with free intellectual enterprise as a razorback sow would be with Keats's 'Ode on a Grecian Urn.'" Football, a matter of high, almost religious import to most Texans, was a topic about which Dobie had decidedly against-the-grain thoughts. Hearing of a coach who led his football team in prayer before every game, Dobie wrote: "Who believes that God cares whether one bunch of young apes or another one has the most success with an inflated pig bladder?" Though Dobie could invoke the deity when rhetoric called for it, he was on the whole a devout agnostic and detested most preachers. At the funeral of Bedichek, in 1959, Dobie sat at the end of a pew and every time the preacher mentioned "everlasting life," he uttered "No, no" in a voice that could be heard all around him. Webb also held a dim view of professional religionists. One time a preacher inveigled him to give a talk on cowboys and religion. Webb appeared at the appointed time, stood up, said, "I have been asked to speak on the cowboy and his religion. He had none," and then sat down.

The most serious public controversy that they all took part in was the acrimonious debate that occurred at the university in the mid-forties over the firing of President Homer Rainey by the board of regents. Rainey incurred the ire of certain regents because he refused to dismiss four economics professors for their "radical" ideas. The

English department also came under fire for including John Dos Passos' novel *U.S.A.* on a reading list for sophomores. One regent even wanted Bedichek cashiered because of a UIL ruling that negatively affected the athletic eligibility of his two sons, who were then seniors at Orange High School. Dobie, Bedichek, and Webb leapt to the defense of Rainey, and Dobie eventually paid a price for it. His drumbeat of Texan foibles had left him vulnerable to attacks from yahoos. Dobie's "radical" politics—which in Texas at that time meant merely being an outspoken New Dealer and civil libertarian—more than irritated the powers that be. In 1945 Dobie had the gall to argue, in print, that blacks should be given full voting rights, and in a speech in Fort Worth, he declared that he would welcome qualified black students to the University of Texas. Opinions such as these drew criticism in the state legislature and anonymous hate letters like one addressed to "Mr. Dopey," calling him a "decrepit, good-for-nothing old fossil and fool." Bedichek, like Dobie an ardent advocate of such unpopular issues of the day as integration and academic freedom, remarked to Webb in a letter: "Dear Dobie works so hard, and smashes so relentlessly in the daily papers at reactionaries in politics, literature and religion that I know the good Lord is laying up a reward for him in heaven if he fails to connect with it here on earth." The university certainly wasn't laying up any reward. When Dobie, who had been granted numerous leaves of absence over the years, applied for another one for the fall semester of 1947, the administration turned him down. George Sessions Perry couldn't believe that the university had "finally turned its back on great, lovable, intractable Frank Dobie, who for so long a time has been the state's and the university's ambassador to the world."

Dobie's conversion to New Deal liberalism also cost him among his old ranching friends. He had, for example, written portions of *The Longhorns* (1941) at the O'Connor Ranch on the San Antonio River, near Victoria, and had inscribed a first edition of the book in fulsome, friendly terms to his friends and benefactors, the O'Connors. Yet when Dobie died, Kate Stoner O'Connor wrote in this same copy of

The Longhorns: "J. Frank Dobie died in Austin Texas Friday Sep 18-1964—unloved and unmourned—because he defected to the enemy—communism."

In the years since Dobie's death, he has also come under attack in certain literary quarters. Andrew Jolly's novel *A Time for Soldiers* (1976) contains a discussion by two students living in Austin in the 1960s:

"I work for J. Frank Dobie. Do you know him?"

"I know of him."

"He's a doll."

"He's a bore."

"You don't like him?"

"I don't like professional Texans of any sort."

Calling Dobie a "professional Texan" would have been fighting words among Dobie's followers when he was alive.

Dobie takes a much worse drubbing in *George Washington Gómez* (1992), a novel by the dean of Chicano studies, Américo Paredes. In Paredes's novel Dobie appears under the thinly veiled guise of one K. Hank Harvey, the "Historical Oracle of the State," a white-Stetson-wearing windbag, and a garrulous, patronizing racist.

Literary assessments aside, the image of Dobie and friends projected at the Barton Springs statue is a powerful and highly public endorsement of the permanent value of their contributions to Texas intellectual culture. It is interesting to speculate what the three friends would have thought about their own apotheosis in bronze. My guess is that Dobie would have loved being immortalized in public, his vanity being no less than and probably equal to that of most people enamored with the blandishments of fame. After all, he didn't get to be Mr. Texas by being a shrinking violet. And Dobie commented memorably on public statuary. The Littlefield Fountain, at the south end of the campus of the University of Texas, for example, offended him mightily. He described it as "a conglomerate of a woman standing up, with arms and hands that look like stalks of Spanish dagger; of horses with wings on their feet, aimlessly ridden

by some sad figures of the male sex, and various other inane para-
phernalia. What it symbolizes probably neither God nor Coppini
knows." A statue of a spraddle-legged braying burro would have been
more natural, he said. Bedichek was no less interested in public statuary. In a 1941 letter copied to Webb and Dobie, he went into rib-
ald detail about a local statue of a fireman that had once adorned the
south entrance of the Capitol grounds but, because of scandal, had
been removed to an obscure spot on East Sixth Street. Bedichek deli-
ciously described the thing that caught everybody's eye:

> Do you remember how this hideous figure of gigantic
> size, drawing a hose over his hip, appeared, at least from a cer-
> tain point of the compass, to be holding not the nozzle of a
> hose, but something else, stiff and straight, protruding at an
> angle of about forty-five degrees from his inguinal region?

He then told how he and other "dirty-minded boys" construed
the fireman's figure as Priapus bent on having his way with the god-
dess surmounting the dome of the Capitol. State authorities agreed
that the statue had an unfortunate sexual subtext and ordered it
removed. When Bedichek rediscovered it in a grass-grown lot on
East Sixth, he was almost nostalgic in noting "the same extension . . .,
the same threat to virginity, the same eternal erection."

The elegant frankness of Bedichek's observations points to another dimension of the circle of friendship. These were men, not
demigods, and theirs is a story of men with the bark on. Like many
phrases from the past, this one may need explanation. "With the bark
on" means "the unvarnished truth." A tree with the bark off (though
the phrase is never used that way) would be prettified, denatured,
inauthentic. Dobie, Webb, and Bedichek all had the bark on.

Their letters are a bountiful index of their wide variety of interests. Birds, for instance. All three of them were as daft as any
Englishman on the subject of birds. Bedichek wrote and received
hundreds of letters about birds. Birds could move him to ecological
passion: "The red-headed woodpecker is getting scarcer and scarcer

here in Austin, since the damned city and thrice damned telephone company began creosoting their ten times goddamned poles."

They also had a rich sense of humor, and that humor was not infrequently scatalogical, bawdy, risqué. On the rock in the afternoon they didn't always speak of high-minded things. Nor did they in their letters always speak of birds, ideas, and current events. Born in the reign of Good Queen Victoria, they carried with them a certain ingrained reticence in the company of women, but in their letters and conversations they relished outhouse and sexual humor to a fare-thee-well. Bedichek and Webb worked for years on a top-secret collection of dirty anecdotes and jokes that they intended to call "The Privy Papers of Sitting Bull." Their chief source was graffiti on the walls of toilets. In one letter to Webb, Bedichek mentioned having discovered a rhyme so foul that he had, against his will, found himself memorizing it. He wrote another friend about the collection: "We got the darndest assortment of it that you ever heard in your life. But we were ashamed to sign our names to it."

But the letters are a rich compost of folklore, jokes, observations. In 1938, for example, Dobie wrote Bedichek about a near sexual encounter between a male deer and a woman. The woman was a "healthy, mature wife," and one morning she walked outside in the presence of a pet buck on their ranch. "He came up, when he got near the woman smelled her, and tried to mount her." Surprised, the woman said, "I don't know what can be the matter with that deer." "Lady," said the foreman. "I do. It's your condition, and you should recognize the fact in dealing with these animals." The letter goes on to relate another deer-human female incident, in which a man claimed that a male deer could always identify which of fifteen girls was menstruating at any given time. Bedichek's last book, not coincidentally, was called *The Sense of Smell*.

It is safe to say that Bedichek and Dobie, at least, were fascinated with the subject of sex. Bedichek hoped that some day Walt Whitman's influence would be so thorough and liberating that "people can write and talk of sex as naturally as they do of other fundamental appetites." Bedichek took a philosophical interest in excretory and sexual functions. He read the *Kinsey Report* with scrupulous attentiveness and concluded that the greater incidence of sodomy in urban centers had to do with the absence of animals for the purposes of bestiality. He raised prescient questions about the nature of scatological and sexual humor. In one letter he asked, "Why is the Anglo-Saxon word for defecation taboo, and why are there so many funny stories about this natural function?" In the same letter he mentions but does not relate a funny story he had told many friends that involved his dog Hobo's interference in Bedi's own amorous relations with his wife. He mentions a friend of his who, like Montaigne, was so struck by the ludicrous aspects of human copulation that he was overcome by the sheer physical absurdity of the act. There is also a charmingly told whorehouse story. It begins with a mild disclaimer of Dobie's assertion that Bedichek was an authority on whorehouses. When Bedichek was a young man, he writes, he visited a local establishment on West Fourth Street, run by one Dixie Darnell. Bedi engaged the services of one of Dixie's young women only to discover, once in the room, a volume of poetry by Heinrich Heine, one of his favorite poets. The prostitute, of German extraction, was a great fan of Heine's, and for the next several hours they discoursed on the beauties of his verse. Bedichek paid for his time, during which the only thing he removed, he says, was his detachable collar.

Bedichek was also a master of the dirty joke. In a letter to Dobie he told the one about the two cowboys who had been together on the range for too long and who were getting mighty tired of each other's company. One night one of the cowboys made some biscuits that the other cowboy couldn't eat, they were so bad. He said they were so bad their hound wouldn't eat them. But the hound gobbled them right up, and the cook, vindicated, said, "You see, he et 'em all right." "Yes," said the other cowboy, "but he had to lick his ass to take the taste out of his mouth." Such jokes endeared Bedichek to Dobie and Webb.

Dobie was every bit as interested in sexual folklore as he was in cowboys and gold-seekers. One of his research habits was to collect items, stories obtained in interviews, anecdotes, scraps of folk idiom, scholarly articles, newspaper stories, anything pertinent to a topic, and place them in an empty typing-paper box. When the box was full, he had a book. Among his archives at the Humanities Research Center at the University of Texas is a box of clippings and related materials collected for a book to be called "Piss & Vinegar." This is not exactly the usual Dobie title, and what he had in mind was something along the lines of his friends' secret "Privy Papers of Sitting Bull." The box contains dirty jokes going all the way back to Sam Houston, who has always been good copy for Texas historians. One tells of how Houston would ride across Texas with an erection and would camp at the spot where the erection fell limp. Obscure informants sent him jokes and stories, and famous ones, too. John Graves, for example, sent along a limerick about a young lady from Bombay. The joke turned upon the c-word. There was a story about a cowboy whose "dingus" was grabbed by a boa constrictor. Dobie's friend Mody Boatright, also a folklorist and English professor at UT, sent him a Texas brag sexual joke. There was a rancher who boasted that his son weighed sixteen-and-a-half pounds at birth. "My goodness, how much does he weigh now?" asked the listener. "Six and a half pounds." "How can that be?" asked the listener. The rancher said, "We've just had him circumcized."

Also in the box are lists of folk expressions based on Anglo-Saxon words for the familiar excremental functions and numerous unpublished essays. The essays bear titles like "Obscene," "F——," "Sexual Potency," "Why Southern Men Fought for Slavery," "On the Size of Pricks," and so on. There is another on that treasure trove of f and c words, Dobie's favorite modern novel, *Lady Chatterley's Lover,* by D. H. Lawrence. There were essays such as "Knowing That He Was Flesh and Bloud," filled with learned citations from ancient and modern writers. This one he submitted to *Esquire* in 1961. One of the frankest essays was titled "C——: The Word and the Thing." It quoted that self-proclaimed expert on the subject, Henry Miller, and told, among other things, of a famous West Texas historian with whom Dobie had roamed in the bramble. Writes Dobie: "I know one woman with a wonderful c—- whom he tried to persuade but could not." There were stories that he told here that he couldn't tell in his books.

Apparently Dobie's research carried over into film as well, as there is an order form from Enjoyment Unlimited, a company in St. Laurent, Montreal, Canada specializing in 8 m.m. black & white films "for your private collection" with titles like "TV Repairman", "Strip Poker," and "Plumber." "TV Repairman" told the story of a young housewife whose TV breaks while her husband is on the road. The TV repairman fixes the set, and then the woman, discovering that she has no money, "decides to pay the only way she knows."

Dobie, ever the moralist, had a serious purpose apart from the thrill of the word chase. The essays, both fragmentary and complete, always pleaded for honesty and frankness in dealing with natural functions and inveighed against hypocrisy, puritanism, and censorship. In "Obscene" he professed, "I can't for the life of me see that a picture or a piece of writing of civilized nature, often beautiful and more often natural, that stirs the sex impulse is obscene." In "Doing Dirt to Sex" he let it rip: "Like Rabelais, I contemplate only with derision some gut-stuffing, fart-stinking, ballicks-sweating, mouth-snoring, piety-intoning priest, smelling terribly of mortality while pretending to have God by the ear because he professes to deny sex." Like "The Privy Papers of Sitting Bull," "Piss & Vinegar" remained underground, scraps in a box stuffed with the blue, the bawdy, the unnamable, the humorous.

In the end, Dobie, Webb, and Bedichek were men, as Dobie would have said, "out of the old rock." They prided themselves on their connectedness with the earth, for which they have been much celebrated, and to that I would add their connectedness to earthiness, a humor that Chaucer, Rabelais, and Henry Miller, among others, would have admired. Their public contribution to Texas culture is perhaps the place to conclude. Webb, a master of the plain style, said: "My theory holds that the true distinctive culture of a region, in this case of Texas, springs from the soil just as do the plants." Dobie eloquently championed the cause of regionalism in an oft-quoted passage: "If people are to enjoy their own lives, they must be aware of the significances of their own environments. The mesquite is, objectively, as good and as beautiful as the Grecian acanthus." And in a marvelous passage from his *Letters*, which represent Bedichek's best work, he speaks with admirable energy of his commitment to the Austin of Barton Springs, of local knowledge: "Personally, if I have to fight for this country, I will not fight for the flag, or democracy, or private enterprise, or the American 'way of life,' or for any other abstractions, which seem cold as kraut to me. But I will fight to the last ditch for Barton Creek, Boggy Creek, cedar-covered limestone hills, blazing star and bluebonnets, golden-cheeked warblers and black-capped vireos, and so on through a catalogue of the natural environment of Austin, Texas."

The books of the triumvirate are there for readers who seek them, and if you happen to journey to Barton Springs, there the men loom, in all their one-and-one-quarter-size glory, intentionally bigger than life, according to sculptor Goodacre. With its anchored solidity and gravity the statue has a reasonably good chance of outlasting even the springs themselves, if ecological jeremiads prove accurate. Under sun and moon there the old three are, eternally sharing some gem of discourse, a passage from Keats perhaps, or the one about the preacher's wife, some moment of pleasure, something natural that amused them.

John Graves
and the Regionalist
Enterprise

W hen Yankee writers began arriving in Austin in the late seventies, the first thing they wanted to do was meet a Real Texas Writer. Dobie, Bedichek, and Webb—the old lawgivers with names linked like a law firm—were dead, and Larry McMurtry had decamped to the nation's capital, but John Graves was here, and he was out of the old rock, he would do to ride the river with. That was how Yankees talked after they read a little Dobie and a little John Graves. Of course Yankees didn't know diddly about Texas. They thought "hard scrabble" was a challenging board game until they read John Graves and discovered it was just a piece of sorry land. Graves made it seem like a virtue, though, and Yankees really liked that, the idea of land possessing some mythic potential. Yankees fresh from Breadloaf, male, female, and undeclared, all sang his praises. In person, Graves filled the bill, too. Kind, modest, well-read, off-the-cuff, informal, he seemed like a benign uncle. One newcomer even put him in a novel in order for her heroine to have an affair with this Lone Star literary icon. Media maven Bill Moyers came down to Graves" actual hard-scrabble ranch near Glen Rose and asked him a lot of heavy questions about Life, Dirt, Art, etc. and filmed it and showed it on PBS so everybody could feel good about regionalism.

So far as I know, John Graves has not written a crime novel with a clever title. This alone is enough to earn him praise in the contemporary climate of Texas writing. As if Graves needed any warrant. Since the publication of *Goodbye to a River* in 1960, he has occupied the high ground in Lone Star letters. In 1995 the poster for Texas Writers Month, an annual spring hoohaw of increasing decibels, featured Graves sitting at his ancient manual typewriter (a Royal?), bespectacled, besweatered, avuncular: The Writer at Work. In the world of Macs and laptops, the typewriter looked as antique as a branding iron or a wagon wheel. It signified Tradition, the Past, True Grit.

This same photograph serves much the same purpose on the cover of *A John Graves Reader* (1996), a 338 page self-selected anthology and a very welcome addition to the corpus that Graves himself has assessed as not voluminous: a handful of books, and now this, the winnowing by the author of work that he values. About one half of the book consists of material familiar to readers of Graves: Chapter 10 from *Goodbye to a River*,"The Last Running," his well-known short story based on the incident when old Kiowa chiefs, former adversaries, came down to Charles Goodnight's Ranch near Palo Duro Canyon and borrowed a buffalo so they could hunt one last time in the traditional way with arrow and lance; several essays from *From A Limestone Ledge*, all originally *Texas Monthly* pieces, including topics such as fly-fishing, favorite dogs, modest stock-farm ranching (in the cleverly titled "19 Cows"), and drinking (Graves is in favor of spirits if not carried to excess); short remembrances of good friends; the oddly titled "His Chapter," a dead-on portrait of a redneck of great integrity named the Old Fart and one of the best pieces in Graves' *oeuvre* (from *Hard Scrabble*); and other bits gathered from hither and yon.

The familiar image of Graves as a regionalist was not how he started out. His conversion to regionalism occurred in the late 1950s after he returned to Texas from living abroad and took a teaching position at TCU. In 1957 he made a canoe trip down a stretch of the Brazos River: it was to be both a rediscovery of Texas' past and a valedictory to a river that he believed was soon going to be dammed and thereby forever changed (rather like the much wilder river in James Dickey's *Deliverance* of a few years later). The Knopf file at the Humanities Research Center at the University of Texas gives a good picture of the evolution of the narrative. It begins on May 11, 1959, when Graves sent his agent, John Schaffner, a copy of the first draft of Part I. In an accompanying letter he set forth his idea of the book's structure: "Its form is more or less that of a string of beads, the string being the trip-narrative itself and the beads the various digressions in the form of anecdotes, tales, historical commentary, essays, etc." Later in the letter, he returned to his idea of the book: "It is not to be a 'thesis' book; it has no particular axe to grind, though maybe a tomahawk or two as it stands just now. I think I will be able to give it a real unity apart from that picaresque unity furnished by the trip-background, by bringing the various themes into organic relationship to one another."

By the end of the year he had finished Part II. His editor at Knopf, Harold Strauss, pronounced the book "wonderful and beautiful," but felt that Part II was a "little less exciting than Part I." In a long reply Graves defended Part II, arguing in his quiet way that its subject matter, the present as compared to the past of Part I, necessitated a different approach. Graves wrote, "The most striking difference is in technique, but when I considered altering the structure of Part II so as to give it the unity of impact that One has, I found that structure—as it usually does—had grown out of subject matter. The 'dying fall' had imposed itself. The later time in Brazos history extending into the present, which forms a background for Two as the

Indians and the first-coming whites did for One, is for me frag-
mented and somewhat degenerate. The old monolithic people and
things went, and what has replaced them is still chaotic" (January 1,
1960).

The manuscripts reveal that very little of the original parts One
and Two underwent change. There are some changes worth noting,
however, and there were some pitched battles over authorial versus
editorial judgment. One of the contested areas was the chapter-head
epigraphs which Graves had placed at the beginning of each chapter. Louis Gannett, an early reader of the galleys who compared
Graves with Thoreau in an oft-quoted blurb, urged the deletion of
"fancy" chapter-heads as well as omitting many of the literary allusions in the text. He objected in general to what he called "hoity-
toity" language and urged the substitution of more common words
for some of Graves' more recondite diction. On this score, Graves
made a fine rebuttal in a letter to Harold Strauss: "I know that in
Goodbye I attempted a stylistic fusion between colloquial and 'literary' English which would leave me free to run with either hare or
hounds as the occasion dictated." Graves won this round, and the
chapter heads and lofty diction remained.

There was discussion about the most minute details. There was,
for example, back-and-forth on how to spell "Goodbye," and Graves
won that victory, too. Finally, near the end of the copy-editing
process, Strauss wrote Graves a long letter detailing forty-odd
queries and proposed changes. These all had to do with diction,
phrasing, and punctuation. Graves yielded on some points, but held
his ground on others. Commas provided the most drama, and in one
letter Graves set forth his philosophy of comma punctuation. In the
end, Graves prevailed, and the book that was published was over
ninety-eight per cent identical to the original manuscript. Most
importantly, Graves left the structures of Part I (the river's violent
human history) and Part II (the present which threatens the river's
existence—pollution, development, dams, etc.)—as he had conceived them. In every respect, the book was wholly what Graves had
wrought—even down to the cryptic encoding of a stylized figure

eight on the title page. Although it appears to be nothing more than an impressionistic design, it held a special meaning for Graves, as he wrote Strauss in 1959: "I have a kind of cabalistic brand or good-luck symbol—from what cabala I couldn't tell you—and wouldn't mind seeing it used in the book as a decoration."

When *Goodbye to a River* appeared in 1960, I was a sophomore at North Texas State University and hadn't a clue as to how books got made. I thought they derived from inspiration, if I thought about it at all. In any case, without really knowing why, I was beginning to pay close attention to the writing of my native state. This meant reading the book page of the *Dallas Morning News* and the *Times Herald* for leads, and in one or both of these papers I became aware of John Graves. There followed a revolutionary act. Instead of requesting shirts or chinos, the usual Christmas fare, I told my mom that what I wanted for Christmas was a copy of *Goodbye to a River*. At that time the only hard-copy books in our house were a complete set of the *World Book*. We owned a Bible of course, but it was a soft copy. I had an aunt who belonged to a book club, but the only books she ever seemed to get were by Thomas B. Costain.

Among the first readers of *Goodbye to a River*, none was more important than J. Frank Dobie, Mr. Texas himself. Earlier in the year, Graves had met Dobie at his home in Austin. They had hit it off, but Graves knew that Dobie wouldn't pull any punches about the book, that is, assuming he decided to read it at all. Dobie was in poor health at the time. But Dobie did read it and liked it very much and he wrote Graves in September, 1960, telling him: "It's a book I've been waiting for. It could do with fewer Comanche episodes, but every line of interpretation talks to me." Dobie also gave the book a glowing send-off in his syndicated column. His admiration meant much to Graves, who wrote Dobie: "I'm solidly gratified by your letter and your article about my book, and can say without hypocrisy that no other person's approval of that book could mean to me quite what yours does."

Graves' book dovetailed nicely with the dominant tradition in Texas writing. In a sense it validated the entire body of work produced by Dobie, Webb, and Bedichek. Bedichek the philosophical observer of nature, author of *Adventures with a Texas Naturalist*, died in 1959; Webb the historian, author of *The Texas Rangers* and *The Great Plains*, died in 1963, and Dobie, the most prolific and best known of the three, author of a whole shelf of books still in print, the pride of Texana, died in 1964. Within five years the Old Three were gone, but *Goodbye to a River* with its loving evocation of the past and its prescient critique of the present was everything Dobie, Webb, and Bedichek required of a book. It was the culmination of a long tradition.

Goodbye to a River weaves together the three main strands of the triumvirate's work: (1) folk memory and oral history tales, (2) frontier history, and (3) vivid, closely observed details of natural flora and fauna. What Dobie most liked about *Goodbye to a River* was not its evocation of the past or even its faithful rendering of the natural world. What he liked was its commentary on the present. Dobie, a keen observer of the contemporary scene, took decline and fall as his theme: the loss of freedom, the passing of the Old Order, the tendency towards a superficial mass-produced culture that led him to lash out against modern follies such as juke boxes and television. Here, for example, is Dobie on contemporary culture, in a 1944 letter to Bedichek: "There is something metallic & barren about an awful lot of American citizens. Their minds are puerile, like the funnies, the pictures, and the horseplay humor they feed on. I always take great delight in people of the soil. Otherwise, I find that more & more I want them to be civilized." Such remarks would have made a fine epigraph for *Goodbye to a River*.

Like most Texas writers at one time or another, Graves pondered the perils of regionalism; he didn't want to be trapped entirely within the provincial ethos of the past. In short, he was worried about the reach his book might have. He didn't want its audience confined to the Southwest, to Texas, to Somervell County. And he certainly didn't want to be locked into some popular misconceptions evoked by the word "Texas." His publisher Alfred A. Knopf wrote Graves in

1959 of an associate who told him that "a book about Texas to be popular has to be very corny."

Graves' book, of course, was anything but corny. It proposed a serious critique of national, not just Texan, culture in the 1950's. *Goodbye to a River*, in fact, belonged in the company of less regional works of that era that sought to define the fifties zeitgeist: *The Organization Man, The Lonely Crowd, The Man in the Gray Flannel Suit.* There was at that time a great deal of fretting about, and fear of, conformity, mass culture, affluence, American smugness, a sense of a vast national lethargy of the spirit. On the cultural front the only counter action was the beatniks. In San Francisco Allen Ginsberg was apt to use four letter words in his poetry and give readings in the nude. The year Graves took his canoe down the Brazos, Jack Kerouac published *On the Road*, the ultimate anti-bourgeois novel of the period. In Texas there were no beatniks. Well, actually there were four beatniks, but they were never together at the same time and in the same place to form much of anything, let alone a literary movement. Young Larry McMurtry, oddly enough, was a beatnik at North Texas State University for a month or so during his senior year, in 1957, when he founded a little journal called *The Coexistence Review* and wrote protest poetry that hit all the fifties themes in lines such as these that attacked the enemies of freedom and individualism: "You who believe absolutely every word of scripture tv commercials the/ reader's digest dale carnegie billy graham and popular songs./ run on to your sleazy heaven and check the trade in on halos for me,/ in case I can't find a flannel suit to match my SOUL." The larger influences of the beatnik revolt were contagious, and you could catch it even if you were a world away, in Texas.

John Graves was by no means a beatnik. He was forty that pivotal year of 1960, a veteran of World War II—a man who had seen more of the South Pacific than he cared to, and who had traveled widely in Europe and lived in Spain and New York and a number of other exotic locales. But Graves' book does carry a critique of American culture in the late 1950s similar to that of the young

McMurtry and the Beats in its celebration of solitude and individualism in an era of self-satisfied conformity. By the time Graves nears the completion of his month-long sojourn on the Brazos made mighty by his imagination, he is by his own account unshaven, a bit ragged-looking, a little ripe, and a kind of down-home, extremely well read, back country figure—all right, a beatnik of sorts—who is almost scary to some of the pampered proto-yuppies along the shore.

In his book the symbol of the new America, to which the lone figure on the river is a living rebuke, is television. Graves sees television as the enemy of lived reality. Near the end of the narrative he describes two old women in an overheated room, their rheumy eyes glued to a television show that, as described, is probably "American Bandstand." Outside is the river, the weather, the primordial reality of nature. Inside is the simulacrum of televised experience, a dazed and glazed mass consciousness supplanting whatever perceptions the women might have been able to muster on their own, a sort of invisible frontal lobotomy that television is performing on what used to be their minds. In the 1950s Americans began to substitute television for the out of doors. They turned up the thermostats and watched weather on TV. *Goodbye to a River,* though, is above all a book about weather. Hemingway once urged John Dos Passos to "put some goddamned weather" in his next book, and it must be said that *Goodbye to a River* has all of the outdoor elements that anybody could want: Weather closely watched, weather thoroughly lived in, weather felt intuitively by the reader.

In his own quiet way, Graves was ahead of his time. In the era of big-finned gas guzzlers, Graves addressed issues that would later become central to the environmental movement. The word he used was "conservation." Later in the decade, writers like Edward Abbey would heat up the discourse, and new words such as ecology would gain hold. Graves was markedly ahead of the curve on these issues, but never strident, never militant in his proclamations.

In choosing to locate his book in an obscure part of the state, on a river largely unknown to outsiders, Graves was performing an act of personal repatriation. For most of his adult years he had lived an expatriate life. Now he was home. Texas writers of that era can be divided into those who left home for good and those who stayed put. Graves was one of the ones who left and then returned. Stanley Walker, a Texan who'd made it big in New York journalism, preceded him in this circular journey and wrote a book about the experience—giving up the fast track in the Big Apple for the quieter rhythms of a ranch near Lampasas. He called that book *Home to Texas.* *Goodbye to a River* is very much in this vein, a point that is made explicit in the full text of one of the drafts of the "Note on the Author" that Graves wrote, at his editor's behest, for inclusion in the first edition. Only a couple of sentences of it were published, but the complete version sums up better than anything else what the author himself thought his book was about:

> *Goodbye to a River* is in a sense a homecoming book, a reexamination of childhood home things seen through eyes sharpened by years and long absence. Having spent nearly a half of his lifetime away from the Southwest, in places as diverse as New York and Spain and Mexico and Paris and the Canaries, its author says that he never managed to rid himself of an underlying, dozing, provincial consciousness of shotguns and fly rods and cedars and live oaks and mesquites and redbirds and Hereford cattle and people who speak with quiet nasal flatness from their palates. When he returned home not long ago, that consciousness came awake. This book is an attempt at its definition.

And it is on the strength of this first book that Graves' reputation has glided all these years, as sure and as reliable as that canoe that he rode upon the river. If *Goodbye to a River* holds the key to all of Graves' other regional work, there is still much of value to be found in his lesser-known writings. Perhaps the best single expression of his affection for nature and the past, linked as they are in his imagination, occurs near the end of "Self-Portrait with Birds," an essay that concludes with these words lamenting the fact that he was born much too late to see what Fitzgerald in *The Great Gatsby* called the green breast of the New World: "What I myself seem to damn mainly, though, is just not having seen it. Without any virtuous hindsight, I would likely have helped in the ravaging as did even most of those who loved it best. But God, to have viewed it entire, the soul and guts of what we had and gone forever now, except in books and such poignant remnants as small swift birds that journey to and from the distant Argentine and call at night in the sky."

In *Goodbye to a River* and his other regional writing, Graves found a way to deal with belatedness—the problem that besets every serious writer. This struggle becomes very clear in the new collection which self-discloses the other John Graves, the internationalist writer, the expatriate. By the late fifties Graves had basically given up on trying to be a big frog in a big pond: meaning Europe, meaning Hemingway, meaning the Major Leagues. Instead he found his usable tradition in his own hard scrabble backyard—Texas regional writing. Here, he could best the Old Fathers. The fact is, the Old Fathers didn't offer that much competition. The best work of DobieBediWebb lay in essays, not in whole books (though with Webb one might argue otherwise, but try reading *The Texas Rangers* sometime as literature). The fragmentary nature of Dobie's accomplishment was particularly striking. For all of his energy and importance, Dobie never produced a book that one could indisputably claim was a regional masterpiece. Nor did Bedichek or Webb.

A John Graves Reader reveals that there have always been two John Graves. One is the Texan described above, the quintessential regional writer. The other is the expatriate writer, following in a grand but decidedly well-marked tradition. Those curious about Graves' earlier career have always known vaguely about the other John Graves, the one before *Goodbye to a River* cast the regional die. Before he wrote about Texas, he wrote about places like Spain and Mexico, and those stories, several of which were anthologized in prestigious collections, could only be read if you took the trouble to dig them out of library stacks. Now here they all are, or rather, the ones that Graves has chosen to bring back into public view. There was also, about that other Graves, always talk of an unpublished novel, maybe two unpublished novels. Graves has decided to include several chapters from one such novel, "A Speckled Horse," forty-six pages in all. All of this makes for very interesting reading indeed.

My favorite of the expatriate stories is "The Green Fly," a well-crafted tale of a graduate student who goes to Spain to write his dissertation. It's a lovely life. He writes in the morning at a hacienda high in the mountains, and in the afternoons he fly-fishes for trout in pure, swift-running mountain streams, accompanied by a dignified old doctor who sided with the anti-Franco party during the Spanish Civil War. In the evenings they dine well, drink excellent wines, and talk philosophy. Into this peaceful ritualistic order comes an American couple, the graduate student's tweedy professor and his perfectly dressed wife. The professor is a pure type of a certain kind of academic: pompous, pretentious, and priggish. The story's climax turns upon the professor's crass attempt to pay the old doctor for removing a fishhook from his hand. At that, the graduate student profanely denounces the professor, and the story ends. Wonderful story. Several of the expatriate stories, as Graves himself notes in a brief introduction, involve an older man-younger man pattern. Graves works some nice variations on the theme of male mentorship in stories like "The Aztec Dog" and "A Valley." In all of these the rhythms and manner of Hemingway are unmistakably present. In an author's note to "In the Absence of Horses" Graves speaks of the difficulty of finding anything fresh to say about bullfighting, the reason being, of course, that this terrain is presided over by "the immense shadow of Papa Hemingway, not a comfortable place to reside, at least for me." Still, this is a fine story about the degradation of bullfighting into an undisciplined communal blood-bath.

Graves says in the introduction that he has taken the opportunity provided by the occasion of this book to make stylistic alterations in some stories, and in particular, of the unpublished novel "A Speckled Horse." In a note to that work, he makes an extremely interesting observation regarding his agent's reaction to some of the material. The agent, he says, was "horrified by the novel when I sent it to him. I had in part expected this reaction, because he was gentle, civilized, and effete, and the book was quite masculine, with hard edges. It also lacked political correctness, and although the growth of that mutation of puritanism into a reigning force was still in the future, its rudiments were active back then, especially in the Northeast." No doubt.

Since we only have pieces of the novel, it is hard to say much definitive about such fragments as Graves gives us of what he calls a "failed, partly autobiographical novel." He has rearranged the chapters into chronological order, he says, having originally planned them to be non-sequential, the result of "an addiction to the work of Faulkner and of Ford Madox Ford." In any event, the pieces as presented here trace the life of a combat veteran named Richard Hill Cavitt, from his wounding in Saipan through rather philosophically bleak post-war musings in New Mexico (with some vividly drawn scenes) through more musings in Mallorca, including a sex scene (rare in Graves, in fact I can think of no other) done overmuch in the Hemingway manner when Hemingway wasn't writing at the top of his form: "Without his willing it Hill's eyes flicked down the length of her body and back up again to her face momentarily, and something moved far down inside him. It had been a long time. He knew that she knew the thing had moved inside of him, and knew that she liked that."

I wish his novel had been published. Somebody—Graves thinks it was Larry McMurtry—once observed that, unlike most writers, Graves hadn't published his failures. Now Graves has answered that charge with what he hopes is the best of his work, published and unpublished, that can be encompassed in a single volume. The resultant book, as I said a few thousand words back, is very interesting indeed.

"Urban by God": Billy Lee Brammer's Texas

For over three decades now, Billy Lee Brammer's *The Gay Place* has carried the aura of a legend. The legend is partly true. Brammer was a supremely talented writer who wrote one very good novel but was never able to write another. Frustration and anxiety dogged his subsequent efforts, and his life ended prematurely at age forty-eight from a drug overdose. According to this version of the legend, he belongs in the company of such promising one-book authors as Thomas Heggen (*Mister Roberts*) and Ross Lockridge (*Raintree County*), novelists whose early triumphs were never duplicated and whose lives came to ruin from, among other causes, the pressures attendant upon their initial successes. Neither Heggen nor Lockridge ever wrote that crucial second book, and both eventually committed suicide.

Like Heggen and Lockridge, Brammer certainly felt a sense of anxiety occasioned by the lofty praise of his first novel. It garnered glowing remarks from the kind of names that matter. Gore Vidal, for example, proclaimed it "an American classic," and David Halberstam ranked it alongside *All the King's Men* and predicted it would be read "a hundred years from now." Such praise registered strongly upon the young author. When Larry L. King read to Brammer Halberstam's rave review from the *New York Times Book Review* in 1961, Brammer responded, "Oh, Jesus, now they'll be waiting to pin my ears back if I can't do it again." But *The Gay Place* was not a commercial success. It went into a second printing—and then onto the remaindered table.

Brammer's decline and death have more to do with the stark and indisputable fact of prolonged drug addiction than with the anxiety of achievement. His second wife, Dorothy Browne, has said: "Tragic? Yeah. But only at the very end. And it certainly didn't have anything to do with Lyndon Johnson. It had to do with addiction." Many of Brammer's friends insist that his life was essentially a happy one. He enjoyed life immensely, say numerous observers. Film director Robert Benton, a long-time friend of Brammer and his first wife, Nadine, says, "I don't think Billy went through the sense of torment that Fitzgerald went through. I never knew him when he was not some kind of extraordinary optimist, or wasn't filled with a kind of hope or generosity toward everyone around him." Journalist Jan Reid reports that Brammer never exhibited any signs of "that tortured writer sense about him." Ronnie Dugger, Edwin (Bud) Shrake, Larry L. King, Willie Morris, and Gary Cartwright all remember Brammer with great respect and affection. Recalling Brammer's habit of staying up all night writing, Shrake has observed: "If it was five a.m. and you wanted company, you could count on Bill." There is also a sense of loss, of wasted gifts. King has written of the frustration he felt upon hearing of Brammer's death: "And I felt, too, a quick surge of irrational anger. But even as I recognized it as such, a part of me began yelling at my old friend's ghost: *Goddammit, Billie Lee, why'd you get yourself so screwed up you only left to the world a fraction of your talent?"*

For Brammer was a card-carrying intellectual and a writer's writer. His conversations were an important part of his influence. Willie Morris recalls that "the long talks we had at his house or under the trees at Scholz's were, along with talks with Ronnie [Dugger], the first real conversations I ever had with anyone about the power and beauty of the written word." Journalist Kaye Northcott has suggested that Brammer "was just as important to the Austin underground as Ginsberg was to the Beats. They were both mentors, teaching the impatient how to cope with an imperfect world." A "middle-of-the-road anarchist" in Gary Cartwright's phrase, Brammer "was always ahead of the game. Instead of writing, he was cueing the rest of us on what to expect."

Born in 1929 in Dallas, Brammer enjoyed a conventional middle class upbringing. He played sports at Sunset High and sometime in early adolescence discovered a life-long passion for books. He attended North Texas State College, which, though no Harvard or Yale, was stimulating enough if you read and yearned for contact with ideas. There Brammer wrote columns for the campus newspaper, adopting a sophisticated, more-superior-than-thou tone regarding such local campus fixtures as fraternity and sorority life, and there he met Nadine Cannon, whom he married in 1950. Following graduation in 1952, he held newspaper jobs in Corpus Christi and then in Austin, where, in 1955, he became associate editor of the sprightly new anomaly in the Texas of that era, a liberal weekly called *The Texas Observer.* Life in Austin in the mid-fifties, by all reports, was pleasant to the point of rapture. The small capital city of some 180,000 citizens had a legislature full of colorful solons and lobbyists, and it had a university growing in prestige. In such a stimulating atmosphere Brammer began to work on a novel called "The Heavy Honeyed Air," set in Austin. It never came together, though. It consisted of isolated pieces and somehow just didn't work.

In 1955, too, the catalytic event in Brammer's life and work occurred: he joined the staff of Senator Lyndon B. Johnson and moved to Washington. The senator hired Nadine as well; hiring couples was a generous Johnsonian habit not without its benefits to the senator; his aides worked very long hours, and this way, it was all in the family. Johnson's vitality energized Brammer, stimulated his imagination, led him to work assiduously on The Novel. Larry L. King remembers those days of intense creativity: "When we were young Capitol Hill flunkies together, Billie Lee wrote *The Gay Place* on candy bars and hot Jell-O water swigged from a milk bottle; he claimed the strange combination gave him 'energy rushes.' He obviously found stronger fuels later on, though I am convinced that in those distant days [1958-1961] Billie Lee was no dopehead."

In 1957 Brammer got a publisher's advance on the basis of "Country Pleasures," a short novel about a governor named Arthur Fenstemaker who visits a movie set in far West Texas, has a fling with a female aide, and dies in bed. The contract was intended to provide the means whereby Brammer would complete a longer novel about the Governor. The result, in 1961, was *The Gay Place*. The title, of course, sounds faintly archaic now, the word "gay" having undergone a permanent sea change within just a few short years of the book's publication. The author's name on the title page is of interest, too. It read "William Brammer," an East Coast emendation of his Christian name, Billy Lee. A letter to Brammer from a Houghton Mifflin editor, Dorothy de Santillane, explained the company's position in detail:

> No one, I repeat no one, up here thinks "Billy Lee" is possible. With all respect to your parents who gave it to you with such evident love (it is a very "loving" name) it has not the strength and authority for a novel which commands respect at the top of its voice.
>
> We are going to call it "by B. L. Brammer" and if we are asked we shall answer "Bill L. Brammer." This is official.

The Texas literati have made much of this change. William Broyles, founding editor of *Texas Monthly*, has remarked that Brammer was "still Billy Lee, no matter if editors in Boston mistakenly believed that people named Billy Lee didn't write great books." Yet in his signed articles for the *Texas Observer* he used the name Bill Brammer. The preference for Billy Lee seems at times something like inverse snobbery to claim him as even more of a down home hipster with a good ol' boy name.

The title page bears a curious subtitle: "Being Three Related Novels *The Flea Circus, Room Enough to Caper, Country Pleasures*." The three novels involve the repetition of characters, settings, and themes. It is interesting that the publisher chose not to call it a trilogy, perhaps because trilogies typically appear in separate volumes (Dos Passos's *U.S.A.*, for example). Shrake has pointed out that if Brammer had published the novels separately, say two years apart, he "would have been a lot better known." That way, he might more easily have had a career. Instead everything was contained in one volume, making it difficult—indeed, as it turned out, impossible—for him to produce the next volume. There is something to this argument. Brammer's "second act," as Paul Cullum has called it, echoing Fitzgerald's famous remark about there being no second acts in American lives, never happened.

After *The Gay Place* Brammer worked for *Time* magazine in 1960. He quit in 1961 to write full time and never held a permanent job again. In 1961 he and Nadine divorced, and in 1963 he married Dorothy Browne. Things looked very promising that year. Columbia Pictures announced plans to make a major film of the novel. Paul Newman would play Roy Sherwood and Jackie Gleason, Arthur Fenstemaker. Eventually the project was abandoned, partly, it is thought, because of the ascension of Johnson to the presidency. That November of 1963, in Dallas, hours after the assassination, Brammer received offers to write magazine articles on the new president. A bit later he got an even better offer, a contract to do the first biography of Johnson. What writer, after all, knew LBJ better than Brammer? But it was not to be. The new president forbade access to Brammer, partly, everyone believes, because the first lady had read the book and was not amused. Johnson himself told Brammer that he had read a few pages and found it too dirty to continue, but there is no evidence that Johnson ever read a novel; he was too busy living one. In any event, the project was dead in the water.

All through the sixties and seventies, friends and admirers expected, hoped, prayed that Brammer would write another novel. And he worked on one for a long time. That, too, became part of his legend. The book was called "Fustian Days," but it never got beyond a mass of pages, revised endlessly, that was never shaped into a coherent whole. Larry McMurtry has claimed that the early sections of "Fustian Days" were the best thing Brammer had written, but that the rest failed to sustain such promise. Larry L. King reports that he read "perhaps 150 or 200 manuscript pages" of "Fustian Days" in 1964 and that they "bordered on the brilliant."

The "Fustian Days" manuscripts survive today in the Southwestern Writers Collection at Southwest Texas State University. There are seven folders of material ranging from a few pages to several hundred. Some sections are fairly clean; others are extensively revised; the sections overlap and repeat each other. But from what remains one can see something of Brammer's unfulfilled intentions. "Fustian Days" consists of three books: "Sonic Goddam Boom," "Secret Muzack [alternately titled "Eatin' Little Babies"], and "And It Don't Hurt the Meat Much." They deal with the lives of Roy Sherwood and Neil Christiansen, the protagonists of the first and second books of *The Gay Place*, now living in Washington, D. C., and somewhat lost and directionless without the spirit of Arthur Fenstemaker to breathe life and purpose into them. A couple of passages are enough to suggest the self-conscious artistry that almost paralyze the fragments. Brammer writes in one section:

> We ought now to be getting round to the *story* part of this
> story: the real and human document part . . . complex,

absorbing . . . leavened with symbol and the subtlest *ennui*
. . . Before we are overrun with the dancing girls I thought-
fully contracted for earlier in the evening in behalf of those
among us whose tastes might run to excess.

A page later in this prolonged meditation on style, he writes:
"Wild prose, hah? I learned how, writing speeches for southern
politicians, whose rhythms are unmatched in all of modern literature."

There were other, far lesser fragments of unrealized efforts. "El
End Zone," dated April 27, 1965, is a wild, obscene, gonzo-style
interview of an author named Maelstrum (obviously Brammer
himself) who at one point lists all the substances fit to smoke,
inhale, or eat, beginning with pot and running through Seconal,
cocaine, ether, "Elmer's goddam glue," and on and on. There is a
one page fragment titled "The Angst Book" or "Avez-vous
Dexamyl?" There are epigrams scrawled on unmarked pages, of
which this one is typical: "Absinthe Makes the Hard Grow
Fonder."

No one was more aware of his problems as a writer than
Brammer himself. He wrote King in 1968: "This is not another of
them pleas begging assistance, so you should immediately relax
the scrotum; lend some ease to your careworn sac. Which is not
to deny the need for help, God wot: wise counsel or some new
miracle drug or just maybe a plain unprettified boot in the arse:
any old damn gesture is welcome currently." A few sentences
later, he summed it all up: "Writing is just so murderously hard for
me in recent years—unaccountably so—though my skull feels
livelier than ever. . . ." The anguished-artist thesis may be the correct explanation; on the other hand, perhaps not. At least one
friend, Gary Cartwright, has argued that Brammer in some sense
"chose" not to write the next novel, that he preferred "living" to
writing and that "everyone who knew the man profited." Perhaps
Brammer himself made the best, most trenchant assessment of
what happened, writing in 1976:

Bestowed from birth with a lucy-in-the-sky twinkle and irreverence for every thing, [I] bounced around the subculture after leaving LBJ, writing unfinished masterpieces by the score, ingesting hogsheads of drugs and acquiring a local image as the best approximation of guru and human wonder around.

The wide open counterculture enticements of the exploding sixties were irresistible to a bohemian, jazz-loving, Methedrine-dependent intellectual of the fifties. The sixties promised everything, and Brammer went hog wild in the decade of revolution. He got on Ken Kesey's bus and schlepped down to Mexico; he journeyed to San Francisco and Europe; he pursued drugs and women and had a long binge of it—in fact on into the next decade. And then, February 11, 1978, the clock ran down. His daughter Sidney, one of his three children to whom the novel is dedicated, remembers the day when she was called away from her classes on the University of Texas campus to claim the body of her father. He had died of an overdose in a ratty apartment where he was living at the time. His last job was as assistant hors d'oeuvres chef at the Driskill Hotel. It would cost about $3,000 for the funeral, and so far as Sidney knew, her father was penniless. She didn't know where the cash would come from to pay the undertaker. But Brammer had provided in a manner that any novelist would appreciate. He had tucked away $3,000—just enough to cover the funeral costs—in the toe of one of his boots.

The Gay Place is the most famous *roman à clef* in Texas writing. That may not be saying very much, but in Texas it matters. Or it used to. Willie Morris, author of a brilliant Texas book himself, *North Toward Home*, has amusingly recounted his experience upon seeing himself in the pages of his friend's novel:

He had this protagonist, Willie England, and I had just returned from England. And he was the editor of a small weekly literary/political journal, in the unidentified capital of the largest state in the Southwest—and I had just taken

over the *Observer*. And I said, "Billy Lee, at least Thomas
Wolfe changed the names and addresses."

With the passage of time, however, the identities of the actual
people grow dim. The most famous *roman à clef* in American writing is *The Sun Also Rises*, yet today only specialists know the names
of the actual people out of whom Hemingway fashioned Lady
Brett Ashley, Robert Cohn, and all the rest. In Brammer's case,
one towering presence comes alive off the page in a novel replete
with the people in Brammer's life: Arthur "Goddam" Fenstemaker,
perhaps the best portrait yet of the *personality* of Lyndon B.
Johnson, the larger-than-life figure who intrigued, beguiled, and
dominated Brammer's imagination until finally Brammer understood the man in a way that biographers such as Robert Caro
seem not to have.

Although it has been widely assumed that LBJ was the sole
impetus behind the creation of Fenstemaker, the character may
be more of an amalgam than previously recognized. Two real-life
governors have been suggested: Earl Long, Louisiana's colorful
governor whose sexual hijinks with stripper Blaze Starr were
widely reported in the mid-1950s, and Beauford Jester, governor
of Texas from 1946 until 1949. The only Texas governor to die in
office, Jester succumbed from a heart attack, on a train on July 11,
1949, in circumstances closely resembling those surrounding the
death of Fenstemaker in *The Gay Place*.

Other characters based upon real-life prototypes include
Sweet Mama Fenstemaker, a weak satirical picture of Lady Bird;
Hoot Gibson Johnson, a right-on depiction of LBJ's brother-in-
the-shadows, Sam Houston Johnson; Jay McGown, Brammer
himself; Ouida, Nadine; and so on, right on down to the children.
Several liberal politicians of the era have been nominated as the
basis for Roy Sherwood, but one leading candidate, Bob
Eckhardt, former congressman from Houston, disavows such
identification: "There's not much of me in there, and I knew
Brammer pretty well." Malcolm McGregor, former member of the

House from El Paso, is another candidate thought by many contemporaries to have been a prototype in the novel. There can be no doubt, however, about the authenticity of the meeting place in the novel where liberals, lobbyists, and university professors gather to talk and drink. The beer garden dubbed the Dearly Beloved Beer and Garden Party in the novel is a meticulous rendering of the site and ambience of Scholz Garten, the famous old German watering hole on San Jacinto Street in easy walking distance from the Capitol and the university.

As to the novel's dependence upon facticity of time and place, Nadine Eckhardt, Brammer's ex-wife, has commented, "Every time I read *The Gay Place* I can't believe how much he got in there. He used everything." Nadine plans to write her own memoirs of that period. About the fifties there is this to be said: there is a secret, as yet unwritten history of the remarkable women of that era, bright and talented women who came to maturity before the women's movement and who often gave up even the idea of a career for the sake of husbands who lived, as the saying goes, in a man's world.

The Gay Place is also a what-if novel that asks the question: What if LBJ had been the governor of Texas? In retrospect, the governorship looks like small potatoes to a man whose ambition was always national. Johnson never aspired to be governor. During the Eisenhower era, the governor of Texas was Allan Shivers, a Democrat who supported Dwight D. Eisenhower, not Adlai Stevenson, in both 1952 and 1956. For this and other sins imputed to him, he was the bete noire of Texas liberals in the fifties. The liberal hero, Ralph Yarborough, was never able to be elected governor, so Brammer made it up: he elected LBJ in the province of his mind and set him at work upon the lives and imaginations of a handful of penny-ante state politicians. The result is a portrait of Johnson that is profoundly true in two respects. Brammer, better than anybody, captures the style and humor of LBJ as well as the authenticity of his commitment to social and economic justice.

The first words uttered by Arthur Fenstemaker evoke the LBJ persona. The governor, like Johnson an inveterate telephonist, rings up Roy Sherwood and identifies himself as Arthur "Goddam" Fenstemaker. Immediately the governor invites Roy to come to the mansion and "break watermelon" with him. It's LBJ to the nth. Fenstemaker's name, incidentally, has provoked some interesting commentary. Lon Tinkle, a well-known southwestern book reviewer of the day, thought the name meant "fence-mender," which is plausible, but Al Reinert, a journalist and friend of Brammer's, convincingly argues that the word derives from the German "window-maker," meaning illusionist or visionary. Throughout the three volumes Fenstemaker speaks in the unmistakable rhythms and tones of a word-drunk southern politician, a consummate rhetorician who is half-Isaiah and half skirt-chasing egomaniac. From many wonderful examples of Fenstemaker as master politician, this one stands out. The governor is explaining his theory of politics:

> "You want to overturn the existin' institution, that's fine. But you got to be sure you know how to build a better one. The thing to do is work *through* the institution—figure a way to do that—to make a change and build a city and save the goddamn world from collapse. You got to work through that institution, Roy. . . ." Then he leaned back and flashed his shark's smile, saying, "An' I'm that institution currently. . . ."

This is Fenstemaker/LBJ, the arm-twisting, snake-charming, "conepone Buddha," the ultimate wheeler-dealer. But there is another side of Johnson that Brammer also captures better than just about anybody. This is Johnson the liberal, the genuine post-New Dealer who wants to improve people's lives and economic conditions. In the novel, Fenstemaker expresses real concern over such issues as integration and education. In the opening chapter he asks his black butler if things are getting any better for his people. And he means it. He energizes Roy Sherwood into passing

an education bill. It's a part-way measure, and the pure liberal ide-
ologues denounce him for it, but, like LBJ, Fenstemaker is a half-
a-loaf politician.

The sincerity of Johnson's interest in improving the lot of
down-and-out Texans is something that Brammer is very con-
vincing about. A little-known radio speech that Congressman
Johnson gave in 1938 sheds some light on the accuracy of
Brammer's portrait. "Tarnish on the Violet Crown," it was called,
an interesting title since Austin had been dubbed "The City of the
Violet Crown" since the 1890s, owing to the twilight coloration
of the hills surrounding the city beside the Colorado River. O.
Henry is credited with coining the phrase. Anyway, here is
Johnson in 1938:

> Last Christmas, when all over the world people were cele-
> brating the birth of the Christ child, I took a walk here in
> Austin—a short walk, just a few blocks from Congress
> Avenue, and there I found people living is such squalor that
> Christmas Day was to them just one more day of filth and
> misery. Forty families on one lot, using one water faucet.
> Living in barren one-room huts, they were deprived of the
> glory of sunshine in the daytime, and were so poor they
> could not even at night use the electricity that is to be gen-
> erated by our great river. Here the men and women did not
> play at Santa Claus. Here the children were so much in
> need of the very essentials of life that they scarcely missed
> the added pleasures of our Christian celebration.
>
> I found one family that might be called typical. Living
> within one dreary room, where no single window let in the
> beneficent sunlight, and where not even the smallest
> vagrant breeze brought them relief in the hot summer—
> here they slept, here they cooked and ate, here they
> washed themselves in a leaky tin tub after carrying the
> water for 100 yards. Here they brought up their children
> ill-nourished and amid sordid surroundings. And on this
> Christmas morning there was no Santa Claus for the 10

children, all under 10 years old, who scrambled around the feet of a wretched mother bent over her washtub, while in this same room her husband, and the father of the brood, lay ill with an infectious disease.

A staff writer for the congressman probably wrote this piece (Brammer, after all, years later, answered personal family correspondence for Johnson when he worked on his staff), but no matter: it came out under Johnson's name; it expressed his sentiments. The 1938 radio address contained the essential premises of the Great Society, Johnson's sixties updating of Rooseveltian liberal policies. Brammer saw and understood this side of Johnson in the fifties when many other liberals did not. Ronnie Dugger, for example, held a quite different view of Johnson. Writing of Brammer's novel in 1966, Dugger remarks,

> From reading an early version of some of the book I knew I would resent Bill's politics in the novel—both his contempt for the Texas liberals, so many of whom I knew to be people I would go to the wall with, and his adulation, a kind of disillusioned hero worship, of his Lyndon Johnson figure, Governor Fenstemaker, with whom I would not.

As a novelist, not an ideologue, Brammer sought to capture the whole complex personality of Johnson. A 1957 memo from Brammer to Senator Johnson suggests the measure of his admiration: "Your strength, as always, again emerges from a joint mutual admiration society: Classic liberals and classic conservatives who can recognize a man for his abilities and honesty rather than whether he fits the mold of their own partisan views." In any case, he got more of Johnson into his novel than many biographers have been able to.

The roots of Brammer's conception of Texas and how it might be corralled in fiction can be glimpsed in the pages of the *Texas Observer*, the liberal weekly founded by Ronnie Dugger in 1954 and for which Brammer wrote a number of pieces in those exciting mid-years of the decade. Typical *Observer* articles dealt with social and political themes of the day: "Negroes Still Take a Back Seat," "Shivers Backs Ban on Integration," "Our Separate But Unequal Schools—Negro Facilities Lag in Some Serious Ways," "Negro Boy Murdered in East Texas," "A Teacher Views Our Schools' Shortcomings—Sees Wasted Time, Effort, Money, Talent, Intelligence," "The Slums of Texas," and "Forgotten Texas—Our Aged Citizens Are in Poverty and Filth." Segregation, education, and poverty were central to the liberal agenda, and each finds its way into the texture of *The Gay Place*, which is sometimes wrongly described as a novel about the ultra-rich or "Super-Americans," the title of John Bainbridge's 1961 book about Texas.

The *Observer* was as interested in the powerful as in those without power and frequently ran knowing articles on the inner workings of the political process. In May 1955, for example, Ronnie Dugger produced a long article titled "Austin Lobbyists at Work—They Inform, Squire, Cajole, and Bribe." At one point he quotes a state senator who sounds as though he stepped out of the pages of *The Gay Place*: "Where's a goddamn lobbyist. I want somebody to pick up the check for my hotel bill, you can't find one around here." In another anecdote Dugger tells of four members of the House who spent an evening dining and drinking at a private club and cheerfully allowed a lobbyist to pick up the tab—a grand total of $20. The earnest young liberals of the *Observer* staff seem to have been fascinated with the simple, eternal fact that people in power enjoy using other people's money and that lobbyists are by nature engaged in precisely this most predictable of transactions.

Brammer himself wrote a series of articles devoted to explaining/exposing another invisible influence-peddling connection, the activities of behind-the-scenes political operatives. "The Political Hucksters—'Hit 'Em Where They Live'" (May 9, 1955) dealt with power brokers such as "Phil Fox, the king of the political hucksters of Texas." This article also records an incident in Dallas in which Barefoot Sanders, a liberal member of the Texas

House, was accosted by an opponent denouncing him as a communist and Sanders engaged the man in a fistfight. This incident seems to underlie the sequence in "Room Enough to Caper" when Neil Christiansen physically removes his red-baiting opponent from a political banquet. Brammer also reported on the visits of the most powerful man in the U.S. Senate to his home state. "The Senator at His Precincts" (May 9, 1956) described Lyndon B. Johnson's convincing grassroots persona at a precinct meeting in Johnson City; "Lyndon Comes Home" (August 24, 1955) described Johnson's loss of weight and fragile appearance following a heart attack; and "Pow-Wow on the Pedernales" (October 5, 1955) offered an insider's view of a political strategy meeting held at the Johnson ranch.

The *Observer* had broader cultural interests as well. Issues in those years were as apt to carry a review of an international work like Simone de Beauvoir's novel *The Mandarins* as of something more locally resonant like Stanley Walker's *Home to Texas*. There were finely honed naturalistic slice-of-life stories about life among working-class Texans, such as Winston Bode's "South San Antonio" (November 14, 1965) and "The Shearers" (November 28, 1956). And there were many pieces that dealt with literary issues pertaining to the Southwest.

In a biting review of a novel about Texas by an "outsider," Robert Wilder's *The Wine of Youth*, Dugger deplored the errors, the reliance upon gross, exaggerated stereotypes, and the general absurdity of passages such as the following, which describes a supposedly typical Texas social event:

> Someone would say let's have a barbeque. The next thing they would be on their way to a ranch a hundred or so miles distant, halting to send telegrams to friends in New York, California, Dallas, Houston, Fort Worth, Beaumont, telling them to hurry on over and eat a piece of meat. Since everyone in Texas knows everyone else, the barbeque might last for weeks. . . .

Dugger denounced such treatment as "inept and inaccurate nonsense." Here was a phony, outsized Texas that had nothing to do with the diverse and complex state that he and Brammer were exploring in their journalism.

Brammer, perhaps inspired by the fact that Warner Brothers was filming *Giant* at Marfa, reviewed Edna Ferber's 1952 best seller, the most famous outsider Texas novel of the era. In "On Rereading 'Giant'" (July 4, 1955) he declared the novel "richly-conceived and rottenly written" and went on to complain of Ferber's distortions: "Instead of portraying Texas as proud, primitive, superpatriots obsessed with sheer bigness and magnitude, which many of us are, she made us out as oil-rich robber barons and feudal lords, buffoons and mountebanks, which, it is hoped, few of us are." Brammer ended his reflections by taking up the question of what the modern Texas novel should be. He cited the recent observations of Harrison Smith, a *Saturday Review* editor, who suggested at a conference in Corpus Christi that Texas fiction had typically dealt with either a mixed population or the very wealthy and called for a writer to deal with "middleclassers who have come from other places." Brammer agreed and concluded: "These are the people who make up the state of mind that is Texas. Miss Ferber failed to sense this. Perhaps the next novelist will."

The next novelist, it seems, was waiting in the wings. His name was William, Billy Lee, Bill Brammer. We know little about the genesis of that first novel, "Country Pleasures." But again the pages of the *Observer* offer clues. Around the same time that he reread Ferber, he visited the set of *Giant* in Marfa and wrote an account of his observations. Most of what he reported in "A Circus Breaks Down on the Prairie" (July 4, 1955) appears in the opening pages of "Country Pleasures." The article begins with a description of the eye-catching false-front Victorian house constructed by the film company:

> Some miles out from town, south on Highway 67, there looms large on the horizon a macabre structure

which should remain for years a curiosity for West Texas cattle and cowpokes. Sticking starkly out of the prairies is a three-storied Victorian mansion, all gingerbread and lightning rods, rococo and utterly inelegant.

In the novel the governor's party first glimpses the house in a passage that owes much to the original journalistic description: "Everyone strained to catch sight of the prefabricated Victorian mansion towering above the floor of the ranchland. The mansion loomed on the horizon like a great landlocked whale, gingerbread bas-relief against the backdrop of bleached dune and mountain and gunmetal sky." Other details in the *Observer* article are woven into the scene in the novel. Brammer reports that the local grass was sprayed with green dye to make it greener, and in the novel the viewpoint character, Jay McGown, the governor's aid, cries: "They even dyed the grass green near the mansion. It wouldn't respond to the water they piped in, so they dyed it green." Another detail that fascinated Brammer the reporter was trucks full of tumbleweed imported from California. In the novel these details are set forth by the governor's colorful brother, Hoot Gibson Fenstemaker. His explanation of how the tumbleweed will be made to perform is a good example of Brammer's perfect-pitch dialogue: "It don't tumble. Even when there's a good wind. It just don't tumble. So they brought out some big blowers—big 'lectric fans—to make the tumbleweed tumble when they shoot the moom pitcher." Curiously, Brammer's central image for describing the spectacle of the movie company that gave the article its title is shifted to another subject in the novel. In the article Brammer writes: "It's as if a vast, traveling circus has broken down in the midst of this desolation and set up shop for some kind of performance." In the novel the circus description applies to the college attended by Jay McGown and his ex-wife, the blonde bombshell Vicki McGown: ". . . you could have mistaken it for a great, shapeless circus that had somehow broken down on the edge of the city."

Clearly the trip to Marfa and the visit to the set of *Giant* stimulated Brammer's creative imagination, as he set to work on "Country Pleasures." There is another tantalizing possibility about the sources of his plot idea of placing the governor in the midst of a Hollywood crowd. There was an immediate precedent for this in real life. That same year, 1955, Governor Allan Shivers appeared in a Paramount Production titled *Lucy Gallant*. Towards the end of the film Governor Shivers introduces the title character, played by Jane Wyman, to an audience assembled to see a Neiman-Marcus-like style show. Brammer would likely have known about this film, and in any case he certainly could have read Dan Strawn's tongue-in-cheek review, "A Gallant in 'Gallant,'" which appeared in the *Observer* in November 1955. There is one odd echo of the Shivers business in the novel. The character who directs the film, based on George Stevens, who also appears in the circus article under his real name, in the novel is named Edmund Shavers.

Brammer's novel remains interesting on both the regional and the national levels. In the Southwest it occupies an important space in the emergence of contemporary fiction set in the region. Published the same year as Larry McMurtry's *Horseman, Pass By* and one year after John Graves' *Goodbye to a River*, it did not, however, reap local rewards. Both Graves and McMurtry received cash prizes from the Texas Institute of Letters. Brammer, in fact, lost out to his friend, McMurtry. The three books and their takes on Texas are most instructive. Graves' book is a nonfiction narrative in the elegaic mode favored by J. Frank Dobie. Old-time Texans loved the book, and still do. *Goodbye to a River* is the culmination of the Dobie-Webb-Bedichek evocation of a pastoral past in decline.

McMurtry's novel is also elegiac. Its portrait of the old cattleman Homer Bannon, whose values derive from the land and are founded on the old West Texas Protestant virtues of work, thrift, and possession of cattle and land, has a deliberate end-of-an-era tone. In McMurtry's rancherly allegory, Hud, the hard-driving, hard-drinking, hard-everything stepson is supposed to stand for an unprincipled modern generation that has replaced love for the land with lust for money, women, and oil. Between them, observing, appraising, judging, is the adolescent narrator, Lonnie Bannon, the sensitive youth, the proto-English major. *Horseman, Pass By* contains some brilliant writing and is the first believable account of a Texas male adolescent in Texas writing. (Katherine Anne Porter's Miranda stories, written in the mid-thirties, are the first great portrait of coming of age in Texas, a fact ignored, however, by both Dobie and McMurtry, between them the two chief progenitors of the patriarchal legend of Texas.)

Dobie admired Graves' book but had deep reservations about those of McMurtry and Brammer. Though he found McMurtry's portrait of the old cowman "good in places," he judged McMurtry overall as lacking in "ripeness." (McMurtry was twenty-four at the time.) Of Brammer's book, however, Dobie had nothing good to say. He inscribed his overall assessment in the flyleaf of his copy:

> Not a character in the thick novel who is not cheap. Some talk about what a great man Governor Fenstemaker is, but he never appears more than an astute fixer, babbling now & then a good phrase. We are in the middle of politics for 175,000 words and nobody actually every [sic] does anything but drink and drink & drink to boredom & screw, & screw & screw to death—the great governor's climax. I expected satire, inside views & a little wisdom at least. Bill Brammer has been with Senator Lyndon Johnson for some time.

Thus the official voice of Texas literary judgment. Dobie said much the same thing about Edwin Shrake's *But Not for Love* (1964), an urban novel inspired by Brammer: "Over drinking of everything but water. Pages & pages of talk that reveal nothing but more drinking, more smoking [sic?], mere facility on part of the author, no character development, no integration with plot." In such reactions it is not easy to tell whether the basis of Dobie's dislike is primarily aesthetic—thus the complaints about length and lack of conciseness—or moral—the degenerate (or is it merely modern?) conduct of the characters.

The Graves and McMurtry books inhabit Nostalgia Ville: a river, a ranch. But not *The Gay Place*. Brammer's vision of Texas is urban, and in this conception lies one of the important insights the novel has to offer. Typically it is Fenstemaker who makes the point. He is fulminating against a right-wing, red-baiting McCarthyite: " . . . what he doesn't know is that most of us came into town one Saturday a few years ago and stayed. . . . We're urban, by God. All of a sudden the people in the metropolitan areas outnumber the rednecks. . . . They come into town—they buy little houses and color television and Volkswagen cars." This is new Texas, ca. 1958, and Brammer's novel accurately predicts the continuing urbanization of the state so that by now, in the mid-nineties, the demographics are around eighty-two percent living in cities and suburbs—urban, by God.

Brammer's novel is also topographically all-encompassing. Its famous opening pages reveal a helicopter-like survey of the variousness and immensity of the Texas landscape. Texas as a transitional region of Gulf coastal lands, Deep South-like pine forests, rocky Hill Country, and western prairie and grazing lands are all caught in the zoom lens of the pictorial imagination. But mostly, Texas is urban in the post-WW II era, and Brammer was the first powerful novelist to make this claim. (There had been earlier Texas urban novels, for example, Philip Atlee's *The Inheritors*, 1940, and George Williams' *The Blind Bull*, 1952, but none had anywhere near the impact of *The Gay Place* upon aspiring young writers.)

Early in chapter one Brammer detaches his novel from the agrarian tradition. Roy Sherwood wakes up in his car with a hangover. (Most of the characters in the novel have hangovers most of the time.) Groggy but in good spirits, he first hears, then sees a family of Mexican-American migrant workers. This family's relation to the land is itself modern in a literary sense, as they are no land-holding farm family with roots in the nostalgic myth of agrarian Texas. And they quickly disappear in this novel, which moves on to its real subject—urban people and political power, not land.

At the national level, beyond Texas, *The Gay Place* is a searching and reflective document of America in the fifties. Brammer touches upon many of the dominant themes of the era, including the conflicts in ending segregation, the role of money and influence in government, and the Cold War atmosphere of lingering McCarthyism. Brammer's fifties are recognizably those of stereotype and legend: an era of comfortable if not bloated affluence, a sense of American power at the apex of its arc, a nation at peace. It is also an era of political quiescence, of liberal paralysis, of what Brammer called, in an *Observer* piece in 1961, "the apathetic conditions that obtained overall." Looking back at the impact of the *Observer* under the leadership of Ronnie Dugger, Brammer characterized the era in extremely negative terms:

> Dugger and the *Observer* survive, and the revolution is on the record for all to see, obvious to anyone who remembers how it was in Texas during that hysterical, No-Think half decade of the early Fifties—our own mid-century Inquisition—when nearly everyone lay torpid and uncomplaining in the clutch of the Peckerwood and the Ignoranti.

"Our Hookworm Belt complacencies," he called the era in another piquant phrase from that article.

At the same time Brammer captures hints of cultural change ahead. Hipsters and politicians talk of Zen and Buddhism and existentialism and jazz. There is a sense of imminent cultural revolution waiting just round the corner. Brammer knew what his old friend David Halberstam has recently shown in his book *The Fifties*, that the Eisenhower era was a lot more complex and interesting than retro television sitcoms would suggest. In "Room Enough to Caper," he also proved prophetic. This story of a young man with good looks, intellectual savoir faire, and excellent political instincts, in short a great campaigner in the coming telegenic age, is ahead of its time. Not until the Robert Redford film *The Candidate* would there be as searching a study of the politician as hollow man, a man capable of winning elections but without any sustaining vision, without any reason or motive to serve beyond ego satisfaction.

Narratively, too, Brammer's book reached far beyond Texas for its models. Brammer was extremely well read. It is hard to imagine another Texas novelist of the period leading off a book with a beautifully apt quotation from Ford Madox Ford's *The Good Soldier.* Though the novel is often compared with Robert Penn Warren's *All the King's Men,* its narrative procedure derives not from Warren's first-person, tough-guy vernacular, but from classical American social realism, the rhythms of F. Scott Fitzgerald, whom Brammer deeply admired, Fitzgerald in turn deriving in part from Edith Wharton and Henry James, novelists who sought to express the manners and morals of the day. In "Room Enough to Caper" and "Country Pleasures" Brammer also incorporates Joycean interior monologue (probably filtered through William Styron's *Lie Down in Darkness*), something else that sets him apart from regional writing of the period. There are stream-of-consciousness sequences in both of these books. There is also a rich allusiveness, from Dave Brubeck to George Orwell to the Bible. Much of Fenstemaker's memorable talk derives from the cadences of Isaiah. Brammer is on record about this influence, remarking in 1961, "The only researching I did for the novels was a re-reading of the Old Testament (in its old-style prose) and I've never enjoyed anything more. . . . "

The most important literary source is T. S. Eliot. The interior monologue section of "Room Enough to Caper," for example, elides the young senator's voice with Eliot's vacillating, indecisive Prufrock and the novel's full-throttled man of action, Arthur Fenstemaker:

Am no presiding officer.
Wasn't meant to be.
I'm the goddamn Prince! An easy tool.

Other specific Eliot echoes from "The Love Song of J. Alfred Prufrock" include "I grow old" in one of Neil's self-reflexive moments and "all those scattered buttends" in Sarah Lehman's stream-of-consciousness reverie in Chapter 15 of "Country Pleasures," which recalls Prufrock's "all the butt-ends of my days and ways." Unmistakable also, and very funny, is the actor Greg Calhoun's pastiche of Eliot's "I will show you fear in a handful of dust" in "Country Pleasures" (which title in turn derives from one of Eliot's favorite poets, John Donne). In the actor's hands the famous line from *The Waste Land* becomes, "I will show you death in a handful of bust."

More importantly than these verbal echoes, the method of *The Waste Land* informs *The Gay Place*. Like many post-*Waste Land* novelists, Brammer adopted the mythic method (which Eliot in turn seems to have taken over from Joyce's *Ulysses*). Put simply, the author underpins the narrative with a mythic substructure, playing off the present against the past. "Room Enough to Caper" makes the most abundant use of the method, as protagonist Neil Christiansen returns home at age thirty-three, at Easter time, to face a crisis of personal belief. Should he run for the Senate or not? Does he believe in anything or not? At one point he ponders Christ's passion: "They just didn't make passion like that anymore. He tried to remember the last time he'd seen real passion, but nothing came to him. It was all a cheap imitation, a fraudulent compound of polemic, spleen, and seasons of rut." Filled with indecisiveness, he thinks at one point: "If I could read that script I just might walk on the goddamn water." Here one of Jesus' miracles is layered with Fenstemaker's signature blasphemy. Later Neil thinks of himself as a "dime-store Jesus." The whole Christian subtext is summed up in the meditation on God of Neil's brother Stanley, quoting from an unidentified source: "Some lines came to him . . . 'For anyone alone and without God and without a master, the weight of days is dreadful. Hence, one must choose a master, God being out of style. . . .'" If *The Gay Place* has a god, it is Fenstemaker, but he proves a completely secular deity, one unable even to save himself from perdition and destruction, no matter how much Isaiah he quotes.

Like the best of novels, *The Gay Place* captures its own era and speaks to ours in rhythms that we remember.

Take My Sequel from the Wall: The Lonesome Dove Cycle

y winning the Spur Award of Western Writers of America, the Texas Institute of Letters Prize for Fiction, and, best of all, the Pulitzer Prize for Fiction, Larry McMurtry's *Lonesome Dove* far outstripped any of his previous ten novels. It also made the Best Seller List of *The New York Times*. Before this megahit, McMurtry had had to depend on the movies to convert the dross of fiction into precious metals. Four of his novels had been turned into films, three of them excellent, the only exception being the execrable *Lovin' Molly*. But it was something new for a McMurtry novel to create such a sensation in the literary marketplace.

Who would have thought that a trail-driving novel would turn the trick? The book appeared in June 1985 poised strategically to capture the summer poolside reading audience and the always rapacious airplane readership. But there was something else either calculated or lucky about its publication; it beat James Michener to the gate by two full months. Did McMurtry have his eye on the Texas Sesquicentennial Sweepstakes of 1986? One can't imagine that he did not.

Career-wise as they say on the coast, *Lonesome Dove* accomplished several things for McMurtry. His lecture fee jumped straightway from $1500 to $5000, his picture appeared in *People* in a story about his close personal friend, Cybill Shepherd, and he was invited to a White House reception for Princess Di. The advance copy of the novel bore portents of his new eminence; his agent was none other the legendary Irving "Swifty" Lazar, who numbered among his clients Richard Milhouse Nixon.

Down Texas way, the most surprising thing about *Lonesome Dove* was that it was written at all. Five years earlier, in 1981, McMurtry had cast a cold eye on Texas letters. In a long article in the *Texas Observer*, he took the measure of his fellow writers and of himself and couldn't find much to be happy about. Texas writers were lazy and unproductive; they were ill-read in the nineteenth century English and European masters of the craft; and they spent too much of their time gazing (and grazing) backwards nostalgically at the vanished and superior past, the days of the cattlemen and the land-centered values of small farmers, small towns, and small Dairy Queens. McMurtry even had a prescription for curing Texas letters. Texas writers should turn to the state's urban centers and explore the "less simplistic experience of city life."

In the meantime, it appears, he himself was carrying out another intention that he had speculated about in 1980. At that time, in an interview he remarked about an abandoned film project titled *The Streets of Laredo*, "I've sometimes thought I might see what would happen if I did it as a novel." The roots of *Lonesome* Dove are clearly traceable to the screenplay, according to McMurtry "an end-of-West Western [in which] three old men stumble into a last adventure, and they're old, and the West is over." Resurrected and fleshed out into 843 pages of nostalgia, nineteenth-century realism, and Hollywood-like heroics, *Lonesome Dove* became McMurtry's signature effort in a lifetime of writing fiction.

The herd doesn't actually hit the trail until page 220, by which point most of the many shoot-em-up paperback western trail-driving novels, from Zane Grey onwards, would have been over, but McMurtry was just beginning in what has to be seen—in length and bulk, anyway—as the *Moby Dick* of the trail-drive saga. The preliminary buildup to the drive informs us of what life is like in a fly-blown dusty little nowhere border town in South Texas where a mixed crew of likely lads, veterans of the Indian wars, aging Texas Rangers, and other assorted types try to figure out what it is they should do. Once on the trail, things pick up considerably, and McMurtry, good popular writer that he is, uses every cattle-drive obstacle ever invented to kick his story along. There are dry drives, wet drives, dusty drives, river crossings with snakes, river crossings without snakes, hail storms, wind storms, lightning storms, Indian attacks, Comanchero attacks, boredom attacks. McMurtry has used this kitchen-sink approach before. *The Last Picture Show* contained everything that had ever happened in every small-town high school in the U.S. and packed them all into the compressed time of that novel. *Lonesome Dove* does the same thing; this is the be-all and end-all of cattle-drive novels.

Clearly, it seems to me, this novel derives from two broad sources: the movies and history. The first does not serve McMurtry as well as the second. But it may well be the element that most caught the fancy of the reading public. To anyone who has never read trail-drive narratives or novels (all those young people sunning themselves poolside), *Lonesome Dove* looks shiny, new, original, cute, and entertaining. To those who've gotten saddle sores reading Andy Adams and J. Frank Dobie, *Lonesome Dove* gives off the scent of research and sources. This is not a criticism; many of Shakespeare's plays ransacked English history and various classical sources for story lines, characters, and flavor.

First, the movies. The figure of Lorena derives from a long tradition in trail-driving movies, from the first, *North of 36* (1924), to

the greatest, *Red River* (1948). To the early romancers, it seemed
necessary to bring a woman along to provide romantic plot interest. History tells us that there were actually women who went up
the long trail. Amanda Bourke was one, and Emerson Hough's
novel *North of 36*, from which the 1924 film was made, was based in
part on her story. In his novel and the film, the woman is young,
beautiful, and plucky but essentially helpless to accomplish the
great task. She can get the cowboys to start the drive, but in order
to finish it, she needs the help of a stalwart cowboy hero. Nearly
all subsequent trail-driving films felt the need of having a woman
along. She could be pure or soiled, but what she offered was
romance. Cows just aren't that interesting for two-and-a-half hours,
not to a general audience. Lorena, who is in the parlance of the
time a "soiled dove," springs from *Red River*, not from history. In the
film the Lorena figure is played by Joanne Dru, who damn near
wrecks the movie when she enters it about three-quarters of the
way through. The dynamics of empire-building, fatherhood, and
patrimony require the presence of a good "breeder," which is the
way Dru's character is presented in the film. Wayne looks her over
like a prize heifer, and Montgomery Clift falls in love with her. The
film recovers, only just barely, and surely its worst moment is the
high-pitched oratory delivered by Dru who has to tell the Duke
and Clift that by god, you big lugs really love each other, don't you
know that. Imagine what the film would have been like if Joanne
Dru had started out with the drive. They'd never have gotten the
herd out of Texas.

Another movie-inspired, or rather, TV-inspired character is the
bumbling deputy of the bumbling sheriff. July Johnson is the sheriff's name, and his deputy by all rights should have been named
Chester. Imagine a *Gunsmoke* episode in which Chester gets laid,
and you have the whole conception of this character in a nutshell.
Fortunately in this bloody book the deputy gets wiped out fairly
early, and we don't have to heed the further misadventures of this
hapless creature adrift on the great plains.

The three main characters, of course, all derive from the movies, as might be expected from a book that began as a movie script. There is Call, taciturn, flinty-eyed, capable, and hard, the strong silent type from a thousand westerns. John Wayne. And there is his opposite, the loquacious, philosophical-minded, and supposedly charming Augustus, who chatters from the early pages until his death near the end. Jimmy Stewart. The third member of this predictable trio is the dandy, and in Howard Hawks' *Rio Bravo* Dean Martin played him to a T. The dandy is a great bore in the novel, and fortunately, he too is killed fairly early in the proceedings. If there is one specific movie source lying behind the novel, it might be King Vidor's *The Texas Rangers* (1936), a quite bad western, or its equally bad remake, *Streets of Laredo* (1949). Both trace the story of three Texas Rangers, all former outlaws, two of whom are converted to truth and justice by the Ranger way, and the third of whom has to be eventually tracked down by his old pals. It's not the plot but the conception of the triad of two good/one bad apples that seems to be reprised in McMurtry's hands.

So much for the movie sources, and there are doubtless echoes of other westerns that may strike you as you read the novel. From history McMurtry has taken details, incidents, and a feeling for authentic recreation of the trail-driving experience. McMurtry has long been conversant with the major historical texts of the cattle-drive era, and I would suggest that certainly one of his sources was E. C. "Teddy Blue" Abbott's marvelous *We Pointed Them North*. This as-told-to narrative has a jaunty tone that makes the book far more attractive than the recognized classic in the field, Andy Adams' *The Log of a Cowboy*. I will quote one passage to give its flavor. Abbott is describing how he and his fellow cowpunchers left Miles City after having spent time and money with the girls they "married" for a week: "I still had Cowboy Annie's ruffled drawers that she gave me that night, and I put them on a forked stick and carried them that way to the mouth of the Musselshell, like a flag. And before we left, my girl took one of her stockings off and tied it round my arm, you know, like the knights of old and I wore that to the mouth of the Musselshell." At its best *Lonesome Dove* does a fair job of capturing the carefree banter and rollicksome ways recorded by Abbott.

As for the numerous incidents of travail, danger, and work practices that inform the narrative and give it an air of dusty authenticity, McMurtry undoubtedly drew upon numerous historical documents. The best single source of such information is *The Trail Drivers of Texas*, a two-volume collection of oral history and written accounts produced in the 1920s and reprinted on several occasions. Many of these first-person accounts are flavored with colorful incidents, but many are narrated in a stiff, rather genteel manner as well. Any novelist wanting to find accounts of incidents that took place on the trail could find plenty in the 1,044 pages that make up the two volumes. Need a good hail story? Here is an account by Jerry M. Nance, who went to Cheyenne, Wyoming with 2,100 cattle in 1877: "There was no timber on our side of the river, and when the hail began pelting the boys and myself made a break for the wagon for shelter. We were all naked, and the hail came down so furiously that within a short time it was about two inches deep on the ground." There are many similar details about stampedes, lightning storms, encounters with Indians, even one incident where a tomboy girl dressed up like a boy in order to go along on a drive. There are also moments of tedium and dry-as-dust accounts of drives that offer little to the novelist looking for action and color. Consider a drive that Jack Potter made in 1882: "There was no excitement whatever on this drive. It was to me very much like a summer's outing in the Rocky Mountains." The only thing that relieved the pleasant tedium was medical in nature: "The itch . . . had broken out on the trail and in those days people did not know how to treat it successfully. Our manager sent us a wagon of kerosene and sulphur with which to fight the disease." The itch might have comic possibilities, but it is hard to see how a novelist would be captivated by this incident.

One surprising detail that McMurtry got from *Trail Drivers* is the name of his magnificently evil Blue Duck, an Indian who is mentioned in passing in one trail driver's account. Blue Duck's death, by leaping from the upper story of a courthouse, appears to have its origins in the suicide of the famous Kiowa chief, Santanta, who leapt to his death from a similar height during his incarceration at the Huntsville (Texas) penitentiary in 1877.

The most moving sequence in the novel, the return of Augustus' body by his old friend Call, also has its source in Texas history. At the point of death Augustus asks to be packed in ice and hauled back to his beloved Texas to be buried. The request seems both absurd and touching. But there is an exact precedent in history. Legendary Texas settler Charles Goodnight performed just such a function for his friend, Oliver Loving. It was Goodnight and Loving, of course, who blazed one of the first cattle trails out of Texas to New Mexico. In 1867 Loving got caught by the Comanches in a skirmish on the Pecos River and was severely wounded. The best account of this episode appears in J. Evetts Haley's biography, *Charles Goodnight: Cowman and Plainsman* (1936). Haley describes Loving as a man "blessed with a constitution of iron." His wounding and eventual death prove that assertion. At one point after he had eluded the Comanches, he tried to eat his buckskin gloves. Later, after he was found and taken to Fort Sumner, New Mexico, where, because of gangrene, amputation of his arm became necessary, Loving realized he might die. He summoned his friend Goodnight to his bedside, and almost the last thing he said to him was, "I regret to have to be laid away in a foreign country." Goodnight made a solemn promise that his remains would be returned to his home cemetery in Weatherford, Texas. On September 25, Loving died and was buried at Fort Sumner. Five months later, in February, 1868, the body was exhumed. Haley's account of the incident is worth quoting in its entirety:

> From about the fort the cowboys gathered scattered oil cans, beat them out, soldered them together, and made an immense tin casket. They placed the rough wooden one inside, packed several inches of powdered charcoal around

it, sealed the tin lid, and crated the whole in lumber. They lifted a wagon bed from its bolsters and carefully loaded the casket in its place. Upon February 8, 1868, with six big mules strung out in the harness, and with rough-hewn but tenderly sympathetic cowmen from Texas riding ahead and behind, the strangest and most touching funeral cavalcade in the history of the cow country took the Goodnight and Loving Trail that led to Loving's home.

In the novel Call's return of Augustus' body is a one-man version of the Goodnight-Loving episode.

In suggesting these combined sources of film and history, I have by no means exhausted the literary and imaginative materials that McMurtry drew upon for his novel. Anybody conversant with the field could suggest other possible influences, including Andy Adams' *Log of a Cowboy* and J. Frank Dobie's *The Longhorns, A Vaquero of the Brush Country*, and *Cow People*. McMurtry, a rare-book dealer of considerable standing, may well have drawn upon less familiar works as well. In part, though, he drew also upon that common fund of cattle-drive lore gleaned from having watched, growing up, hundreds of western movies. As a writer with a keen eye for the marketplace, McMurtry must have been concerned with the problem of keeping his largely urban readers turning the pages and believing they were getting the straight stuff and not Louis L'Amour. The reviews suggest that he was very successful indeed. But few of the reviewers seemed aware that there have been other trail-drive novels. Two from Texas seem especially worth mentioning. One is Benjamin Capps' *The Trail to Ogallala*, a straightforward novel with no women characters along for the ride. Capps' theme is the nature of leadership, of what is required to trail a herd of some 3,000 cattle from south Texas to Nebraska. The second is Robert Flynn's *North to Yesterday*, a serious novel with comic overtones. It traces a cattle drive undertaken fifteen years after the cattle-drive era had closed due to barbed wire, increased settlement, and the extension of railheads into Texas. Its end-of-the-West feeling in particular seems to anticipate McMurtry's belatedness. Placed in the context of such novels, *Lonesome Dove* begins to seem at times like a novel too crowded with incidents, with everything that could possibly happen on one drive but never did. Still, it's a rollicking read, and that apparently was McMurtry's main goal from the beginning.

In the past few years Larry McMurtry has been recycling himself like an aging TV producer trying to capitalize on past successes. We've had sequels to *The Last Picture Show, All My Friends Are Going To Be Strangers, Terms of Endearment,* and now *Lonesome Dove.* What's next? *Hud Goes To Hawaii?*

Nonetheless, *Streets of Laredo,* son of *Lonesome Dove,* stands as the best of McMurtry's sequels. Although it is not quite as long as its predecessor, it is twice as bloody. Many familiar characters from *Lonesome Dove* reappear in the new novel. Chief among these is Captain Woodrow Call, Augustus McCrae's taciturn, violent friend and sidekick. (Gus, of course, does not reappear, having been buried at the end of *Lonesome Dove.* Several characters recall his memory throughout the new novel, creating a significant absence.) Call is near the end of the trail, seventy now, and afflicted with arthritis and failing eyesight. Still the most famous lawman in Texas, he is called upon (many are chosen, but few are Call) one last time to bring to justice two of the most savage threats to the women and children of the frontier.

Lorena, the good-hearted prostitute, is back too. She's now married to Pea Eye (one of McMurtry's most boring creations) and is a mother of five (plus two more whelped in this novel) and a schoolteacher who may, if she ever gets the time, take up the study of Latin (as her old friend Clara urges her to do). Other minor characters are reprised from *Lonesome Dove,* along with numerous passing references to its characters and incidents. Reading the new novel is sort of like looking through old yearbooks of Lonesome Dove High.

There are, of course, a number of new characters created especially for *Streets of Laredo*. Brookshire is a likable and therefore doomed tenderfoot from Brooklyn, sent to Texas by the railroad that employs him to hire Call to apprehend a deadly train robber. Brookshire, however, is only a moderately interesting personage, and as a traveling companion for Call, nowhere close to Gus McCrae in garrulous affability.

Two other new characters are Joey Garza and his mother Maria. Joey is nobody's pal, a certified sociopath who hates his mother, her four husbands, and her two other children—a blind girl and a retarded boy. He also hates all Anglos and anybody who has something that he doesn't. Joey begins his career of mayhem by amputating the feet and hands of his mother's fourth husband. He goes on from there to a career of robbing banks and shooting innocent pilgrims.

Joey Garza, unfortunately, reads as a very contrived character, like somebody in a demented dimestore novel. He has a rifle with a telescopic sight and can kill people at great distances. He has a cave in which he hides his loot. He dresses like a dandy and is very handsome, though deadly as well.

His mother Maria is a kind of down-and-out madonna. Nearly every man she's known has, in some way, done her wrong, and yet she loves men, even her psychopathic son. But it is difficult to believe in this character either. Credibility is stretched when she kills a giant, corpse-eating pig that has proved impervious to all previous attempts upon its life. It appears that McMurtry is striving for a fabulous quality here, and something nightmarish as well.

Another new character in *Streets of Laredo*—one that although Lorena remembers him from Blue Duck's gang (and she should know, she's in that novel), I don't recall from *Lonesome Dove*—is Mox Mox, who, if anything, is even more psychotic than Joey Garza. Mox Mox gets his kicks from burning people alive, especially women and children. What he most enjoys, in fact, is roasting a child in the presence of its mother. So when Mox Mox, who was thought to be dead, turns up in West Texas at the same time that

Call is chasing Joey Garza, West Texans have much to worry about. Lorena, for example, is so afraid of Mox Mox that she ships all her children to Nebraska to stay with Clara until Mox Mox is killed or brought to justice.

Thus in the Trans-Pecos region of Texas some unspecified years after the end of the cattle drive to Montana in the first novel, the frontier is in a sorrier state than anybody could imagine. Joey Garza and Mox Mox are running completely amok, and on their trail is beat-up old Call with a ragtag posse. Eventually Lorena joins him, bent on finding her husband Pea Eye (a member of the posse) and at the same time compelling Call to eschew police work in favor of family life, something he wants to do anyway.

In fact, one theme running throughout this novel is the struggle between the claims of heart and home versus those of nomadic derring-do and violence. Hence for a woman to stand by her man, she sometimes has to take to the trail herself. Lorena, as we know from *Lonesome Dove*, can endure anything a man might, and more.

The death toll in this novel is so great that you wonder how anybody west of the Pecos ever survived to build a Dairy Queen. There are plenty of other assorted disasters that befall peripheral characters, including a rape, a suicide, and—in the case of one beloved character—being kicked to death by a horse.

For the sake of historical interest, McMurtry also introduces several real, legendary figures into his novel. The gunfighter John Wesley Hardin, a ruthless killer with a bad skin condition, appears in several scenes where we are convinced that he will shoot anybody at any time on any pretext.

Then there is Judge Roy Bean, famous self-proclaimed "law west of the Pecos." He's presented as a dangerous, rambunctious sort, as unstable as John Wesley Hardin and just as likely to hang a citizen as Hardin is to plug one. Bean gets his comeuppance, though, when Joey Garza hangs him in front of Bean's saloon qua courthouse. For the unwary reader, McMurtry is playing fast and loose with history, and the revisionism is unsettling. It's as though the exaggerated dime-novel villains have taken over and are rewriting the history of the region.

Roy Bean actually died from lung and heart complications in 1903. According to Bean himself, he did undergo one hanging experience, but that was back in the late 1850s, and he was cut down at the last minute by his Mexican girlfriend (he complained of a stiff neck for a long time afterwards). If McMurtry wants to hang him, that's his novelistic prerogative, I suppose, but consider the implications. This is an important point: if Bean dies here before 1896, that means the famous Fitzsimmons-Mather heavyweight prize fight that Bean staged near Langtry on a sand spit of the Rio Grande didn't take place. How would Fitzsimmons feel about his two-minute pugilistic triumph being stolen from him by a capricious novelist?

The best-drawn and most appealing of the real-life characters is Charles Goodnight, famed plainsman, settler, and eminence grise of the Panhandle. McMurtry has long been an admirer of Goodnight, evoking the Old Man's spirit in his first novel, *Horseman, Pass By*, and addressing his legacy even more directly in some of the essays of *In A Narrow Grave*, in which Goodnight is viewed as some sort of demi-god of the old ranching ethos. (Incidentally, one of the characters in *Streets of Laredo* is buried "in a narrow grave," a small bit of self-reference for which one tips one's Stetson to Larry.) Goodnight's portrait is splendidly drawn, though when he sets out on the trail to capture Mox Mox, one begins to pray that McMurtry's darkening imagination won't let the grand old man of pioneer Texas fall prey to a pyromaniac's machinations. But Goodnight, thank goodness, is allowed to return to the Palo Duro Canyon where he belongs and can live out his ninety-three years, well beyond the boundaries of this novel, dying at that ripe old age in 1929.

Perhaps with the title *Streets of Laredo* McMurtry merely sought to evoke the memory of the famous ballad: "Bang the drum slowly . . ." and all that. Being something of a literalist, I kept expecting the novel to focus on Laredo, but it doesn't. One of Zane Grey's

Texas novels was titled *West of the Pecos*, and that would make a more accurate title for this work than McMurtry's own. Only a few scenes actually take place in Laredo, and most of the action occurs in the trackless wastes between Fort Stockton and northern Mexico. Although the book covers a desolate, far-flung area, much of the time the bulk of its characters remain in surprisingly close proximity to most of the other characters. The plotting is some-what reminiscent of James Fenimore Cooper's *The Prairie*, in which the entire history of the Trans-Mississippi West seems to unfold in a space no larger than the Astrodome. McMurtry's empty West Texas is crowded with villains and varmints who, by their frequent interaction, might as well be living in a tenement house in Stephen Crane's Bowery.

And after the violent climax—actually, there are two climaxes because there are two villains—the rest of the novel consists of very short chapters, many only a page long, which either continue the saga of some lives or extinguish, rather capriciously at times, the lives of others. There probably won't be a sequel to this sequel, as the old *Lonesome Dove* cast has, by book's end, been pretty severely whittled down. In the case of Captain Call, who has lost an arm and a leg and walks on a crutch, "whittling" is not a metaphor.

Streets of Laredo seems to summarize several recent tendencies in McMurtry's career. One is the self-reflexive reinvention of previous characters and themes. Another is the relocating of his vision of the West in the late nineteenth century, the very terrain of romance and myth that McMurtry spent much of his earlier career seeking to avoid. The Thalia trilogy posited, in varying lyrical and satirical tones, the eclipse of the ranching West by changing times, the onset of urbanization, and a kind of realism—of language, espe-cially of sexual reference—that differed greatly from the genera-tion of the grandfathers. Dialectically, McMurtry set himself against the sexless ranch romanticism of J. Frank Dobie and Company, and Dobie and his generation got the point. For instance, my freshman English professor at TCU, a venerable pioneer of southwestern literary scholarship, checked out the library copy of *Horseman, Pass By* on permanent faculty loan in order to keep it out of the hands of innocent TCU students, of whom, of course, there were none.

After the three Thalia-based novels came his goodbye-to-all-that book of essays, *In A Narrow Grave*, in which the enfant terrible of Texas letters kicked dust on the graves of the Texas trio of Dobie, Bedichek, and Webb. He also froze the livers of his fellow Archer Countians by ticking off every four-letter expletive ever uttered in that bleak Protestant country, and generally declared that he was through writing about the rural beatitudes and would henceforth decamp from Nostalgiaville to train his guns on modern city life. It was his end of "Old Texas" and the beginning of "New(e)rotic Texas," as found in the Houston trilogy: *Moving On, All My Friends Are Going To Be Strangers*, and *Terms of Endearment*. Amazingly, two of these books have already had their sequels, and only the most perverse reader would wish to find out whether Patsy Carpenter of *Moving On* is still crying at the turndown of a bed sheet. But even though *Moving On* is interminable and tedious in some places, it's the closest anyone in Texas has come to doing a Trollope number on the petty miseries of graduate student life, and for some readers, like myself, it's strangely addictive.

All My Friends demonstrates McMurtry's versatility and the desire he once held not to repeat himself. A road novel, it draws on one of the young McMurtry's major influences: the writings of Jack Kerouac. McMurtry has noted how Kerouac's *On The Road* opened up American fiction by slashing through the stodginess of American formalist prose in the fifties, and *All My Friends* moves like a roller coaster as it traces the fortunes of its feckless hero, Danny Deck, a young, lonely, horny writer whose first novel, *The Shallow Grass*, sounds a great deal like *Horseman, Pass By*. But where *All My Friends* differs from McMurtry's previous fiction is in its tendency to veer into areas of exaggerated comedy to the point of testing the reader's credulity. The scenes set at his Uncle Laredo's monstrous, gothic ranch house in West Texas are cartoonish and in fact owe more to Yosemite Sam cartoons than to *Giant*. As an ironic, self-reflexive portrait of the perils of regionalism, *All My Friends* stands as one of the oddest and most likable productions from McMurtry's pen.

Its sequel, however, is something else again. *Some Can Whistle* resurrects Danny Deck from the Rio Grande , where he was last seen trying to drown his manuscript, and places him in a mansion in Thalia some twenty-odd years later. Now fabulously wealthy, he is also a boring eccentric. Future psychological interpretations of McMurtry may view this 1990 novel as offering insights into the author's mid-life mind-set following some health problems, including a heart bypass. In any event, this novel is certainly haunted by the notion of mortality, and its death toll parallels that of his novels set in killer country in the Old West. It used to be that when McMurtry couldn't think of anything to do with his characters, he'd have them hop into bed with the nearest available prospect. Now he subjects them to death and destruction. If you get to liking somebody in McMurtry now, watch out. Few of them ultimately survive.

Sequels followed upon sequel: *Texasville* (*The Last Picture Show*); *The Evening Star* (*Terms of Endearment*); *The Late Child* (*The Desert Rose*). All seemed attempts to capitalize upon McMurtry's new eminence as a Brandname Author seeking to join the company of such immortals in the marketplace as James Michener and Danielle Steele. Other nineteenth-century westerns followed: *Anything for Billy* and *Buffalo Girls*. The Billy the Kid book, a send-up of the dime novel, was thankfully short and has provoked a fair amount of ridiculous overestimations by academicians of a postmodern bent. Of *Buffalo Girls* I cannot speak because I do not read books about (1) forts, (2) madams, or (3) Calamity Jane, the latter of which is the hermaphroditic subject of this excursion into western mythology.

So far none of McMurtry's sequels and forays into western fairyland have enjoyed the success of *Lonesome Dove*. *Streets of Laredo* is his most honorable effort to return to the mother lode itself, the "ore in the whore" as it were, and gives us, as we have seen, Lorena redux. But not Blue dux. If the novel is out of Gus, there are still enough fumes in the tank to get us if not to Dodge then at least to somewhere near Laredo.

McMurtry Recycling, Inc., has just released its new fall model, the prequel to *Lonesome Dove*, the company's best-selling western of a few years back. In *Dead Man's Walk* Augustus McCrae, who died so affectingly at the end of *Lonesome Dove*, reappears as a young man, along with his pal Woodrow Call who, in *Streets of Laredo*, the sequel to *Lonesome Dove*, had lost an arm and a leg. In the new novel both young heroes are fit as fiddles and ready for adventure.

There is, of course, plenty of precedent for resurrecting dead heroes. James Fenimore Cooper, for instance, killed off Hawkeye in the third Leatherstocking novel, then brought him back on stage for two more novels. McMurtry may well have several more Gus and Call novels left in his Olivetti. Texas history between 1842 (approximately the time of *Dead Man's Walk*) and the late 1880s (*Lonesome Dove*), is rich with possibilities: the 1848 war with Mexico, the Civil War, and Reconstruction Texas. Heck, that's three novels right there. Then there's always the possibility of "Romper Room Rodeo: Gus and Call, the Nursery Years."

In *Dead Man's Walk* McMurtry continues his recent trend of rewriting history. The history that he draws upon needs a little explanation first, because there are quite a few people who make up the current 18.4 million citizens of the Lone Star state who haven't had the privilege of studying Texas history in our public schools. The historical events underpinning the novel are those doomed expeditions into New Mexico launched in the early 1840s by the brash, cash-poor, imperialistic, and ambitious young Republic. Texas' record of achievement in the various filibustering assaults on Mexico and New Mexico is so poor that one wonders how the state ever achieved its braggart status.

The main goal of these ventures was Santa Fe and the lucrative fur trade that fueled the economy of that ancient village. Santa Fe had always been on President Mirabeau B. Lamar's mind. The second president of the republic, Lamar selected Austin as the site for the capitol because it formed, as he saw it, an axis between Houston (the city) and Santa Fe. Lamar's middle name, incidentally, was Bonaparte, and he wasn't named after Napoleon for nothing; his ambitions were about that size.

In point of fact, Lamar was right. Texas would have done well to have taken and held Santa Fe. There are several advantages to this proposition. First of all, if we had it, it wouldn't look like an adobe theme park. Second, there wouldn't be any blue Mexican food. Third, we'd have our own ski slopes, which we could really use. Now we'll never have them unless somebody like Ross Perot stops wasting his time running for president and builds some snow-capped mountains out near Amarillo or some other empty flat place in Texas that could use the tourist business. 'Cause it's way too late ever to get Santa Fe now. The Californians have it—and the next thing you know Santa Fe will be home to earthquakes, mud slides, adobe meltdown, and celebrity murder trials.

But back to the past. The Santa Fe Expedition, launched in 1841 with President Lamar's full support, was doomed to an humiliating surrender and capture without a shot being fired. This expedition got off to a bad start, when the party mistook the Wichita River for the Red River and spent a great deal of time headed in the wrong direction. McMurtry has clearly borrowed from this event, because his contingent of two hundred adventurers that leaves Austin headed for New Mexico does exactly that, confuses the Wichita with the Red. Here McMurtry brings in Charles Goodnight for a cameo appearance. The ever sensible Goodnight points out their error and laughs at the folly of their notion that Santa Fe is a paradise of gold and silver there for the taking.

The Somervell Expedition of 1842 was also ill-conceived and quickly ended in abject failure. Many of its adventurers immediately joined forces in what would turn out to be an even greater disaster—the Mier Expedition. It is the Mier Expedition that McMurtry draws upon most heavily. Yet another filibuster, the Warfield Expedition (1842-1843) was intended as a retaliatory mis-

sion to invade New Mexico. The Texans captured one little flea-
bitten town, Mora, but were routed when Mexican troops stam-
peded their horses. Some elements of this folly also find their way
into the novel.

The Warfield contingent then joined up with one Jacob
Snively, a leader with not the most heroic-sounding moniker, who
had formed an expedition said to have the support of Sam Houston
himself. Styling themselves the "Battalion of Invincibles," they
proved anything but. In Kansas, where they sought to capture
lucrative caravans on the Santa Fe Trail, Texas troops ran afoul of
the U.S. Army, which sent them packing.

The history of ill-fated Texan efforts to obtain the plunder of
New Mexico is almost farcical in its total repudiation of their
grandiose dreams. Many Texans perished, and those that did not
had to suffer a forced march to Mexico, imprisonment, privation,
and the sheer misery of being held captive by hated enemies whom
they considered inferior.

Into this historical mess enter Gus and Call, as young Texas
Rangers who have signed on to see the world, make a living wage,
and have some rowdy adventures to boot. Gus will disappoint, I
believe, those readers who loved him in *Lonesome Dove*. All the
young Gus talks about is "poking" whores. Call, on the other hand,
is trying to learn how to survive on a bloody, merciless frontier.
Taciturn as ever, Call is still more interesting here than Gus.

After much suffering caused by bad leadership, nasty weather,
and nastier Comanches, Gus and Call and a handful of stragglers—
most notably the legendary Bigfoot Wallace—are taken captive by
the Mexican army and marched through the Jornado del Muerto,
from which the novel takes its title. Eventually the captives are
taken to a small village in the vicinity of El Paso, where the novel
reaches its conclusion with a retelling of the most famous incident
of the Mier Expedition: the "decimation."

Every Texas schoolchild used to know the story of the drawing
of the black and white beans. When the Mier Expedition collapsed
and the Texans surrendered, they were put in chains and marched

into the interior of Mexico, all the way to Perote Prison in Mexico City. The few survivors languished in captivity for nearly two years, before finally being released to straggle back to Texas. But before that outcome, the prisoners were subjected to the decimation. Near Saltillo, all the Texans were blindfolded in turn and forced to draw beans from an earthen pot. Those who drew white beans were spared; the seventeen who drew black beans were stood against a wall and shot. The decimation did not do much to improve relations between Texas and Mexico.

The most detailed historical account of the black bean episode appears in John C. Duval's *The Life of Bigfoot Wallace*. Bigfoot Wallace was a real person, one of those outsized figures that tended to turn up on the western frontier. Texas had a bunch of them: Davy Crockett, Jim Bowie, John Wesley Hardin, Sam Bass, hellcatters like that. Wallace's account of how he survived is compelling. According to Wallace, he thought he detected a difference in size between the white or smaller beans and the black or larger ones. When it came time for him to draw and the blindfold was in place, he tried to calculate by touch the size of the beans and eventually settled upon one that he hoped was white. "It was a white one, of course, or I should not now be here to tell my story," he writes, but "not a very white one, and when I cast my eyes upon it, it looked to me as 'black as the ace of spades.'"

In McMurtry's hands, however, the wily old frontiersman draws a black bean and dies. (Gus and Call, by the way, draw white beans.) Cut down in the prime of life, McMurtry's Bigfoot Wallace is not allowed to live out his historical life. The real Bigfoot died in 1899, and his life as told to Duval is one of the classics of early Texas literature. We wouldn't have that book if he had drawn the black bean.

So I don't get it. Why does Bigfoot die in McMurtry's novel? Is there some anti-bean gene in McMurtry? He prematurely killed off Judge Roy Bean, remember, and now Bigfoot Wallace gets it because of a bean. Or is it that McMurtry dislikes certain storied figures from the mythic past and wants to pare them down to size?

Or is it that he wants to join the postmodernist camp and treat historical fact irreverently and irresponsibly? I don't know. It's all very deep or very shallow.

That McMurtry is wallowing in postmodernism would appear to be the case given the circumstances he invents surrounding the decimation episode. First of all, it doesn't take place in Saltillo; McMurtry's characters never cross the Rio Grande into Mexico. Secondly, he stages the whole scene at a leper colony. That's right, a leper colony, something we haven't seen since Lew Wallace's popular novel of 1880, *Ben Hur*. The leading leper is a British lady named Lady Carey, who has for retinue a "Negress" and a chipper son, the young viscount Mountstuart. Lady Carey needs an escort to Galveston and enlists the services of the handful of surviving Texans.

And so they set off. Call and Gus are especially pessimistic about their chances. Throughout the whole trek they have been under constant, murderous harassment from Buffalo Hump, a fearsome Comanche skilled in the ways of torture and dismemberment (there was an actual chief named Buffalo Hump, by the way). Sure enough, only a few days after leaving the leper colony, they come upon B.H. and the boys. Things look really bleak until Lady Carey takes over. She strips off her clothes and rides among the Comanches, singing an aria from a Verdi opera, in pure, thrilling Italian. The Indians, of course, not having been previously exposed to Italian opera, light out for the mountains, and all are saved. I can't help wondering what Charlie Goodnight would have thought about this turn of events.

Polemics

Palefaces and Redskins:
A Literary
Skirmish

*It is quite all right to regard me as a Southern,
specifically a Texas, writer.*
—*Katherine Anne Porter to George Sessions Perry,* 1943

The Texas literary scene reminds me of the skirmish line a famous critic once observed in the landscape of American literature. Philip Rahv said it was the Palefaces versus the Redskins, Henry James vs. Mark Twain. On one side, culture, refinement, and technique; on the other, raw life, realism, and maybe something less than art. In Texas terms, Katherine Anne Porter vs. J. Frank Dobie. Such polarities are of course complex when you get down to actual cases. In a work like *Noon Wine* Porter wrote about the Redskin side of Texas experience with consummate power; and Dobie, who devoted a lifetime to studying the Redskin past—Old Texas, the ranching tradition, cowboys—loved Romantic poetry and lusted after Paleface status.

Today the Paleface-Redskin issue is plainly present, and the sides are clearly lined up. The Palefaces are all those folks who stand ready to rescue Texas writing (and indeed Texas itself) from its provincial, embarrassing, and nativistic roots. Many of the Palefaces are èmigrés, recent arrivals, but many are homegrown, too. All are the literary equivalent of Yuppies: upscale, well-educated, fern-bar writers. The Paleface world view is pretty simple, and it looks like this:

EAST	TEXAS
Ideas	Prejudices
Sensitivity	Crudeness
Art	Ort

Palefaces tend to cluster in the major cities and many earn their bread in the academies teaching creative writing. Houston is probably the capital of Paleface Writing Culture, though Austin is not far behind. In the 1980s Houston managed to lure back to Texas the best of the Paleface writers, Donald Barthelme. Now Barthelme is a very fine writer indeed, and any state ought to be glad to claim him. But with two or three tiny exceptions, none of Barthelme's work takes the measure of Texas—or tries to—though it does do an excellent job of capturing the frissons of upper Manhattan.

Redskins, on the other hand, tend to live out where the screw worms kill the cows. Elmer Kelton, for example, resides in San Angelo where, at one time, the best steakhouse eatery in town billed itself as "The Dinning Room." Kelton is the puredee Redskin author: his fiction is always and only western, and it's nearly always about cowhands, drought, and squintin' into the sun. Elmer probably couldn't be dynamited out of San Angelo. But you don't have to live in Texas to be a Redskin. Dan Jenkins and Larry L. King have lived out of the state forever, it seems, and have made semi-serious fortunes recycling their increasingly nostalgic versions of Redskin culture. Vide *Semi-Tough* and *The Best Little Whorehouse in Texas*.

Maybe where you drink is a better index than where you live. In Austin the ultimate Paleface-Yuppie drinking hole is a eucalyptus bar overlooking Lake Travis, with a multi-tiered, many-splendored view of the lake, the circling buzzards, and the falling waterline. Here, every sunset, the pilgrims from California and Colorado come to sip their Perriers and strawberry daiquiris and genteelly applaud the sinking of the sun in the west. In old-time Texas drinking establishments you never saw the light. Dark, dank, and choked with smoke, such bars featured people hunched over their drinks, getting up only to punch B-16 or the guy next to them. The only green thing was the felt on the pool table. An actual plant wouldn't have lasted two days. Sometimes the barmaid, usually named Brenda, might consent to add a plastic plant or two, but even these lost their glossy sheen in short time amidst all that smoke and hacking.

Who's winning the culture battle? asks the erstwhile novice. The Palefaces. In the end they nearly always win. They've already taken over the Texas Institute of Letters. In the early eighties the top prize ($5,000 cold American) went twice in a row to books that have absolutely nothing to do with Texas: the 1981 winner dealt with bachelor life in New York City, the 1983 winner with the international tennis circuit. Mr. Bachelor had barely touched down at the Houston airport before the prize was his, and Mr. Tennis, who taught in Austin for a while, has lived in Rome the last three years. TIL membership has tilted, too. Of late, the fern-bar, emigré, or carpetbagging crowd has been admitted by the gross, while outsiders, native Texans writing in and out of the state, languish at Dairy Queens and honky-tonks, internal exiles in their native land. Brie anyone?

The Palefaces are bothered most by Texas "vulgarity" and "anti-intellectualism." From similar misapprehensions, I think, most writers don't like being labeled as Texas writers or even regionalists for that matter. They just want to be called writers. Fine. But still, I think, there's something to be said for looking at writers within the context of a culture, a place. This was the whole point of the Dobie-Bedichek-Webb project, bringing Texas into literature. Bedichek put the whole matter best, in a letter to Dobie in 1946: "Don't, I beg you, become expatriated. The mind and the emotions have to have a home, just like the body. For better or for worse, in health and in sickness, etc., etc., a man is born into (i. e., married to) a country, and with all her faults, he must love her still. Think of your brush country and of the paisano, and of the friendly people who talk with just your own accent, and of the good and noble things your countrymen have done and said. As Whitman said, 'report everything from an American point of view.'"

Today, in the post-Dobie era, it is possible to ask if there is a Texas literary tradition. I think there is, but it exists apart from the knowledge of the writers themselves. Writers have other fish to fry, they read eclectically, and often they haven't read the work of their predecessors and peers, for dozens of good and sufficient reasons. If you look at the responses of Texas writers collected in Patrick Bennett's *Talking with Texas Writers*, it becomes overwhelmingly obvious that most of the writers Bennett interviewed have not read very widely in the imaginative literature produced by earlier Texas writers.

Where does this situation leave us? With plenty to do. The task for academics is to do what they do best, to uncover, sift through, evaluate, and redeem from the past, writing which is valuable and worth knowing. The task for Texas writers is to stop worrying about Texas as a provincial tag, a handicap, a brand. The task for publishers is to take chances, print original new Texas fiction, and reprint the classics. Newspapers and magazines need to review Texas books, and here the record is extremely spotty. Too many Texas newspapers carry no book reviews at all, or devote all their space to printing canned reviews from East Coast papers on national authors such as Joyce Carol Oates, while allowing good Texas fiction to sink into obscurity. Finally, the public needs to buy Texas fiction, add new titles to personal southwestern libraries, and stop depending on the bestseller lists to tell them what to read.

With increased knowledge instead of fifth-rate opinions based on cultural differences, brie vs. barbeque, maybe then the Paleface-Redskin controversy can level off, TIL can start operating the way it should (or else drop Texas from the name of the organization), and everybody can recognize that Texas, a big country, has room for every kind of writer under the sun.

Postscript, 1987

When my remarks on the Texas literary scene appeared in 1984, I received several postcards from writers scattered hither and yon— one, I recall, was postmarked London, England—and all said they considered themselves in the Redskin camp. Then silence, the usual response, set in, and I went about my business, going for whole weeks without ever thinking about Texas literary skirmishes.

Imagine my surprise, then, when Donald Barthelme, two years later, in 1986, took out after me in *Texas Monthly*. My portrait of the new Texas writers provoked him to inquire, "Did he mean faggot homosexual queer pansy fairies? And if so, why didn't he say so?" Very odd, this sexual reading of my argument. It seemed obvious to me that all I had meant by "fern-bar" writer was the kind of writer who lacked any close or meaningful relation with a place, namely Texas. Deracination (a nice Paleface word) was the point of my argument. It had nothing to do with anybody's sexual inclinations.

It's probably time to drop the armed-camp metaphor. Most native Texans have their feet in two worlds: Redskin past, Paleface present. I don't want to turn the clock back, return to live on a starve-out farm or in a small town where there are no libraries, no theaters, no museums, no restaurants. Nor, in reading, do I want to have to choose between George Sessions Perry's Rockdale or Bud Shrake's Dallas. Country, town, city—Texas regionalism can encompass them all.

Postscript, 1997

This little essay, which appeared in the now defunct *Texas Humanist*, acquired a life of its own. People still mention it to me— writers, I mean. Without belaboring or rewriting the whole piece, I want simply to make a few addenda here and then let it rest.

1. The Barthelme sexual misprision of my point was oddly reinforced by one of the writers whom I mentioned in the original piece, Mr. Bachelor. An editor at a university press in Texas once showed me a letter that she had received from Mr. Bachelor, denouncing me

for various literary sins and, something I really found astonishing, claiming that his private parts were bigger than mine. Mr. Bachelor's last book (he's been back in New York for years) contains a paean to his own navel. Enough said.

2. Many of the points raised in the paragraph about the tasks awaiting various groups, academics, writers, etc., have largely been realized. The eighties proved to be a rich period of academic conferences, dissemination of information about Texas writers, and publication of out-of-print works. Several Texas newspapers have done an excellent job of increasing the number of reviews of works by local authors. In the nineties, with the decline in academic funds, independent chain bookstores have played an increasingly important role. There are far more readings, signings, and other locally based cultural/literary activities for Texas authors than ever before. The creation of Texas Writers Month gets the word out, too. The Texas Literary Festival, under the auspices of First Lady Laura Bush, also gives Texas writing a high-profile venue.

3. Ironically, many of the writers seem to have abandoned serious Texas fiction for the quicker returns of film scripts and genre novels, chiefly crime and detective novels. It may be that just when Texas literature is being celebrated the most, it is dead. Only nobody seems to have noticed.

4. The advent of Cormac McCarthy to Texas is the single greatest literary plus of the last decade. McCarthy's three Texas-based novels show what can be done with formulaic western materials in the hands of a serious, dedicated artist. McCarthy's creative appropriation of Hemingway, Faulkner, Crane, and Melville, among others, puts him far ahead of provincial, formula-bound genre writers. One page of a McCarthy novel offers more rewards than entire novels by many Texas writers.

5. I now think that I was wrong to suggest that Texas writers need to read more Texas writing. What I find most striking today is the sheer provinciality of much Texas writing. This is a point that Larry McMurtry made, rather forcefully, back in 1981.

6. Counting Texas as a nation-state, a world in itself, or "a whole

other country," as a recent tourist ad puts it, Texas comes up quite short in the literary department. By comparison, our population is about the same as that of Australia, but that country, connected through literature with three great traditions—British, European, and American—has produced a Nobel Laureate, Patrick White, and a host of astonishingly good writers. Texas literature sometimes seems too absorbed, in the most limited way, with its history, with accounts of the Alamo, cowboys, and put-on local color. Allusions to Lone Star Beer, armadillos, and Willie Nelson are not enough to make a novel authentic or, for that matter, good.

Land Without Myth, or, Texas and the Mystique of Nostalgia

....

lmost a dozen years later, it's possible to look back on the Texas Sesquicentennial with something considerably less than awe. The Centennial, in 1936, had been a watershed moment in Texas cultural history. A whole book has been written about that congeries of events, but when the history of the Sesquicentennial is written, it won't take a book. Perhaps a few paragraphs will suffice.

The only stimulating thing about the Sesquicentennial was its ironic timing—it came right in the middle of plunging oil prices. So instead of celebrating the rich panoramas of the past, some of the rich spent much of 1986 hiding out on their ranches and attending auctions; only they weren't buying, they were selling.

Still, there were a few lame attempts at celebration, self-evaluation, and the sort of backward glances that are supposed to accompany events such as a 150-year milestone. James Michener, for example, signed on to help us out, delivering his Lone Star opus even before the calendar year 1986 began. The result, *Texas*, was like a giant oil spill off the fair coast of Texas literature. A television station in Corpus Christi mounted a PBS-style documentary called *Lone Star*. It recycled all the old myths: Texans are strong, Texans are independent, Texans are blah blah blah. What the series really said is that Texans are male, minorities are either invisible or colorful, and women are best seen in short skirts on the sidelines of football games.

Larry Hagman, dressed as J.R. Ewing, introduced the series, standing on the beach in back of his adobe palace at Malibu, a Texas flag waving in the gentle California landward breezes. The *merde* in *Lone Star* was deeper than the sand at Malibu. Jimmie Dean, the mythic sausage maker, squinted into the camera and said, "Ah know the meaning of temporary setback, but Ah don't know the meaning of defeat." Travis couldn't have stated it better.

All through 1986 the myth was showing signs of strain. A wagon train with a bunch of pioneer-style senior citizens, early retirees dressed up in leggings and calico, was supposed to travel all around the state, but by early spring they were out of money and nobody gave a damn.

In the eighties I'd been writing about Texas' propensity to advertise itself at the expense of facts. In three books, one about movies, one about literature, and one that was literature—an anthology of Texas short fiction—Texas was depicted as little different from the one celebrated in film, song, beer commercials, and the *Lone Star* television series. What I quickly learned, though, was that the media preferred the stereotypes. At various times I was interviewed by the media—by CBS during the Republican convention in Dallas in 1984 ("Morning in Texas"), for example, and by *USA Today*. I'd answer their questions as truthfully as I could, and then they'd edit my answers to fit their needs. As a result I always came out sounding like (1) a fatuous spokesman for the Sweetwater Chamber of Commerce, or (2) a fatuous spokesman for the Republican party.

My message is simple. Texas is a land largely without a "land myth." In modern Texas, where I live, the land is almost wholly given over to malls. What hasn't been malled or condoed o'er awaits the next boom. In Austin we're said to be in that boom even now. Eventually we'll pave the rest of the state that's inhabitable.

Needless to say, I don't own a foot of land. I'm afraid if I did, I'd start writing like John Graves, one of the state's more treasured writers. Graves is a landowner who feels compelled to write about it. He won't let anybody alone about his land; it's his only subject and has been for nearly thirty years. Herewith, a typical passage from one of his books:

> . . . inside me somewhere there has always been the incipient disease of the land. . . . I had never managed to purge myself of the simple yeoman notion, contracted in childhood from kinsmen looking back to a rural past, that grass and crops and trees and livestock and wild things and water mattered somehow supremely, that you were not whole unless you had a stake in them, a daily knowledge of them.

Anytime somebody calls himself a "simple yeoman," you know you are listening to a landowner and not a simple yeoman. I guess if you own land, it means something to you. Not being given to mysticism—my forebears had all of that stamped out of them when they stopped being Catholics and started being Protestants on the way to being Nothing—I would have to say, in the lingo of the region, land don't mean much to me in and of itself.

The most land in Texas is in West Texas, if you are talking about empty land, and I wouldn't give a dime for most of it. Oh, the Big Bend country has its pleasures, and the Palo Duro country is very fine, but the land around Midland, Odessa, Abilene, Lubbock? One time I flew over West Texas in a small plane, and a historian on the trip with me, looking down on that vast and thinly populated flatness, said he figured if the water gave out like the oil had, and all the kids kept moving to Dallas or Houston, which they have been doing pretty steadily since World War II, then in the future West Texas might become like the Australian outback—desolate, which it already is, and empty, which it almost is. (Except at night. At night

West Texas is amazingly aglow with electric lights. From Abilene to Austin there's a solid connecting grid of lights on the land.)

So I think the only people who care about land in Texas are those who own some. It helps if you own a ranch and have read J. Frank Dobie. If you come from cotton farming country, you may not have so much land lust. Maybe if my dad had owned several counties and had a big plantation house, I'd have stuck with the cotton way of life. But he didn't and I didn't. He didn't stick with it either, for that matter. He couldn't. When cotton played out, small farmers like my father were forced to find other means of survival. The tendency in Texas in our time has been always towards the cities, where the jobs are.

With a few exceptions such as George Sessions Perry's *Hold Autumn in Your Hand*, land in Texas literature acquires what force it does for me through ironic portraits of space and, conversely, limitations.

Larry McMurtry, the best-known Texas writer since Dobie, has a nice ironic touch when he writes about the land. In *Horseman, Pass By* there is a fine moment that shows what I mean. The boy Lonnie is dreaming, and in his dream he and his grandfather, a throwback to the old wild days, sit on their horses on a ridge overlooking some rolling country. McMurtry writes, "There below us was Texas, green and brown and graying in the sun, spread wide under the clear spread of sky like the opening scene in a big Western movie."

Notice how the western movie reference frames the scene. What would have been nostalgia is undercut just enough. The country is beautiful in a minimalist sort of way, but it's seen through the controlling, ironic lens of a movie; also, it's a dream. In McMurtry's Sesquicentennial-inspired novel *Texasville*, there's a very funny bit of landscape description that shows he can still work that side of the street. He's describing the results of a boomlet in Thalia, his fiction-alized Archer City: "Across the street were the new municipal tennis courts, the latest addition to the Thalia skyline. The west edge of town was so flat and ugly that a tennis net could legitimately count as an addition to the skyline." Yet, as McMurtry knows better than anybody, what readers want most is not the real landscape but dreamscape. In other words, *Lonesome Dove*, set in a time before there were fences, oil derricks, Dairy Queens, or high-rises.

Dobie, McMurtry's famous predecessor and still much beloved by Texans, wrote only about the landscape of nostalgia, and he believed it would never end. Here is Dobie celebrating the place where he was raised:

> No matter what is discontinued, the land remains. A thousand years, ten thousand years hence, the Dobie ranch will be where it was before the Ramirez Grant took in a portion of its pristine acreage. It will have other names, be divided and then be absorbed. The land will always be grazing land, for neither soil nor climate will permit it to be anything else.

In less romantic terms, what Dobie is really saying is that the land is so sorry, it will escape all the ravages of possible change and transformation. It will endure because it is so sorry. (The word "sorry" in Texan speech means worthless. It 's what one says about something or somebody that's no good.)

John Houghton Allen, whose 1952 book *Southwest* deserves to be better known than it is, has a fine description of sorry country: "For this is hard country, brush country, mean country, heartbreak country. Ugly in summer, drought-stricken, dusty, glaring, but in winter it is hideous." He was talking about South Texas, but I think he meant most of the state. He said all you could do in such country was drink and fornicate.

Richard Harding Davis, that intrepid reporter-adventurer, now largely forgotten, viewed Texas from the window of a train car on his trip to the West in 1891. South Texas, along the border, he called the "backyard of the world"—a country, he said, "where there are no roses, but where everything that grows has thorn." These observations inevitably bring to mind what General Phil Sheridan said about Texas: "If I owned Hell and Texas, I'd rent out Texas and live in Hell."

Land so desolate, so empty, has provoked a kind of wonder in some writers. One is Loula Grace Erdman, whose novel *The Edge of Time* (1950) evokes all those moments, in western and in Texas literature, when a woman from a more sheltered environment confronts her fate—displacement and disorientation—because of a marriage:

> The first thing Bethany saw was nothing. Nothing at all. She pitched her mind in nothingness, found herself drowning in it as a swimmer drowns in water too deep for him. Here was more sky than she had ever seen before. That was all there was— sky. No houses, no trees, no roads. Nothing to break the landscape. She shrank back from it as one draws back from sudden bright light.
>
> "Aren't there—aren't there any trees?" she asked Wade.
>
> "Not on the high plains. Too dry for them. They grow down in the breaks though."
>
> She thought she could not bear a place without trees. They broke up nothingness. They cut a land down to something you could stand to contemplate.

This same Panhandle landscape—or skyscape, one might better call it—inspired some of Georgia O'Keeffe's most daring early work. And that painterly writer Gertrude Stein, on a swing through the state, put it this way in *Everybody's Autobiography* (1937):

> Texas is a level surface . . . We saw the flatland and we saw the cattle not so many of them it had been a bad year for cattle as there had been too much cold weather and too much dry weather and as they do not in any way protect them they all died not all of them but a lot of them still it was a pleasure to see them and even see some cowboys and one cowgirl go toward them.

Stein saw the level surface of Texas from an automobile window, and that is the way most Texans relate to the land—by driving across it as fast as they can.

So Texas, I insist, has no land myth that empowers or nourishes its devotees. In Texas the "remembered earth" is the land the family sold to make a killing on, or is the property used to hunt deer on, or is something one wished to escape from because it was so harsh and unforgiving. Myth in Texas is either (a) a system of belief in profits, development, and expansion that is commercially defined and perpetuated through advertising, self-promotion, and politicians seeking simple iconographic symbolism—Stetsons, Lone Stars, the state's distinctive shape, etc.; or (b) a monolithic Anglo interpretation of the past that begins at the Alamo and ends at Southfork; or (c) an anti-myth in which the world, to use Mircea Eliade's terms, is profane rather than sacred. I don't think that eighty-two percent of Texans, the proportion that currently live in cities, spend much time at all remembering the earth. Perhaps they should, but they don't.

History, in Texas anyway, is on their side. There is no model in Anglo Texas culture for thinking about Mother Earth. Early on, Native Americans in Texas were either killed or driven out of the state, so that in contrast, say, with New Mexico, there never was in Texas a civilization of Indian culture approaching the complexity and richness of Pueblo culture in New Mexico.

But I am always reluctant to generalize too much about such matters. What I want to suggest instead is a point about the selectivity of all myths, all systems that are designed to transmit a structure of beliefs and values from the past to the present. Myth-making is a very selective process, and if you are looking for Native Americans to emulate, I offer for your edification the following examples, from Cabeza de Vaca's great narrative, *La Relacion* the first southwestern prose work of art. (I quote from the English translation by Cyclone Covey, *Adventures in the Unknown Interior of America.*) De Vaca is describing the quaint practices of some people he called the Mariames, whom he encountered in Texas sometime around 1535:

> They cast away their daughters at birth; the dogs eat them. They say they do this because all the nations of the region are their enemies, whom they war with ceaselessly; and that if they were to marry off their daughters, the daughters would multiply their enemies until the latter overcame and

enslaved the Mariames, who thus preferred to annihilate all daughters [rather] than risk their reproduction of a single enemy. We asked why they themselves did not marry the girls. They said that marrying relatives would be a disgusting thing. It was better to kill them than to give them to either kin or foe.

To which the only appropriate response might be: it takes a pillage. De Vaca's bit of amateur anthropology serves to remind us that in all times and all places there may be forms of behavior that seem troubling to the liberal humanist eye.

The absence of an Indian presence in Anglo Texas, is, then, one of the possible sources of the missing mysticism about the land. What about the Hispanics? There, too, it seems to me, Texas is fundamentally different from other, more exotic southwestern locales. Texas Hispanic authors such as Tomás Rivera and Rolando Hinojosa have as little mysticism in their works as any of the Texas Anglo writers, which is to say none at all. I can't explain why, except perhaps that in Texas, unlike New Mexico, for example, where several cultures coexist on their own autonomous terms, in Texas the Anglo commercial view has dominated to an extraordinary degree. And that view holds that land is personal property and not the sacred body of Mother Earth. Those of us who live in cities and own no land, I repeat, spend very little time thinking about land. And never mystically.

In modern Texas the ideal is Las Colinas, an upscale mixed residence/business development on what was once raw prairie just north of Dallas, near the Dallas-Fort Worth Airport. Las Colinas is a twenty-first century suburb, reported an article in *USA Today*. And in a post-modernist description worthy of Donald Barthelme, we learn that "a third of Las Colinas is open space. Flowers are changed five times yearly." In Texas, land—and its corollary, nature—must be harnessed to meet prevailing economic needs.

Postscript

This essay is one of those that seem to irritate some readers. I wrote it originally for a conference held at Tucson in 1987. I was on a panel with writers famous for their portrayal of mystical Kiowas and magical carp, and I found I had no magic baggage to draw upon. Some readers liked it, though. A reviewer in *The New York Times* in 1994 cited it as his favorite essay in the collection, *Open Spaces, City Places*, calling it an act of "witty deconstruction." This pleased me inordinately—as the idea of deconstruction had always seemed unintelligible. To learn at this late date that I was a deconstructionist? Well, I couldn't have been prouder.

Anything for Larry

··

The last time I saw Larry was in 1988 when he came to the University of Texas to give a talk. Actually give is not quite the word. Larry is not *into* giving, as they say. I don't even want to know how much he was paid to give this talk. But he was still riding the crest of *Lonesome Squab* and I know the amount was in the neighborhood of five thousand plus. Anyway, I was asked to give the introduction, which I had no choice but to do. And do happily, I might add, because that is what I do when the administration asks me to do something: I do it for free and hope for a crumb later. It's called Being a Professor.

Anyway, during my brief and incredibly witty remarks which I read with studied casualness, a front tooth that I'd forgotten had even been capped fell off in mid-sentence, clattering onto the slanted podium in front of me and rolling down to the bottom where, covertly, I managed to snare it. A faint odor of decay filled my mouth, like the opening of an ancient, long-sealed tomb, but the worst problem was that my voice began to emit a low whistle, and the louder I talked, the more I sounded like a wind tunnel where they were testing a new supersonic jet. I staggered through to the end, once again humiliated in the presence of the august and fabulously wealthy Larry McMurtry.

Larry's speech that day was one of those off-the-cuff, thinking-out-loud deals. He doesn't have to prepare anything; he just talks for a specified time and they write him out a check. It was sort of interesting, though, when he said he was tired of writing novels, that men over fifty-five or so, whatever age he was at that moment, couldn't write novels anyway (the thought of Tolstoy, Saul Bellow, and John Updike momentarily flickered across my mind as, furtively rubbing my tooth like a talisman of failure, I sat sunken and dejected beside the president of the university). Larry went on to state that he was perhaps going to write some travel books in the future but he certainly didn't intend to write any more novels. Since then, he has published five or is it six novels and signed a $10.2 million contract for four novels. That they seem to be getting progressively worse is perhaps a point of interest to some readers, though I wonder whether Larry cares or not.

The truth is, though Larry's much on my mind, I haven't read all of his work. I've read only two of the what is it now, five sequels that he continues to bring out like an aging TV producer hoping to hit pay dirt one more time; these novels that are beginning to feel like one of those reunion shows, the Waltons twenty years later, the Brady Bunch reassembled, etc. Still I think about Larry all the time, though I'm sure he never thinks of me except when he reads one of my brilliant, insightful and less than charitable appraisals of his recent work, and then I know what he thinks, he thinks: "It's that dipshit Graham again." I know he thinks of me as a dipshit because that is the word he used to describe David Koresh in a marvelous meditative essay on the Branch Davidians that he wrote for the *New Republic* (Larry is a wonderful essayist) in which he called David Koresh a "dipshit guru," which is a phrase I wish I'd written in an essay I wish I'd written but if I had it wouldn't have been published in *The New Republic* for $1,000 to the delight of every intellectual in the country, but in *The Texas Observer* for $75 and the total oblivion that a $75 royalty can guarantee.

Although I call him Larry, I probably shouldn't. What shall I call him? I've met him enough over the years to feel awkward calling him Mr. McMurtry, and in a rambling bit of post-modern memory criticism like this, I must eschew the rather cold lit-crit convention of "McMurtry," and since this is an entirely imaginary journey—well, almost—I feel most comfortable with Larry. Were he to knock at the door of my modest domicile someday soon—though I'm certain he won't—he never has—I'd probably avoid calling him anything until I was sure "Larry" wouldn't seem too familiar. But since this is my story, not his, and therefore home court advantage is mine, not his, "Larry" it is.

The first time I actually spoke to Larry was in Houston, in 1980, at the MLA meeting. Larry was on a panel with William Goyen and some other Texas writers. I don't recall what Larry said during what must have been a scintillating discussion of regional writing, but after the panel broke up I made an effort to speak to him for a few moments. I held out my hand, told him who I was—rather breathlessly, because in these brief sound-bite celebrity encounters you have to make your pitch succinctly, grippingly, or not at all—and Larry simply looked at if not through me and muttered something, and then walked almost through if not over me to get to Grace Paley, who, it turned out, was standing behind me. I know this because I glanced at her name tag and it said "Grace Paley." They knew each other; they were buddies. Of course. I left them engaged in voluble discourse while I slunk away down some sterile corridor feeling like nothing so much as an academic with nothing better to do than attend some unspeakably boring session on Jacques Derrida and the ideology of advanced obfuscation. Instead I entered the forlorn, empty streets of downtown Houston and found a quiet, impersonal bar and had a stiff one.

What you have to realize is this: Larry is a brand-name author, has been since the runaway success of *Lonesome Dove*, a book I reviewed, back in '85, for an obscure, now defunct local magazine (I have written for more defunct magazines than I would like to admit). I missed the boat completely on that book. How was I to know that yuppies across the length and breadth of this great land would spend their poolside summer enchanted by the dusty adventures of Gus and Call and Blue Duck? How was I to know that for the next three years, every time I got on a plane, and I got on a lot of them, seats would be littered with well-thumbed copies of *Lonesome Dove*. On the other hand I never saw anybody with a copy of *No Name on the Bullet*, my biography of Audie Murphy (see, I have to explain it), and probably never will, unless it's some gimlet-eyed *Soldier of Fortune*-type clutching a greasy, broken-backed copy stolen from some public library in some god-forsaken midwestern state.

You see, Larry has reached that level of eminence, public approbation, all right, love, where anything he publishes automatically enters the best-seller list at No. 7. He could publish a book I had written and it would soar to No. 7, which is saying a lot. Larry's like that oil you hear the price quotations for on the stock market that you can't afford to invest in: he's Texas Sweet Crude, and you just pump it out of the earth and reap the profits.

The whole Larry-Don situation can be summed up by a little anecdote of something that never happened. Sometime in the early nineties Larry decided to take unto himself a partner, a writing partner. This sidekick would carry the load, share the burden, tote that bale, perform heavy lifting. I was ready. I sat by the phone waiting for the call. Let's go, Larry; let's take 'em to Missouri. It never happened. He never called. Instead he picked somebody else, a woman, a friend. Then they signed a four-book $10.2 million dollar deal.

My only real phone conversation with Larry was, of course, about money. This was sometime in the early eighties. The administration wanted me to find out what Larry would charge to come to campus and share his wisdom with us. When people ask me what I charge, on those increasingly rare occasions now that money seems to have dried up for conferences and talks, I hem and haw, because I don't know what fee to set. I don't have a set fee. Of course Larry does. Or did that time I called him. "It takes $1,500 to get me on a plane," he said. That was a good deal more than I had ever received for a talk, and I would get on a plane for the promise of a bottle of Fundador (a cheap Spanish brandy that I learned to like from reading *The Sun Also Rises* by Mr. Ernest Hemingway). After *Lonesome Dove* the cost for getting Larry on a plane jumped to $5,000. Among other things, this is what a Pulitzer Prize can do for you. I don't know what his fee is currently, lo these many books later. I would like to know, though, because whatever Larry gets is a benchmark for the rest of us to aim at. Larry's the man. He bats cleanup.

Over the years I have taught Larry on three continents—North America, Europe, and Australia. I would teach him on others if I had the opportunity. I like teaching Larry, especially *Horseman, Pass By*, his first novel and one he has never said anything good about. He always dismisses it as juvenilia. Yet this is the one that most people who teach Larry like to teach. I know it's my favorite, though I've taught several other of Larry's novels as well. Fact is, over the years I've moved a lot of Larry's books—in three currencies. So that is a part of the record too, my sponsorship and patronage of Larry, going into the third decade now. I have also, I have to confess, made a small amount of money off Larry. I'm like some kind of pilot fish that trails along behind Moby Dick in that novel by Mr. Herman Melville—a symbiotic relationship on a very low-level frequency. A strict accounting of my pilot-fish earnings is not possible, because I keep terrible records, but here is a reasonable approximation of profits and losses.

1974: "Is Dallas Burning? Notes on Recent Texas Writing," Texas State Historical Association, Waco. $00. Net loss: $250 air fare, $200 hotel, $100 bar bill; fine for drunk & disorderly conduct, $75.

1985: "Lonesome Dove," *Texas Humanist*. $100.

1986: *"Lonesome Dove*: Sources Real and Imagined." Popular Culture Association Meeting, Atlanta, Georgia. $00. Net loss: $400 air fare, $300 hotel, $200 bar bill, including table dance. No arrest.

1989: "Filming McMurtry: The Regionalist Imperative" in *Taking Stock: A Larry McMurtry Casebook.* $50.

1989: "Blood on the Saddle," *The World & I.* $800.

1993: "Trail to Texas," *Entertainment Weekly*. $350.

1993: "Way Out West," *Entertainment Weekly*. $1100. Big one.

1993: "Take My Sequel from the Wall: McMurtry Revisits McMurtry," *Austin Chronicle*. $250.

1994: "Pretty Boy Floyd," *Dallas Morning News*. $150.

1995: *"Lonesome Dove*: Butch and Sundance Go on a Cattle Drive," *Southwestern American Literature*. $00.

1995: "Dead Man's Curve: Gus and Call Pay a Revisionist Visit to Texas History," *Texas Observer*. $75.

1995: "Dead Man's Walk," *Entertainment Weekly*. $200.

1995: "Anything for Larry," Austin Culture Bash. $00.

1995: "Anything for Larry," Fall Literary Festival, Denton, Texas. $00. Net loss: $200 hotel; usual bar tab, etc.

1995. "Anything for Larry," *Texas Observer.* $75.

1996: "Waco/Taco: Remarks on Regionalism," Spring Writing Conference, Sydney, Australia. $200 (Australian) Net loss: Thousands of dollars (US)

1997: "Anything for Larry," Benefit for *Texas Observer.* $00.

Paris, as in Texas

At the UCLA Student Union the two English majors at the next table were growing animated. The topic wasn't politics or money or sex; it was the film *Paris, Texas.* "You've got to see it. It's a great film. It's about these abysses, right? It's German expressionism." Then the one who loved *Paris, Texas* told his pal about the key scene. Harry Dean Stanton is in this weird sex shop in Houston where the deal is you can see them but they can't see you. Stanton sits in a room talking by telephone to the young woman inside, through the glass partition, but she can't see him. Definitely an abyss.

Sipping coffee at the next table, I remembered the scene well because that was the moment when I had walked out of the movie, something I rarely do. The English major omitted an essential point. The woman in the film, played by Nastassja

Kinski, says I think I'll take my sweater off, and ol' Harry Dean says no, no, don't do that. Tears slide down his weathered cheeks. Tears almost slid down mine. One hour and forty-five minutes into this interminable film, and the only boobs in sight are these two characters.

There were plenty of other reasons to take a walk. *Paris, Texas* has the single stupidest premise behind it that I can remember in any film. It makes *Porky's* look smart. Stanton has been wandering in the deserts of the Southwest for four years, suffering from amnesia. Amnesia! When was the last time that one was hauled out of World War II movie mothballs? Worse, he suffers from an obsessive fixation upon the *place where he was conceived*. He believes that this great event occurred in what is now a vacant lot in Paris, Texas. They should have called this film *Vacant Lot*. I've taken a poll of my friends, and not one of them has ever been moved to wonder about where his mama and daddy did it. It's just not a big issue in the Sunbelt at this time.

They could also have called the film *Terlingua, Texas*, because that's where the vast empty landscapes were found, not in Paris, Texas. Terlingua is southwest of nowhere, in the remote Big Bend country. Every year they hold a chili cook-off; pilgrims and celebs fly in, cook the stuff, get drunk, then get the hell out. Paris, on the other hand, is a nice little town with a junior college, fast-food deco, and enough banks to finance two or three Third World economies. Paris is northeast of Dallas about eighty miles: farming country, or used to be. The countryside is green much of the year, winters are brief, and if there's enough rain the land-scape at ground level is quite lush. Nice country, but not very mythic. I know because I grew up in the same part of Texas.

Why does the film *Paris, Texas* have so little to do with its name site? Because certain intellectuals think it's funny that a place like Texas—all those cowboys, don't you know—would have a town named Paris. But we do. We also have towns named Athens, Troy, and London.

Europeans—this film was directed by Wim Wenders, a

German—are not the only ones to blame for *Paris, Texas*. Two Americans are also indictable: Sam Shepard and L.M. "Kit" Carson. Shepard came up with the original story idea, and Carson did some rewrites. The trio improvised as they went along, and it shows. Nobody had a story to tell. They just planted this guy in the middle of nowhere and then tried to figure out what to do with him. If they had wanted to admire some majestic John Ford scenery they could just have looked at back issues of *Arizona Highways* and spared the rest of us the agony of a phony existentialist quest for meaning. But no, that wouldn't have led to a film that most reviewers in the United States flipped over. You expect this kind of film to cop a Cannes Prize, which it did, but then you hope for some homegrown sanity that won't fall for the Cannes game every year. I've never seen such inflated reviews as those sparked by *Paris, Texas*. From the *L. A. Weekly*: "Wenders' vision of family, of human relationships, is almost unbearably bleak. Yet he faces the abyss with such vulnerability, such openness (not to mention a camera eye worthy of a Japanese landscape master) that we feel the truth of what he sees, and with it the beauty." Dozens of reviews soared into similar empyreans of intellectual eyewash. Can they all be wrong? Yes. There's a rule among some American reviewers: if it's long, boring, and foreign, it must be great.

The promoters of *Paris, Texas* were not short on pretentiousness themselves. Before the film opened in Austin, where I saw it, there appeared in local bookstores a thick, oversized book called *Paris, Texas*. It contained not one, not two, but three versions of the script: in English, French, and German. Abyss, abime, der Abgrund. There, that's it, the perfect title: *Der Abgrund*.

The main fault of *Paris, Texas* is its failure to see the state afresh. The director and writers came to the subject with a host of stale, preconceived notions; they might as well have made the movie in Germany. You can see the problem in books like Shepard's *Motel Chronicles* (1982), which is said to have been the starting point for the film. In one section datelined San Marcos,

1979, Shephard's hero is brooding (the favorite indoor sport of such heroes) in the night. Images of Texas flicker through his mind: "He could feel the presence of the automatic pistol, of cattle, of barbed wire, of dice, of riding the night range without a flashlight, of bars plunged into prairie night." Reading this, I can feel the presence of clichés. San Marcos is a little college town on the edge of the Hill Country, thirty miles south of Austin. The motels in San Marcos are all on I-35, and instead of cattle, cowboys, and western saloons, the traveler sees sights indistinguishable from those on any other interstate corridor in the United States: Great Western Motels, Sizzler Steakhouses, Red Lobsters, Chevrons—neons ablaze. Writers like Shepard, with their tired, ersatz sensibilities, can't see Texas or the Southwest accurately; they're too busy seeing it symbolically. Perhaps Shepard has a better sense of Texas today. I saw him recently at one of Austin's trendiest new watering holes; the scene was indistinguishable from a bar in Malibu or Manhattan; everybody was very upmarket and the women, nary a cowgirl among them, were enjoying expensive cigars right along with their yuppie boyfriends. The hottest topic was the rise in techno stocks.

When moviemakers take Texas on its own terms, the results can be wonderful. *Tender Mercies*, shot in Waxahachie in 1983, comes to mind. Directed by Australian Bruce Beresford, it catches the look and feel of rural and small-town Texas and manages, with the help of Robert Duvall, Tess Harper, and the rest of the cast, to capture the style of the people as well. Pauline Kael didn't like the country-music simplicity of the lives portrayed in this little film, but even she couldn't fault the rightness of a place perceived in accurate images. From a native Texan's point of view, *Tender Mercies* is valuable because it's true to the landscape, the weather, the inflections of the native idiom wrought by soil and sky. Someday somebody ought to make a picture about Paris, Texas, on location, there, in that specific and complex place. Then what Anna Thomas, maker of *El Norte*, calls the "voodoo of locations" might happen, and we might get something far better than we got with *Paris, Texas.*

Puerto Vallarta
Squeezed

....

Reviewer walks through the door, sits down. Has a review to write. Trying to remember the wind, how it feels to have been out there. Has known a lot of sorrow but never faced anything this tough before, trying to say how it is, this novel by a man called Robert James Waller.

The novel called *Puerto Vallarta Squeeze* takes an aging Kincaid-like hero from the novel called *The Bridges of Madison County* and, instead of making him a photographer, makes him another kind of "shooter": a professional sniper-assassin. Clayton Price is a guy from Brooklyn, though it's hard to imagine a less Brooklyn-sounding name. Name like that, he ought to be an oil man, a governor. No matter. As a boy, Clayton Price wanted to be a mountain man, as we learn in this marvelous sentence: "He'd read about them [mountain men] in a library book, and after that wanted to be one and having the freedom to go where wind took you and coming back only when you felt like it."

Although it is unclear which he most wants to be, mountain

man or library book, Clayton Price eventually becomes something very male and hard: he becomes a Marine sniper in Vietnam, where he kills hundreds of Viet Cong, including a woman whose head "exploded like a cantaloupe." Later, liking the life, Clayton Price becomes a mercenary. Now, in his fifties, he is simply a free-lance hit man who can still kill truly and well.

The story begins in a colorful Mexican village of "expats" (expatriates), Puerto Vallarta, where Danny Pastor, dropout journalist and author, is wasting away in his own private margueritaville, hanging out with Luz Maria, a beautiful girl up from peasant Catholic poverty. They spend their days drinking tequila and beer and their nights making endless whoopee. In a bar one night, Danny sees the "shooter," Clayton Price, drill two Americans.

After the hit, the shooter persuades Danny to drive him to the U.S. border, many miles to the north, and Danny, hard up for cash and fearful that Price knows his secret, agrees to take him in his battered Bronco. Luz goes along because she has always wanted to go to *El Norte*.

From then on, the novel moves from village to village with Clayton doing what he does best, knocking off bandidos and federales. Meanwhile a massive chase led by a CIA hardcase pursues the threesome into the mountains near Mazatlan.

Reviewer doesn't know what to make of Mr. Waller's prose, thinks it's strange, sort of dyslexic Hemingway, this need to drop subjects. The second sentence of the novel begins: "Had a partner name of Willie Royal. . . . " Later: "Had a gun under the fold . . . . " Mr. Waller's characters have the same habit. Says one: "Got divorced a while back. Running from her and the memories, not the IRS. Looking for warmer weather. Just drifted down here."

Reviewer also puzzled by the author's tendency to rev up meaning where there is none. The "Bronco called Vito," for example, is worn, its paint flaking or missing, its metal wearing out. Where you can't see rust you see holes and "after holes, infinity."

This is more meaning than any Bronco can sustain, even one called Orenthal.

But Mr. Waller's fans don't care about such niceties of language and precision. They can't, because if they did, they couldn't read a Waller novel. No, in Waller-Waller Land the plot is everything, and the plot is actually a scenario, an outline for a movie. Reading the novel, you start casting it. The reader is the director of the movie. In a script novel like this, you always think first of the Sheen brothers—which is never what you want to think of first.

In this kind of novel-outline for a screenplay, the main structural principle is sets of two. Everything happens twice. An example: During a stop at one village Danny, Luz, and the shooter think about setting free a caged ocelot and regret that they don't, and at the end Danny returns and frees the animal. It's a symbol, all right? It's about freedom and wildness, all right?

Novel lacks a Francesca to pull in the women's audience. Would be surprised if it stayed on the best-seller lists forever, but reviewer has been surprised before.

What the World
Wants to Know

....

In Terlingua a man walked up to John Grady Cole and said without preamble, my name is Perez, and I am Commander of the Chili.

My name is John Grady Cole, said John Grady, and this is my bosom waddy and chief all-around bottle washer, Lacy Rawlins.

Lacy? That is no name for a man, said Perez.

Look, Mister, he's kindly touchy about that.

Bastante de las maricones, said Perez. Let us have a philosophical conversation about chili.

Suit yourself, said John Grady.

What the world wants to know is whether your chili has *cojones*.

Say what?

The world wants to know whether your chili has *cojones*.

Do you have to repeat everything you say?

Yes, it is my way, for I am Commander of the Chili.

Now what's this about *cojones?* John Grady asked.

Cojones, testicles, I believe the surgeons call them. In your country. In my country, we call them *cojones*.

You mean to tell me that to win this contest we have to put *cojones* in our chili?

In a manner of speaking, yes.

Perez walked away, and John Grady turned to Lacy, who was busy setting up the cooker.

Lacy, did you hear that?

No, I didn't, John Grady. I was setting up the cooker.

Our Lord Jesus Christ, Lacy, it don't take your entire mind to do that. Or does it.

What did he say? Lacy asked.

He said we need *cojones* in our chili.

Well, you ain't using mine, said Lacy, so don't go getting no ideas.

Lacy, do you remember that road kill we saw a ways back where they have that sign saying EXOTIC ANIMAL RANCH.

No.

Never mind. Anyway, I saw laying over there in a bar ditch what looked a whole lot like a giraffe. A male giraffe.

Yeah?

Yeah. You didn't see it? Good Lord, Lacy. An eighteen-foot spotted animal with a neck from here to Albuquerque? Anyway, I want to you to go back there and cut off that animal's gonads and bring them back. We're gonna make us some real chili, ol dad.

Aw, John Grady, do I have to?

Yes, you have to, idjit. Cause if you don't I won't let you drive the Nissan with the cooker any more. I'll just tow it behind the RV. How'd you like that?

Okay, okay, I'll go get the gonads.

Perez pronounced their entry tasty enough for Third Prize. First Prize went to a transvestite couple from Austin with an excellent tofu recipe that Perez said was the wave of the future. Only he said it in Spanish, and John Grady thought, I've had enough of this chili shit.

Lacy, let's go into another line of work. I been thinking about hiring out to be a literary consultant. Find a writer somewhere and fill him in on everthing that happened to us down in Old Mexico that time.

Can I go with you, John Grady, please, please.

Course you can, darlin. Course you can.

Winner, 2nd Place, Bad Cormac McCarthy Contest. El Paso Public Library, November 1996.

Pictures

Moo-vie Cows:
The Trail to
Hollywood

*"As we heard some one say, this picture is all very well if
you like cows."*
—*The New York Times* review of *Sundown*, 1924

irst there were cattle drives and then there were cattle-drive
movies. The time span between the end of the trail drives and
the beginning of motion pictures was surprisingly brief: about
ten years in all. As early as 1898 the essential elements to make
a trail-drive film were in place. That was the year Thomas
Edison produced segments of film portraying typical ranching
activities. The titles indicate the subjects: *Branding Cattle*, *Calf Branding*,
Cattle Leaving the Corral, *Cattle Fording Stream*, and *Lassoing Steer*. All that
was needed to make a narrative film of these segments is a commanding leader, some cowpokes, including a garrulous cook, a hot-
head, and a green kid, and maybe toss in a fragile beauty who has a
slightly tarnished past, a couple of stampedes, a soupçon of water

moccasins (for the Cattle Fording Stream scene), and you've got a Trail Drive Epic. You've got, in fact, *Lonesome Dove*.

A mere five years after the Edison documentary footage, the first successful narrative film, *The Great Train Robbery*, appeared, making the western the first popular genre of the nascent art form. That same year (1903), Andy Adams published *The Log of a Cowboy*, his classic account of trailing cattle from Texas to Montana, but it would be a while yet before a big cattle-drive film would be made. For one thing, there were as yet no exciting narratives of the cattle-drive era. *The Log of a Cowboy* was too authentic to offer much in the way of cinematic whoop-ti-do. Adams hewed hard to factual authenticity and refused to inject romance and shoot-'em-up elements to spice up the story. He scoffed at the suggestion that he add a female to his list of characters, and without a lithesome young thing along for the ride, there wasn't going to be any romance. Zane Grey, who always used sex to spice up his plots, didn't get around to writing a cattle-drive novel until 1936.

Instead, it was another writer, Emerson Hough, not much remembered today, who breathed life into the cattle-drive narrative and gave it epic proportions. The novel was *North of 36*, published in 1923. It was an epic sequel to his big-canvas novel of the Oregon Trail, *The Covered Wagon*, which had itself been made into a significant popular and critical movie that same year.

North of 36, released in 1924, was shot on location on a ranch thirty miles from Houston and in many frames carries a very authentic flavor. In one shot, for instance, the cattle are being driven through a shallow dry arroyo and in the background are trees with Spanish moss, something you don't see in those "Texas" films shot in Arizona where you do see a lot of saguaro cactus, those great tall crooked-cross-like cacti that do not in fact grow in Texas. The other authentic element of *North of 36* is the cattle themselves, the five thousand longhorns that were used in the making of the film. J. Frank Dobie, no admirer of shoot-'em-ups, liked the realistic manner in which cattle were handled in this film, as he wrote in *Cow People*: "Often in recollection I see the lead steer, Old Alamo, a mighty longhorn, dun in color, standing at the edge of a lake where the other steers were standing, watering. They looked serene, as cattle at water naturally are. Those in the picture had been furnished by Bassett Blakeley from herds on the prairies of the Gulf Coast in the region of Houston. To be sure, there was a stampede, but the picture furnished views of the herd quietly grazing along and strung out in a long line behind Old Alamo."

Apart from location and bovine authenticity, *North of 36* introduced themes that would reappear in most cattle-drive movie epics. One was the presence of a woman, a heroine, on the long drive—that figure spurned by Adams. The film works hard to make the willowy young beauty, Taisie Lockhart, integral to the plot. Miss Taisie loses her father to a Yankee carpetbagger's cowardly bullet, leaving her with a ranch, thousands of cattle, but no money, not a cent. She's so broke she can't pay the ranch hands—the year is 1867, the era, Reconstruction Texas—but the cowpokes admire her so much they're willing to work for nothing, willing to risk everything on a trail drive north to railheads in Kansas, north of the 36th parallel. So Taisie puts on her best trail-driving outfit, saddles up her pinto pony, and with an old geezer sidekick and a band of loyal cowboys, sets out to find new markets for Texas beef. The unmarked prairie trail is long and filled with danger; it's clear from early in the film that she's going to need the gunfighterly skills of a tall, dark, handsome hero to help her and the herd out of various jams. But she misunderstands the hero's intentions, and so for most of the drive he has to provide help sort of in absentia, operating on the fringes, doing what he can to erase difficulties and obstacles. The biggest obstacle is the state treasurer of Texas, a Yankee carpetbagger appointed by an unforgiving Yankee government, and the very same man, it turns out, who murdered Taisie's father. He wants her ranch and will stoop to anything to accomplish his nefarious ends. Pardon the melodramatic language, but with fat oily villains who wear black suits and smoke big cigars, you find yourself falling back on adjectives like nefarious to describe them. This villain is so despicable that in a sub-plot, he comes upon two Comanche women bathing nude in a stream (they really are nude: the silents took a sort of *National Geographic* view of undressed native women), and he rapes one of them. The title for this sequence is "Virgin Wilderness." Later at film's end, after the cattle have been safely escorted to Kansas and the hero and heroine are properly squared away, the villain is turned over to the Comanches, who promptly make fajitas out of him.

The grand intentions of *North of 36* at the thematic level are what make it the archetype of all subsequent cattle-drive epics. *North of 36* wants nothing less than to make its story—the taking of cattle to market—the saga of a nation's destiny being made manifest by means of a sizeable achievement that has its origins in both economic need and ideological necessity. Among the prologue titles to *North of 36* was a quotation from historian Phillip Aston Rollins that might have explained every cattle-drive movie: "The Texas Trail was no mere cowpath. It was the course of Empire." According to standard southern interpretations of the Reconstruction era, carpetbaggers came south after the war to plunder a ravaged and defeated nation. In Texas, people had no money, they only had land or cattle, neither of which was worth anything. The solution lay in new economic opportunities: cattle could be driven to railheads in Missouri and Kansas, to Indian reservations in Nebraska and Montana. Cattle drives, so the myth went, redeemed Texas from a bankrupt economy, allowed its citizens to believe and take part in an epic enterprise, contributed to the economic well-being and health of the rest of the country, and made money for cattlemen.

After overcoming the standard number of obstacles, including a grass fire, crossing a river, stampedes, attacks from Comanches and outlaws, Taisie and her cowboys, with the help of the two-gun hero, Dan McMasters, reach Abilene, Kansas, and deliver the first herd to that emerging boom town, driving the wild cattle down the middle of the street. The epic drive accomplishes exactly what the young hero foresaw: "The North and the South are going to build a new world above the old slavery line! It will be the West—the heart of America." Reviewers to the contrary (they didn't like this Hough-based film as much as they had *The Covered Wagon*), *North of 36* was truly a pioneering movie.

It wasn't the only cattle-drive movie of 1924, however. That same year there appeared a film called *Sundown* that, though lost today, seems to have been a notable effort to capture the majesty of the trail-drive enterprise. Filmed on location near El Paso, *Sundown* contains some of the best landscape shots from a time when there was still a great deal of empty country available to a discerning cameraman. One still photograph is simply remarkable: a herd of cattle is stretched across the plains in a kind of leisurely line, issuing out of nowhere and headed to some remote destination. There are no cowboys in the picture, no barbed wire, no 7-11, no mobile homes, nothing but land, sky, and cattle.

Regardless of its superlative visual elements, *Sundown* apparently suffered from the same plot problems as *North of 36*. The *New York Times* reviewer put it succinctly: "But as soon as one gets back to the story in this production it becomes unusually boring." The reviewer did enjoy, however, the "impressive scenes of thousands and thousands of cattle which are photographed from the mountains and from the plain level." He also liked other scenes of the cattle (much as Dobie did in his remarks on *North of 36*): "It is interesting and satisfying to see the steers and cows plunging into the river and enjoying the water."

When the talkies came along, the cattle-drive film followed—now audiences could hear the cattle lowing and the cowboys singing. *North of 36* was remade twice in the 1930s, as *The Conquering Horde* in 1931, and as *The Texans* in 1938. *The Texans* had a solid cast (Randolph Scott in the lead, with Walter Brennan as the crusty sidekick, a role he would reprise beautifully in *Red River*), and it had location-shooting—at a ranch near Cotulla, in South Texas—but neither element was strong enough to overcome other problems. *The Texans* rode the Reconstruction myth hard and added a racist dimension missing from *North of 36*. Said the prologue: "The South was ruled as a conquered enemy. Northern politicians wallowed in an orgy of power—of plunder by organized mobs—of tribute and tyranny and death." In one early scene drunken black soldiers bully defeated Confederate veterans, while white straw bosses make Anglo Texans perform "nigger work" unloading cargo at Indianola, a port on the Gulf Coast. After this sensationalized historical frame, the film goes on to tell the familiar story of Texas frontier enterprise overcoming the oppressive policies of northern Reconstruction rule by forging a new market for Texas beef.

Contemporary reviewers gave *The Texans* a failing grade on two counts: history and form. Philip Hartung in *Commonweal* called the film "sugar-coated History" and felt that the Reconstruction period in Texas "deserves better treatment," something, incidentally, that could be said of virtually every western ever made about the state. Frank S. Nugent in *The New York Times* criticized the movie's pretensions: "Theoretically it's 'epic,' that convenient Hollywood word for any Class A picture filmed on location, but practically it is just another romance." But give J. Frank Dobie the last word on *The Texans*. As he reports in *Cow People* he happened to be in Los Angeles at the time the film was released: "I saw a sign announcing it, 'now running.' I bought a ticket and went inside. I wanted to see the A and B brands on La Mota cattle. I wanted to be back home. I looked and listened through the entire film. The only glimpses of the cattle I got was while they were running like scared jack rabbits. I tried another cattle picture or two. Had I not known better, I might have concluded that a herd bound for the Blackfoot Indian Agency on the Canadian-Montana line crossed the Rio Grande in a run, slept in a run, grazed in a run, drank in a turmoil, and never quit running over the entire two-thousand-mile trail."

Between *The Texans* and *Red River*, a decade of westerns used cattle-drive sequences as a constant ideological reference point. A standard opening scene showed cowboys leisurely riding along accompanying a vast herd spread across the terrain. In such *de rigeur* cattle-drive sequences, the ideology was always the same: this was America's epic moment, the creation of its historical and commercial destiny, the act of empire.

During the late thirties and forties empire was not a word that embarrassed Americans; in fact the country liked the idea, in this "American century," of being reminded of its grand designs. But even so, there were dissident strains apparent in films ostensibly endorsing the concept of empire building. In a 1942 film called, inevitably, *American Empire*, the idea of empire was perfectly acceptable, but the trouble with building an empire was the effect upon the builder. As long as the enterprise was linked with national aims, it was laudable. In *American Empire*, the original intention is noble. A verdant valley encircled with mountains and teeming with cattle provides the "biggest job in the U.S." That the valley and mountains are located along the Sabine River in East Texas is something that would bother only people who know what Texas east of I-35 looks like—wooded flat farmland giving way to piney woods and lakes and marshes along the Sabine. In any case, the prime motive for marketing prime beef in this film is spelled out as part of a national agenda. "We must get beef to all parts of the U.S., North and South," says one of the men who claim the land, found the ranch, and trail the herds north to Kansas.

The noble purpose soon changes to selfishness and greed, however, which undermines the larger social vision. One of the two ranchers begins to translate their success into personal despotic terms and refuses to cooperate with neighboring ranchers who need to send their herds across his land to reach market. He orders barbed wire to close off his lands and refuses to grant the railroad the right-of-way it needs. Such anti-social and anti-progressive actions represent the opposite of the pragmatic optimism that launched the original venture. Eventually the bad rancher sees the error of his ways: he builds gates in his fences for his neighbors to use and he accepts the coming of the railroad. The cattleman must give way before the inexorable march of progress. Although in no sense a memorable movie, *American Empire* is instructive in its themes and its forecast of the end of the open-range cattleman.

In 1948, with *Red River*, the cattle-drive movie achieved its apotheosis. *Red River* could easily have been called *American Empire* since it too traces the imperatives and consequences of empire-building. *Red River* utilized more successfully than any of its predecessors the drama of the cattle drive to stand for the American epic experience. It opens with a historical scroll, a sure sign that something significant is afoot, then moves swiftly into the primal act of Tom Dunson's seizing the land and holding it. His purpose, announced in Dunson's own words, is to grow beef for America. But the way he says it indicates a potential problem. In a rhapsodic peroration, the egotism of possession is apparent: "Wherever they go, they'll be on my land. My land! I'll have the brand on enough beef to . . . feed the whole . . . country. Good beef for hungry people. Beef to make 'em strong . . . make 'em grow."

After the building up of his bumper-sticker empire ("Good Beef for Hungry People"), Dunson—John Wayne—is thwarted by the Civil War and its attendant post-war crisis: in Reconstruction Texas, Dunson owns plenty of land and cattle but he has no money, no currency. A pioneer, a builder, Dunson doesn't understand money or the new economic forces in the postwar world. All he knows is that he must get his cattle to market in Sedalia, Missouri. But even this is wrong and backward-looking, because the real future is in Abilene, Kansas, where the railroad has already established a beachhead on the twentieth century. Too fearful, Dunson lacks the necessary confidence to trust in an unseen future. His adopted son, Matthew Garth (Montgomery Clift), has to wrest control of the herd from the tyrant Dunson in order to lead the Texas cattle industry—and cattlemen—into the modern era. Dunson's empire was feudal in conception, hardly different from that of the previous Mexican grandees from whom he took the land by force. Garth's method involves cooperation, teamwork, and good faith in society and its citizens. Garth offers a benign corporate model; Dunson, a rugged individualist one. But rugged individualism is no longer enough; in *Red River* as in *American Empire*, it leads to tyranny and cruelty.

Red River is deeply indebted to *North of 36*. Tom Dunson, the economically desperate rancher, is a male version of Taisie Lockhart; and

Old Groot (Walter Brennan), Dunson's cook and conscience, recalls Taisie's faithful comic foreman. The arrival in Abilene, with the cattle flooding into the overjoyed and surprised town, is strikingly similar, too. But the chief advance of *Red River* over its forerunner is to replace the external melodramatic Reconstruction villain with interior psychological obstacles. Dunson himself becomes the villain. His ruthless commitment to empire leads him to ignore the claims of others; he hardens himself and cuts himself off from common humanity. Fortunately his "son" is strong enough to bring him back into the human fold.

You will notice that throughout these comments I have accepted unquestioningly that the Red River of the title designates the actual river that separates Texas from Oklahoma. This is how all the actors in the film regard the River as well. After all, they have to cross it; for them and for the real cattle drivers of history, the Red River was there, an indisputable geographical fact. Imagine my surprise, then, when I came across Jane Tompkins' discussion of the film in her book *West of Everything: The Inner Life of Westerns* (1992). To Tompkins "Red River" refers to something else entirely. To her it stands for the blood of the slaughtered animals. That Tompkins is a self-admitted vegetarian may account for her reading of "red" as blood, first the blood of slain Mexicans and Indians, of Dunson's cowboys and of his sweetheart, but most of all, she says, red "stands for the cattle." In this kind of criticism the floating signifier of semiological criticism falls into the Grand Canyon of indeterminancy—thirteen ways of looking at a longhorn.

Although Tompkins also hints at some sexual implications of the text, pointing out that Dunson's sidekick Groot's first name is Nadine—an unusual name for a male, surely—she does not pursue these implications. Allow me to do so. If "red" can refer to the cattle's blood, why can't it refer to menstrual blood? Hear me out on this. At the film's beginning Dunson, the male principle, abandons his sweetheart, named Fen. A fen, of course, is a bog—wet, sodden land. Fen doesn't want him to leave. She says she has "knives in her knees," obviously a displacement of pain from menstrual cramps. He leaves her on the Oklahoma side of Red River; Oklahoma with its soft, lilting vowelization, is obviously a feminized and softened sign, while Texas is: Tex As—Land of Possibility, or Tex Is—Land of Macho Assertion. .

With Fen gone (now she probably has arrows in her chest), Dunson has no counterbalancing female principle. Not, that is, until the curiously androgynous boy, Matthew Garth, shows up with a cow to complement Dunson's bull. The symbolism here is pretty direct, but what do we make of the fact that one of the other gunfighters is named Cherry (John Ireland) and admires Matthew's "gun" and wants to see it? Or that Cherry is actually a womanizer and Matthew is virginal?

Once on the trail, Dunson's patriarchal nature takes over; he becomes a relentless and obsessive trail-boss bent only on achieving his goal. In the process he alienates himself from his feminized son, whose own masculinity is much softer, more pliable than Dunson's. But once again the dynamics of gender takes over, and a "soiled dove" named Tess Millay (Joanne Dru) comes temporarily between the two male friends. Dunson looks Tess over like a prize Jersey heifer and makes her an offer to produce, as she says, a "Dunson out of Millay." Now that he has lost his "son," he needs a biological heir to his dynasty. But at the same time, this "son" is realizing his own gender and phallic destiny, spurred on by a very sexy scene—for the forties—when he sucks the poison from a wound in Tess' shoulder, an area just north of what Zane Grey would have described as her "swelling breasts." Thus the suppressed and denied feminine blood reenters the story in a big, dramatic fashion. So Matt and the soiled dove fall in love, but the real love story is one between the two men, and they have to transact this love through the body, as it were, of the woman who loves one, the younger, and who will bear the sons of the now thoroughly masculinized and "legitimate" heir to the Dunson fortune. In the *Saturday Evening Post* novel from which the script was conceived, Dunson crosses the Red River on the trip back and dies. In the film he remains alive and reunited with his "son" at the end, thanks to the wisdom and intervention of the female principle that he has so many times repudiated in his quest for empire.

Most films following in *Red River's* wake offered nothing more than postscripts to its operatic working out of the implications of empire-building. In *The Longhorn*, 1951, William Elliott played a Texas rancher with the foresight and conviction necessary to lead the Texas cattle industry into its next phase. Elliott drives a herd of Herefords from Oregon to Texas to prove that this breed of cattle can flourish as well as the longhorn. Then there was *The Rare Breed* (1966), a minimalist variation upon *The Longhorn* and the entire cattle-drive movie tradition. The cattle in this film consists of exactly one Hereford bull named Vindicator! The bull is walked down to Texas from Kansas (again reversing the historical formula) and is delivered to a ranch in the Panhandle where it will have to prove its ability to survive a hard, cold winter. Although it doesn't survive, its semen does, because before cashing in his chips, Vindicator plants his lusty seed in a longhorn cow. The purpose, of course, is to sire a new kind of bulkier, leaner beef for discriminating Yankee palates. *The Rare Breed* is the first low-cholesterol cattle-drive film.

The most recent cattle-drive epic is, of course, *Lonesome Dove*, a monumental TV miniseries that has become a standard crowd-pleasing allusion in the speeches of Texas politicians.

Lonesome Dove's indebtedness to movies is most apparent in its reliance upon female companionship to spur the narrative along when sandstorms, river crossings, stampedes, and Comancheros are thought to be growing a trifle tedious and repetitious. With its constant sexual concerns regarding the favors of Lorena, often purchased at discount prices—sort of like Attention, Lonesome Dove Shoppers—this film (and book) adds a whole new dimension to the meaning of the word cowpoke.

Indeed *Lonesome Dove* might be seen as the culmination of McMurtry's career-long effort to humanize, or should one say, in current academic lingo, to empower the gender-specific hegemony of the cowboys of Dobie and a host of other Western writers who present us with cowboys as sexless as newts.

I don't know how to account for either the novel's or the film's achieving hit status. I can't explain why yuppies read the novel poolside all through the summer of 1985 and are still reading it. The novel was one thing; filming it was something else altogether. The big western movie had been dead since the $40 million debacle of *Heaven's Gate* in 1980 and when the galleys were making the rounds of producers on the Left Coast in 1985, there were no takers. Not only that, television miniseries were thought to be fading fast. So to combine two losers—the western and the miniseries—looked like a dumb idea. Nobody optioned it until a woman producer at Motown Records, in Detroit, took a chance and bought it for a song— $50,000. The rest is show-biz history: *Lonesome Dove* drew rave critical reviews as well as much popular support. It finished number 14 on the all-time list of successful miniseries.

Why was the TV film so popular? The quality of certain performances, those of Robert Duvall and Tommy Lee Jones in particular, is, of course, one explanation, as is the superior adaptation by Bill Wittliff, but there must be something else at work. Harry F. Walters of *Newsweek* made an astute point when he called *Lonesome Dove* the "first buddy mini-series," seeing in the complex, well-acted relationship of Gus McCrae and Woodrow Call the key emotional appeal of the film. That could be part of the basis for its popularity; certainly *Red River* owed much of its power to a relationship between two men (although there the interest derived from generational differences). Linked with the buddy plot-line is nostalgia for an earlier time, when men were men and women were women and both genders knew the difference and not *le differance*. Part of the appeal of *Lonesome Dove* must be that the problems of getting the cattle to market, difficult as they are, are mostly external—outlaws, Blue Duck's assorted depredations, natural obstacles, weather, etc. Compared with problems in the '90s—AIDS, terrorism, television talk shows—*Lonesome Dove*, though filled with violence and death, seems to offer a simpler world where the heroic act and its attendant suffering still mean something, where dignity can still be observed in human tragedy.

Or it may be that *Lonesome Dove's* appeal lies in its structural similarity to a baseball game, or, because it's so long and because one doesn't want it to end, a baseball season. To see *Lonesome Dove* as a baseball game, all you have to do is follow the bouncing ball. First, there's the playing field: a green and brown pastoral setting. Second, there are the players, the line-up: a garrulous, philosophical player-manager in the twilight of his playing days (Gus), a heavy-hitter (Call), a rookie (Newt), a former star whose career is ended because of an addiction problem—gambling and girls (Jake Spoon), a talented black player cut down in the prime of his career (Deets as Roberto Clemente), and a groupie—Lorena—who follows the team rather like the woman in *Bull Durham* or the woman in the Wade Boggs story. Third: the opposing teams: we might call them the Texas Rangers and the Cleveland Indians. Fourth: the drive/game is a team effort in which each player has his turn at bat and either does well—Call or Newt or Deets, for example—or fails: the kid who strikes out at the river crossing. Fifth: the pace and rhythm: Part of the charm of a baseball game—if you like baseball—is that the game theoretically has no ending; it can go on forever. Fortunately one never has, but as I said, theoretically, it could. All the great cattle-drive movies reach a point in the narrative where the players feel that the drive is all, that it will never end. But it does end, and the team that delivers the most runs with the fewest errors wins; and the Indians or outlaws lose. Very satisfying, this narrative thrust, its exciting periods of intense action punctuated with leisurely moments, those seventh inning stretches in which a couple of cowboy teammates amble along on horseback smoking and chewing tobacco and scratching their privates and thinking deep philosophical thoughts about life and death and wimmin, whom they like to call fillies— such moments comprise the perfect expression of a male world of fantasy and escape, equally evident in a cattledrive or a baseball season.

After the surprising success of *Lonesome Dove*, we might well ask whether Hollywood will react, as it often does, to TV hits and revive the trail-drive western. So far the only response has been the comedy *City Slickers* (1991), which combined the dude-ranch motif of the 1930s and '40s with the cattle drive framework. The result was a poorly made but highly popular film that was meant to serve as a kind of allegory of reclaimed yuppie manhood beset by urbanism and feminism. Much ado is made about nursing a baby calf in this film, and lest anyone imagine that this motif is original, forget it. In 1924's *Sundown* a calf's mother is killed, leading one of the cowboys to feed the cute little critter with condensed milk run through a hole in the nipple-like finger of a glove.

A cattle-drive film that showed a great deal of promise is one that never got made, that never even came close to getting made. During the summer of 1986 Ben Johnson, that superb actor in many John Ford westerns and an Oscar winner for his role in *The Last Picture Show*, told me about his plans to film Clair Huffaker's novel, *The Cowboy and the Cossack*, which is a story about a Russian prince who buys longhorns in the American West and transports them to Russia where cossacks and cowboys join together for a long drive across the steppes of that vast country. Johnson wanted to shoot on location in Russia, wanted to hire a train to carry all the tenderfeet while real seasoned cowboys drove the herd to the cattle pens in Moscow. I was ready to go with him, to write a book about the making of an epic, but Johnson died before he was able to bring his dream to fruition. The costs, one imagines, would be staggering. The first post-Gorbachev, post Communist western would be something to see. Until then, we will just have to settle for reruns.

The Big Show:
Autry's Artful Oater

....

I grew up seeing big-budget A westerns at the Ritz Theater, on the square in McKinney, Texas, but on Saturday afternoons I also saw a lot of double-feature B westerns and serials, cheaper, cruder fare for kids and die-hard adults in a seedier venue, at the Texas Theater, off the square. Looking back, I don't feel any great welling up of nostalgia about all those long forgotten oaters that formed, even for an artless young viewer like myself, a more or less nonstop barrage of chases, comedy relief, and blazing six-guns. Still, viewing the genre from an adult perspective, you can find amongst all the forgettable flikkers an occasional gem. Such is the case with Gene Autry's *The Big Show*, a film I happened to stumble upon in the early eighties. Since this film was released a number of years before I was born, I am fairly certain I did not see it as a child. If I had, I suspect I wouldn't have liked it very much. It possessed too much artifice, and I wanted my westerns as authentic as possible. I worried a lot about the number of times a six-shooter was fired—that kind of realism. Yet I was a complete sucker for a good tune, never being bothered whether real cowboys could actually sing like Gene Autry or not.

The Big Show is unusual for many reasons, not the least of which is that, unlike ninety-nine percent of the Bs, it was shot partly on location. I say partly because there is some confusion on this score. In his autobiography, *Back in the Saddle Again*, Autry downplayed the location aspect, claiming that although lobby posters advertised that the movie was filmed on location, it in fact was not. He explains, " . . . we did the background shots and some of the specialty acts—Sally Rand (yes, that Sally Rand) and the SMU band—in Dallas." Yet in his history, *Republic Studios: Between Poverty Row and the Majors*, Richard M. Hurst calls *The Big Show* a "landmark" because "it was filmed at the Texas Centennial in Dallas which gave the production added gloss and values." A contemporary account in the *Dallas Morning News* of September 16, 1939, is helpful. According to the newspaper, on the previous day, the fifteenth, a convention of motion picture exhibitors meeting at the fair grounds were treated to visits by several movie actors, including Gene Autry. Autry was in Dallas, the story said, to film "a western with the Centennial Exhibition as a background setting." Rain delayed some of the shooting that day, and prevented an appearance by Texas Governor, James V. Allred. However, some background footage pertaining to the Cavalcade of Texas was shot. (The Cavalcade figures importantly in the finished film, but Governor Allred does not appear.)

Internal evidence from the film suggests a stronger location factor than Autry indicates. The art deco buildings of the Texas State Fair Grounds are clearly visible in many scenes; the long shallow pond that greets visitors upon entering the fair grounds is the setting for the final showdown, when Autry captures the villains in a rousing chase scene; the midway is visible in several scenes; there is a parade featuring the SMU marching band; and there are scenes of considerable duration dealing with the Cavalcade of Texas, as well as shots of the contemporary audience in the bleachers watching the cavalcade's spectacular show. The sense of location shooting is so strong that *The Big Show* has a documentary value today: it is a vivid record of the Texas Centennial as witnessed by the thousands of people who thronged there daily. Of course, given the fact that Republic was famous for its technical expertise, some of the location ambience may be the result of skillful back projection.

The Big Show is unusual for other reasons as well, reasons that have to do with artifice and creativity, qualities we don't often associate with B movies. *The Big Show* is truly and wittily funny at times, containing a level of sophistication that cannot be the result of mindless luck. Of course the film has the usual number of low comedy techniques: especially pratfalls, most of them performed by Smiley Burnette, Gene's sidekick. Smiley wants to be a stunt man like Gene, but he can't mount a horse properly because he's too fat. Such physical comedy runs all through the film, as we would expect. But there is other comedy as well, that points to another level of discourse in a film that contains enough self-reflexivity to make a French structuralist sit up and take notice.

The Big Show is unusually complex for a B western. The movie opens in California, at an outdoors movie location, probably in some place like Griffith Park in Los Angeles where films were routinely shot. In any case we realize in the first few moments that we are watching a western movie in progress, a B western it is almost unnecessary to point out. The star of the movie being made is Tom Ford, played by Gene Autry. Gene also plays the stunt man and double for Ford, only the third time in his long career that he played characters with names different from his own. Ford is a prima donna on the set, a "kind of snooty film actor" as Autry remembered in his autobiography, and Gene is his nice, talented, and underrated stand-in. Gene is obviously superior to Ford in every respect except status and social identity. Ford is the star; Gene is a nobody. All that will change. Quickly the film establishes its parodic and self-reflexive stance. In a close-up embrace with the heroine, Ford rudely asks her if she has been eating onions! Then his horse bites him on the rear end.

When the film is completed, Ford the spoiled star takes off on a hunting trip and refuses to honor the studio's commitment for him to make a personal appearance in Dallas at the Texas Centennial. The studio manager, a comic figure with a beret and a manic, exaggerated style, pleads with Gene to stand in for Ford in Dallas. But Gene is reluctant; he doesn't want "to make a big show of himself," he says. But, nice guy that he is, he is finally persuaded to go to Dallas to represent Mammoth Studio. The name of the studio is obviously satirical. Republic doubtless intended to satirize the major studios, given its own status somewhere between Poverty Row and the majors.

On the way to Dallas there is an episode that also reflects this constant self-reference. After a near collision with a cattle truck, the cattle break loose and scatter across the countryside. Gene and Frog (Burnette's nickname) unload Champion from the horse trailer, and Gene sets out to round up the cattle. So in the midst of automobiles and highways, there is time for a little old-fashioned cowboy work. Gene performs his cowboy duties to refute the charge made by the young woman who owns the cattle, who claimed that Gene's duds made him look like "a drugstore cowboy." He has to prove he's the real thing.

In Dallas things get further complicated as Gene attempts to play his role while remaining true to himself. Dressed in a resplendent white outfit and looking "just like a star," Gene rides in a parade featuring the SMU marching band and famed exotic dancer Sally Rand (dressed chastely in a businesswoman's dress suit). Gene is made an honorary Texas Ranger by a representative of the governor. When the parade breaks up, a mob of girls, bobby-soxers, storm Gene, seeking autographs. They tear off his pants. Alarmed at the price of stardom, Gene declares, "When a bunch of women tear my clothes off, I quit." But he doesn't, of course. The studio needs him.

The best self-reflexive humor of all is built out of what happens next. Invited to sing, Gene gives a fine rendition of a song that is itself mocking and parodic: "Have you heard the story about the wild and woolly West?" A radio announcer hears him and invites him to sing on a show broadcast at the fair grounds and beamed around the nation. (This is accurate: the centennial broadcasts were a major means of achieving national publicity.) On the radio Gene does a Jimmie Rodgers-style song to perfection: "Come Sit by My Side, Little Darling." Gene Autry's ability as a singer is much underrated. He could sing Rodgers-style country ballads, crooner-type songs (which he also sings in *The Big Show*), and smash novelty hit numbers such as "Rudolph the Red-Nosed Reindeer" and "Here Comes Santa Claus." Autry's singing was always one of the strongest sides of his appeal.

In the movie, the radio broadcast precipitates trouble for the real Tom Ford, who can't sing a lick, and trouble for the false Tom Ford. The real Tom Ford, holed up in a mountain cabin, is furious, and the false Tom Ford is now the target for reprisals against the real Tom Ford. Ford the actor owes a gambling debt of $25,000 to some thirties-style urban bad guys led by a gangster named Tony Ricco (a reference to the famous Edward G. Robinson character?). When Ricco and his boys hear someone whom they presume to be Ford on the radio (everybody listens to the radio!), they rush to Dallas to collect. On the studio front, things are getting sticky, too. The studio manager is sweating bullets because Gene sang on the radio, but the head of Mammoth Studio, a stereotypical mogul named Schwartz, loves it. He tells the worried manager, "From now on we're making nothing but musical westerns."

At this point the manager and Gene engage in one of those playful verbal moments that all too rarely are there to reward the faithful viewer of B westerns. The manager moans aloud, "Oh, why was I ever born?" To which Gene, who knows his Sophocles, replies, "This is no time for riddles." You can see hundreds of B westerns and never hear an exchange to match this one.

The centennial background provides another layer of cross-referencing. The most popular event during the centennial celebration was the Cavalcade of Texas, a lavish spectacle featuring 300 actors in an historical pageant designed to reveal the "glamour of Lone Star

State history" from "conquistador to cowboy, from the quest for gold to the discovery of oil." The cavalcade dramatized Texas under six flags and featured a cattle drive and other stirring renditions of frontier episodes. In *The Big Show* the cavalcade offers a kind of Texas subtext to the film proper. Gene performs one number that is particularly worthy of comment. In a chase scene he and Champion pursue outlaws over the sham plains and mountains. Here, again, the idea of theater and illusion is part of the *mise en scene*; we see the creation of illusion while the thirties audience sitting in the bleachers sees only the illusion. Near the end of the chase, Champion falls, his leg apparently broken. Gene sings a farewell song to his beloved horse: "Old Faithful, we rode the range together." Gene points his six-shooter at Champion's head, ratcheting up our emotions; it is as though we were watching an opera. The audience is moved by the performance; the gangsters, too, as their chief tells them to be quiet until the song is over. Then just when it looks as though Gene is going to kill his faithful steed, Champion playfully wags his head and rises, while the audience breaks into relieved applause.

The cavalcade continues. Gene carries the Stars and Stripes in the climatic number of this pageant of "Texas under six flags, an empire on parade," as the public address system describes it. In the meantime the gangsters have dropped their urban style for a western one. They have stolen 25,000 grand and, seeking to escape, don western-style duds and flee on a stagecoach. Gene, alerted to the theft by the P.A. system (in this film electronic communication is everything), rides after them. The chase, a staple item for both B and A westerns, recalls an earlier stagecoach chase at the beginning of *The Big Show*, back in California in the opening minutes of the film. In that chase Gene showed off his stunt abilities in a falling-under-the-speeding-stagecoach scene that is itself interesting in light of the famous and dangerous stunt performed by Yakima Canutt in *Stagecoach* three years later. (The stunt in *The Big Show* is obviously achieved by back-projection.)

The final chase in *The Big Show* is composed of a wonderful layering of genre elements: an honorary Texas Ranger, Gene Autry, is impersonating western actor Tom Ford and pursuing urban gangsters dressed as western cowboys riding a stagecoach alongside a man-made lagoon on the Texas State Fair Grounds in 1936. His sidekick follows in a rickshaw, to complete the levels of artifice and absurdity. The scene ends with some bloodless gunplay, fisticuffs, and the capture of the crooks. Then Gene delivers them into the custody of a real Texas Ranger.

The film then returns to its movie origins, to a movie set in California where a new western is being filmed, a musical western need it be added. Gene is the leading man and Ford is his double. Gene sings the song "I'm Mad About You" to his leading lady. This was one of the songs that launched his rise to stardom back in Dallas. The movie ends with the new star embracing the heroine, and there is no mention of onions on anybody's breath.

The Big Show charms us with its playful mix of on-location color, genre commentary, and sly industry humor. It stands as a triumph of low-budget studio inventiveness and a rebuke to anybody who wants to dismiss the lowly B western out of hand. And for Texans, the film has special historical value as a documentary picture of what the Texas Centennial experience was like. Not bad for a B western.

Remembering the Alamo: The Story of the Texas Revolution in Popular Culture

....

Republic. I like the sound of the word. It means people can live free, talk free. Go or come, buy or sell, be drunk or sober, however they choose. Some words can give you a feeling that makes your heart warm. Republic is one of those words.

John Wayne's Davy Crockett, *The Alamo*, 1960

In thinking about the Texas Revolution we would do well to heed the advice of English novelist Henry Fielding, who long ago urged the importance of scrutinizing popular materials in order better to understand a culture. Wrote Fielding: "I must blame you for taking so little notice of our Diversions and Amusements; tho' these may perhaps be called the best Characteristics of a People. They are, indeed, the truest Mirrors . . . ."

The output of popular materials about the Texas Revolution began almost concurrently with the events taking place in San Antonio, Gonzales, and Washington-on-the-Brazos. The first Texas novel to treat these events was *Mexico versus Texas* (1838), which, with slight changes, was reissued in 1842 under a new title, *Ambrosio de Letinez*. *Mexico versus Texas* used historic events such as the massacre at Goliad and the battle at San Jacinto as background for its twin themes of romance and theological debate set against the conflict between progressive Anglo-American civilization and a retrograde Spanish-Mexican civilization.

In the dedication to the 1842 edition, the author of *Ambrosio de Letinez*, presumed to be Anthony Ganilh, elucidates the overriding meaning of the historic epoch under examination: "The Texians may be considered as leading a crusade in behalf of modern civilization, against the antiquated prejudices and narrow policy of the middle ages, which still govern the Mexican Republic." What Ganilh expresses indirectly, many other novelists named outright as the scourge of Catholicism. As a somewhat disaffected member of the Catholic priesthood, Ganilh offers many criticisms of Catholic abuses in Mexico and Texas, but his criticism is mild compared to that of later novels. In these novels the Texas cause is championed chiefly on religious grounds, and the image of the Republic is that of a new government founded to relieve its citizens of the dark designs of priests and the hierarchical and undemocratic structure of the Catholic Church. Ganilh exempts from calumny those priests who practice charity and endure hardships for the sake of their flock, but in many of the novels the main villain is a priest. In Augusta Evans Wilson's *Inez* (1855), for example, Father Alphonso Mazzolin craftily converts the Anglo heroine to Catholicism and tries to force the titular heroine, Inez de Garcia, to marry a cousin for whom she has no love. Father Mazzolin, typical of the evil priest type, possesses "cunning, malignity, and fierceness." His counterpart appears in Amelia Barr's *Remember the Alamo* (1888) as Fray Ignatius, who has a "dark, cruel face" and is "immovably stern." Ignatius spends much of the novel trying to

force the Mexican-born wife of the hero to sign over their property to the church. His hatred for Americans is all-consuming: "If
these American heretics were only in my power! . . . I would cut a
throat—just one throat—every day of my life."

In the struggle between the forces of light and the forces of
dark, the meaning of the Texas victory is the same in novel after
novel. Perhaps *Remember the Alamo* best summarizes the issues: "For
the priesthood foresaw that the triumph of the American element
meant the triumph of freedom of conscience, and the abolition of
their own despotism." Such anti-Catholicism sometimes finds
innovative and sinister imagery in these novels. In *Remember the
Alamo*, for example, the Bowie knife receives a kind of ironic religious sanction. A Mexican who is partisan to the Texan cause calls
it a "knife of extreme unction—the oil and wafer are all that
remains for the men who feel its edge." And in *The Lost Gold of
Montezumas* (1906) Davy Crockett approves of lead ammunition
derived from the ornaments of church windows: "Church lead is as
good as any other to kill Greasers with."

Such rabid hatred is nearly always the handmaiden of racism.
Racist themes are developed chiefly by two means: stereotypes and
overt statements. Stereotypes are ubiquitous and involve a system
of classes based upon purity of blood lines. On the Mexican side,
at the top, are those of Spanish descent. They do everything better than their inferiors, the mestizos. The depiction of manners in
Anglo-biased novels reveals some amazing niceties of superiority.
In *La Belle San Antone* (1909), for example, the heroine notices such
marks of caste as this one: "She told herself it was only the true
Mexican of high caste who could handle and dispatch the tamale
with such deftness and neatness as did the senior [sic]." The presentation of mestizos, however, is systematically reduced to such
formulas as this one, from *Guy Raymond* (1908): "Gambling among
Mexicans is only a degree less natural than dancing, with them
dancing is one of the necessities of a contented existence."
Raymund A. Paredes has defined these two predominant types
thus: "The *mestizo* was physically unattractive, dirty, cruel, and

supremely treacherous . . . The second variety of Mexican was predominantly of Spanish ancestry, a pathetic, anachronistic figure in the manner of Don Quixote but with few of his saving graces." In many novels racism takes virulent forms. In the dime novel *The Trapper's Bride; or, Love and War: A Tale of the Texan Revolution* (1909) Mexicans are branded as cut-throats, "greasers," and "infernal imps." The scurrilous epithet "greaser" receives a full explanation in *Bernard Lyle* (1856):

> An American whose ill fortune has made him, for any number of days, a sojourner in the city of Metamoras [sic], can have no difficulty in tracing the origin of the term "greaser". . . . Narrow, muddy, filthy streets, swarming with men, women and children as filthy. . . . The people look greasy, their clothes are greasy, their dogs are greasy, their houses are greasy—everywhere grease and filth hold divided dominion, and the singular appropriateness of the name . . . soon caused it to be universally adopted by the American army.

It is rare indeed when the opprobrious term is used with anything other than loathing, but a positive instance does occur in Joseph A. Altsheler's *The Texan Star: The Story of a Great Fight for Liberty* (1912). A character named Obed says with grudging respect: "Greasers or no greasers. Those are men of courage!"

Racism infects the juvenile novels as well, those written, need it be added, expressly for the edification of Anglo children. Everett McNeil's *In Texas with Davy Crockett* (1908), which enjoyed four reprintings through 1918, sprinkles the epithet "greaser" on nearly every page. Even Jim Bowie, who married a Mexican woman, speaks of "Santa Anna and his army of Greasers." And Davy Crockett, when he hears of an account of the early Texan victory over General Martin Perfecto de Cos in San Antonio, calculates the odds in familiar racist arithmetic: "If it takes three hundred Greasers to get two Texans, how many Greasers will it take to get all Texas?" In the celebrated comic strip *Texas History Movies*, which has been oft-reprinted, including a recent bowdlerized version to eliminate racial slurs, racist exchanges between the opposing armies—"Gringos," "Greasers"—do much to create the flavor of enmity.

Like Catholicism, racism provided a convenient platform for dismissing Mexican civilization across the board. In *Guy Raymond* a familiar generalization occurs: "Mexican treachery was but one degree removed from savage barbarity. . . ." Even when Mexico is depicted in more temperate terms, the dismissal is still apparent. In Frances Nona's verse drama *The Fall of the Alamo* (1879) a long paean to Texas contains this characterization of Mexico:

> Save but a few enlightened of their people,
> They all behold with eyes of livid envy
> Our industry and our prosperity.

If the general populace is so contemptible, one can imagine how the military is presented. In *The Trapper's Bride* the Mexican army is one "whose savage legions were given to every kind of horrible excesses, and whose arms were deeply stained with the blood of helpless old men, feeble women and innocent children." The head of this army, Santa Anna, is an opium user (true: so was Sam Houston), tyrant, and ravisher of fair Anglo-Saxon womanhood. Davy Crockett calls him an "old coon" in Hiram H. McLane's play *The Capture of the Alamo* (1886). In *Guy Raymond* we learn that "sensible Mexicans detest him." Only rarely is Santa Anna raised above the level of cardboard tyrant and abuser of everything civilized. In Nona's play Santa Anna gives a vigorous speech castigating the opposing claims of his Anglo antagonists:

> . . . What is this Texas, speak!
> A dreary waste, a desert territory
> Of Mexico not worth the name of State.
> With outlaws filled and refugees from justice,
> The scum of the depraved society
> Of the United States.

Here Nona invests Santa Anna with some of the energy of the truly great villainous characters in literature, such as Milton's Satan. More often than not, however, Santa Anna is simply the "Herman Goering of the Texas Revolution," as one writer noted in the 1940s.

While anticlericalism and racism are used to denigrate the Mexican side of the Texas Revolution, historical analogies are enlisted to elevate the Texan side. A passage in *Ramrod Jones* (1905) is typical. Here the Texan cause is linked to the long tradition of political liberty that began in England and was brought to fruition first in the American Revolution and now in the Texas Revolution—"the rights that have been fought for ever since King John placed his seal upon the provisions of the Great Charter." In *Margaret Ballentine* (1907) other, more interesting historical parallels are cited to explain the power of resistance demonstrated by the Texan colonists: "It is kin to the fanaticism that inspired the Moslems in their holy wars, that made the psalm-singing followers of Cromwell believe they were serving God, and enthused the followers of the medicine men, or prophets of our Indian tribes."

But the favorite, overriding parallel is classical. *The Texan Triumph: A Romance of the San Jacinto Campaign* (1913), the third volume of Joseph A. Altsheler's juvenile trilogy, contains a nice summary of the classical analogy with its most familiar allusion: "Santa Anna is like that old Xerxes . . . The Alamo was our Thermopylae and Goliad was the sack and burning of Athens. But we'll beat him yet, as the Greeks beat Xerxes." (Imagine a book written for juveniles today that would deploy such an array of classical references—impossible.) Invocations of Thermopylae are so pervasive that it almost seems a law that each novel, drama, or poem must contain its own Thermopylaen echo.

This all-purpose allusion receives slight changes in each work. In *Bernard Lyle* the narrator imagines a commemorative statue being built at the site of the Alamo: "Over that spot someday, a monument will rise to meet the skies, with proud inscription, 'Thermopylae had one messenger of defeat, but the Alamo had none!'" In *Inez* the allusion becomes part of Fanning's [Fannin's] inner debate at Goliad: "What am I to do? Make this a second Thermopylae?" In Nona's play *The Fall of the Alamo* the honor devolves upon Travis to make the utterance, notable here for its inversion:

> "Thermopylae one herald had of death,
> The heroes of the Alamo had none!"

Verse about the Alamo—and there is a great deal of very bad verse on the subject—abounds with references to the Greek story. Frank B. Crockett's poem "The Texas Thermopylae" makes the allusion explicit in its title. An even better example appears in Horace Chaflin Southweek's Kiplingesque poem "The Alamo." The first twelve lines are enough to give the flavor:

> Say, you talk of Balaklava,
> > And the bloomin' British Square,
> Of Waterloo and Ballyhoo,
> > Why, that's nothin' but hot air;
> Like the story of Thermopelae [sic],
> > An' yarns about the Greeks,
> An' Persians and Egyptians—
> > Not to speak of other freaks.
> Why, sonny, down in Texas
> > Not so very long ago,
> They had a scrap with Greasers
> > At a place called Alamo . . . .

Finally, the Thermopylae parallel persists into our own time in the verse of the distinguished Argentine writer Jorge Luis Borges. In his sonnet "Texas" he calls the Alamo "that other Thermopylae."

The original utterance of the comparison was a memorable and effective piece of rhetoric that sprang from public oratory, not from attempts at imaginative storytelling. Exactly who authored the sentence remains a matter of conjecture. J. Frank Dobie assigned the honor to General Thomas Jefferson Green, a soldier with a classical education who participated in the Mier expedition. In any case the inscription, which Dobie dates from 1841, eventually found its public enshrinement on a monument at the Capitol in Austin. The

carved version reads: "Thermopylae had her messenger of defeat—
the Alamo had none." This ringing sentence and the cries of
revenge said to have been uttered at San Jacinto—"Remember the
Alamo, remember Goliad"—are, according to Dobie, the "two
thoroughly Texas sentences destined for immortality."

In the final analysis the story of the Revolution is the story of
the Alamo. Goliad, San Jacinto, and annexation have had their
singers, but the Alamo has garnered the lion's share of attention in
popular culture. As early as 1882 humorist Alex Sweet noted the
commercialization of the Alamo in the city of San Antonio:

> From where I stood I could see the Alamo livery-stable, the
> Alamo cigar-store, and the Alamo tin-shop. I was told that
> around the corner I could find the Alamo bakery, the Alamo
> brewery, the engine-house of the Alamo Fire Company, and
> the rooms of the Alamo Literary Society. The aged gentle-
> man said there was some talk of building an Alamo monu-
> ment, that the name and fame of the historic spot might be
> kept before the people; and I could not detect any sarcasm
> in the tone of his voice when he said it.

When Stephen Crane visited San Antonio in 1895 he felt
obliged to relate the story of the fall of the Alamo. He joked about
the burden: "Statistics show that 69,710 writers have begun at
the Alamo." A few years later Crane's contemporary, Frank
Norris, called for a serious, epic treatment of the West by
American writers. He made special mention of the Alamo, con-
trasting heroes such as Travis with the outlaw breed that populated the dime novel. Said Norris: "And the Alamo. There is a
trumpet-call in the word; and only the look of it on the printed
page is a flash of fire. . . . Yet Thermopylae was less glorious, and
in comparison with that siege the investment of Troy was mere
wanton riot." Half a century later Sylvan Karchmer, a Texas-born
author, wrote a short story about a writer torn between a commitment to artistic truth and commercial success. In the story the
writer is urged by his agent to do a "costume novel about the

Alamo." The scene continues with the writer musing: "I might even work in the Alamo heroes—Bowie, Fannin, Crockett. 'You've got a fistful of personalities,' he said. 'The material has never been touched.'"

If the fictional literary agent means that the Alamo story has never been captured effectively, he is correct; if he means it has been neglected, as Frank Norris believed, then he is as wrong as Norris was in 1902. For by the turn of the new century the Alamo had already been treated extensively in fiction, drama, and poetry. And even as Norris wrote, a new medium, the motion picture, was coming into being. Down that flickering road lay many Alamo movies and several film biographies of Sam Houston.

The Alamo story appealed to filmmakers early in the century. In San Antonio, Gaston Méliès, brother of the famous French pioneer filmmaker Georges Méliès, filmed the Alamo story in 1911. Although no print of *The Immortal Alamo* has yet been uncovered, extant stills suggest an early appropriation of familiar visual signs. Davy Crockett, played by Francis Ford, John Ford's older brother, wore a coonskin cap and carried a long rifle. In one action still, a Mexican officer prevents his soldiers (played by students of Peacock Military Academy) from slaying a couple of women and an infant held in the arms of one woman—obviously a representation of Susannah Dickinson's story.

The Martyrs of the Alamo, the first full-blown epic version of the Alamo saga, was filmed in 1915. Directed by W. Christy Cabanne and supervised by D. W. Griffith, it bore close resemblance to *The Birth of a Nation*. Walter Long, the actor who played the infamous mulatto in that film, played Santa Anna in *Martyrs*, which is as thoroughly racist as *Birth of a Nation*.

Like many novels of the nineteenth and early twentieth centuries, *Martyrs* offers a simple racial paradigm: the Alamo defenders are upright Anglo-Saxon heroes, and the Mexicans are craven violators of everything that is good, pure, and decent. The action turns upon such racial contrasts despite the usual avowals in the prologue that the Alamo is a tale about tyranny and freedom. In the buildup before the battle begins, Mexican soldiers in San Antonio split their time among hat-dancing, cockfighting, and insulting Anglo women. No woman is safe from the Mexican threat. One title sums it up nicely: "Under the dictator's rule the honor and life of American womanhood was held in contempt." With each affront to womankind, the Texans grow angrier, more rebellious.

Once the battle begins, the racist interpretation is sustained at every level. Mexican soldiers are portrayed as cowards; their officers shoot those who try to run away, forcing the others to scale the walls. The most sensational vilification occurs in the mopping-up actions, when a Mexican soldier hurls a little blonde Anglo-Saxon girl against a wall, killing her instantly. Not surprisingly, the commander of such troops does not come off well. Santa Anna is depicted as "an inveterate drug fiend" and a "Dictator . . . also famous for his shameless orgies." In the closing scenes of the film, at San Jacinto, Santa Anna's dissolute behavior is partly responsible for the Mexican defeat. Before the battle, he entertains a woman in his tent amidst much revelry and debauchery, an incident based upon the story of Emily Morgan, the "yellow rose of Texas."

The Anglo heroes in this film are a blur of coonskin caps and virtue. Davy Crockett is quite young, an historical inaccuracy in a film admittedly concerned with spectacle and melodramatic oppositions, not with truth or accuracy. The other Anglo heroes perform as expected. Bowie, in one of the film's better action sequences, dies in his cot, his chest impaled by two bayonets and his bedside littered with a dozen or more slain Mexican soldiers. The whole flavor of the film's cheerful Anglo-Saxonism is caught in one scene before the final Mexican assault. Two Alamo defenders shake hands and then prepare to die. The film ends with a series of flag images: 1824, Lone Star, Confederate, U.S. On the surface the film sports a strong patriotic message, standard fare for all the Alamo movies through the 1950s; but its real text, its pattern of action and character, is thoroughly racist. Nor was this fact lost upon contemporary audiences. Re-released in the 1920s under the Griffith-like title

The Birth of Texas, it provoked a Mexican-American audience in
Baytown, Texas, to walk out.

In the next decade there was one Alamo film, *Davy Crockett at the
Fall of the Alamo* (1926), but since only one reel is extant, it is difficult to say what this film accomplishes. On the basis of the first
reel, it seems to be a very mediocre melodrama. A young maiden
and her father's land are imperiled by the wily schemes of a rapacious villain; Davy Crockett comes to set things right. A critique of
this film appeared in a surprising context, in Harvey Fergusson's
novel, *Footloose McGarnigal,* published in 1930. Fergusson's hero
spends a few days in San Antonio, where he attends a "bad" film
entitled "The Fall of the Alamo." Fergusson recounts the film's
action in considerable detail and, despite the slight difference in
titles, the film his hero watches must be the 1926 one. Fergusson's
rendition of the final climactic battle scenes is the best account we
have of this obscure film:

> The fight was really impressive. The man who took the part
> of Crockett had shortcomings in the emotional parts but in
> slaughtering Mexicans he displayed an incredible activity,
> serving three cannon at once until the enemy breached the
> walls and then fighting hand to hand against hordes of them.
> Drenched in his own blood, with musket, pistol and Bowie
> knife he piled up the swarthy dead. Colonel Bowie himself
> was seen making his last stand from under his blankets and
> fairly blocking the door with slain enemies before he finally
> died with a bayonet through his heart and a smile on his lips.

The next Alamo movie, a low-budget production released in
1937 to take advantage of the national attention accorded the
Texas Centennial, borrowed many of its action scenes from
Martyrs, particularly those of the Mexican assault on the Alamo
walls. A B western with no name actors, *The Heroes of the Alamo*
received praise from contemporary Texans such as Leita Small, cus-
todian of the Alamo, and Governor James V. Allred. In all respects
Heroes of the Alamo is an odd film, and one of the most original of the

Alamo movies. It focuses on Almeron Dickinson instead of the usual triad of Crockett, Bowie, and Travis, and it approaches the Alamo story from the angle of the small landholder, not that of an adventurer-hero or a military leader. Dickinson is portrayed as a common man who wishes to till his fields and enjoy the beatitudes of hearth and home. But duty whispers low, "Thou must," and Dickinson, like every Texan worth his salt, rallies round the emergent flag and goes to the Alamo to die.

Although everything about this film smacks of low-budget considerations, the results are far more stimulating than those produced by most of the A-budget pictures. The main reason is that, whether intentionally or accidentally, the story develops an odd slant. This is particularly evident in the manner of the triad's death scenes. In most Alamo films Crockett, Bowie, and Travis are given special send-offs, like gods, like Greek heroes, but in this one Crockett, for example, dies almost as an afterthought. As the battle is winding down, a Mexican soldier spots a wounded coonskin-clad Texan crawling away and casually finishes him off with his rifle butt. The figure is none other than Davy Crockett, thereby anticipating by several decades the fiery controversy over how Crockett actually died—heroically or by firing squad after surrendering. Bowie and Travis die in similarly undramatic fashion. By trying to make the common man (Dickinson) the center of the film, it levels the loftier heroes, thereby accomplishing a democratic presentation of death: in this equation all defenders of the Alamo are equal. The film is also worth mentioning for its creative use of anachronism. The night before the final onslaught the Texans sit around a campfire singing "The Yellow Rose of Texas," which was not written until long after the fall of the Alamo. But emotionally, this is the song, the national anthem of Texas as it were, that the Alamo defenders should have had in their repertoire.

The 1950s saw presentations of the Alamo story reach the height of earnestness and flag-waving. The three Alamo films of this decade were variously ambitious, expensive, and uneven in accomplishment. The first, *The Man from the Alamo* (1953), had promise but was compromised by timidity, genre limitations, and other intangible factors. Even so, the Daughters of the Republic of Texas were alarmed when word reached them that a film about Moses Rose was to be made. The president of the organization said in a letter: "I am very distressed that the Motion Picture fraternity has scraped the barrel to the point they have to use Moses Rose as the hero of a picture." But she felt that a campaign by the DRT would only give free publicity to the motion picture company.

The promise of *Man from the Alamo* lay in its focus on the one taboo figure in the Alamo legend: Moses Rose. A film examining this veteran of the Napoleonic wars, widely regarded as the only man who declined Travis's invitation to cross the line and die defending the mission fortress, offered a real chance to explore the central power of the Alamo story, the decision to cross the line. Instead, John Stroud, the Moses Rose character in the film, played by Glenn Ford, wants desperately to stay in the Alamo but is forced by bad luck to go on a courier mission. He draws a black bean— an unhistorical appropriation of the Mier Expedition legend to a new context. As a result of leaving, he becomes a pariah, the only man who didn't stay and fight. Throughout the rest of the film he has to suffer the scorn of his fellow Texans, who believe him a rank coward.

The film turned out to be as centrist as the most ardent Texas chauvinist could hope for; and the enigmatic figure of Rose was converted into a legitimate hero who, though misjudged and maligned, manages to save a wagon train of settlers from the depredations of outlaws. These same outlaws killed Stroud's family while he was away fighting for the Texan cause. Disguised as Mexicans, they were actually renegade whites. Mexicans receive patronizing treatment in this film, different but no less stereotypical than the harsh negative portrayals seen in *Martyrs of the Alamo.*

The refusal to confront the Moses Rose question in this film is highlighted by a more original approach to his character that appears in Ramsey Yelvington's play *A Cloud of Witnesses* (1959). Here Rose takes the part of the Devil and raises major questions about the Texan stand for freedom. Arguing according to Reason and Nature, Rose champions an ethic of self-interest: "Live out your life and champion no cause that cannot be defined as 'bread,' and 'bread' alone." But his most penetrating question, the one that all Alamo movies seek to explore, is: "Hasn't Freedom changed?"

According to all Anglo interpretations of the Alamo story, the answer to such a question is a resounding no. Yelvington's play states the theme thus:

> The mammoth Thing, Freedom,
> Received a forward thrust
> That has continually reverberated.

Virtually all the works about the Alamo express this meaning: at the Alamo the Texans acted on behalf of freedom against tyranny, and therein lies a lesson for all future ages. Of course this formulation is that of the ultimate victors of the war, the winners writing history as they are wont to do, history (and land) being the most lasting fruits of victory. The lesson has a particularly American focus in most versions. The prologue to *The Man from the Alamo* (1953) states the point succinctly: "The story of Texas symbolized the spirit of independence so close to the heart of all Americans."

During the Cold War era especially, filmmakers sought to hammer home the message that freedom was an unchanging principle for which one must be willing to die. To John Wayne, the Alamo story had to be retold in the post–World War II era in order to insure the preservation of the meaning of freedom. In an interview Wayne said:

> It was not a story that belongs only to Texas; it belongs to people everywhere who have an interest in a thing called freedom. I think we are all in danger and have been for a long time of going soft, of taking things for granted; neglecting to have an objective about the things for which we stand and forgetting the things that made this a great nation.

Wayne's first assumption, that the Alamo is a tale of universal significance, is one with which all the filmmakers who have attempted the subject would agree. His second, the "danger" of "going soft," seems tied to the Cold War zeitgeist.

The most popular Alamo film of the decade was easily Walt Disney's *Davy Crockett, King of the Wild Frontier* (1955). The movie, the song, and the product—the coonskin cap—swept the U.S. and the world. Documentary filmmaker Brian Huberman, a youth in Britain at the time, was so caught up with the romance of the Alamo that years later, in 1974, he made a fascinating documentary film called *An Alamo Scrapbook*. It paid homage to the children's version of the Alamo story developed in the Disney vehicle. Huberman constructed a scale model of the Alamo, as accurate as he could make it, complete with toy soldiers representing the opposing armies. Against this deliberate attempt to treat the story as fantasy (but rigorously authentic and true at the same time), Huberman employed a sort of march-of-time narrator to describe in somber, thrilling tones the essence of the story being enacted by the toy soldiers. Between these two modes, the documentary historical voice and the sense of fabrication, fall most of the attempts to tell the Alamo story.

The Disney film is better than one might be inclined to think at first blush. Crockett's arrival at the Alamo is especially effective. With his ridiculous entourage—his garrulous sidekick, a carryover from western movies; a diminutive Indian; and a posturing aristocrat—Crockett races into the Alamo, chased by Mexican cavalry. As the horses gallop across the prairie, the camera angle, from above, creates the illusion of flying. It is as though the hero and his compatriots fly into the Alamo as in a dream. And that is precisely the point: the Alamo is as much a dream of history as it is a well documented historical event. Thus the cinematic liberties taken by the Disney film are emotionally right, like the anachronistic song introduced into *The Heroes of the Alamo*.

The leveling lesson of the Alamo is also effectively rendered. The absurd aristocrat becomes a far, far better man because of the encounter with death. The ending of the film is perfect, too, with

Crockett in full swing with his rifle Old Betsy, the music swelling. We leave the heroes poised in mid-myth. All in all, the Disney version, seen as a juvenile romance, is one of the more effective translations of the Alamo story into film.

The next Alamo movie of the decade, *The Last Command* (1956), veered in the opposite direction from the Disney film, toward historical accuracy. Filmed on location at Brackettville (in the town, not at the Happy Shahan ranch outside town where *The Alamo* was filmed three years later), *The Last Command* featured meticulous research and gained some good effects as a result. Most notable is the portrayal of Santa Anna by J. Carroll Naish. His Santa Anna is a man with some flaws, too much vanity, too much political ambition but nonetheless a man and not a blustering cartoon, someone that Jim Bowie could respect, talk to, and finally disagree with strongly enough to oppose in combat. This Santa Anna is a far cry from the degenerate opium fiend of *Martyrs*. Yet *The Last Command* is not the ultimate Alamo film. It errs in part by returning to the fixation on the triad, in this case Jim Bowie. Part of the problem, too, is Sterling Hayden's wooden-Indian portrayal of Bowie, a performance so solemn, so reasonable, so careful that the audience has trouble staying awake until the final conflict. Hayden's Bowie hasn't a spark of passion or romance about him, and the Bowie legend is sacrificed to humorless understatement. Davy Crockett, however, receives a fresh interpretation by Arthur Hunnicutt. Here Crockett is drawn correctly as an older man (older meaning just under fifty and not some dewy-faced youth). Hunnicutt's grizzled, rather seedy, and truly humorous depiction of Crockett as a man who loves to spin windy yarns is one of the best Crockett representations on film. By contrast Richard Carlson's Travis is like Hayden's Bowie—understated and colorless.

In staging the most famous moment in the Alamo story, this film errs, too. The drawing of the line is done during a pelting rain storm, and one wonders, watching it, why the Texans haven't the sense to get in out of the rain.

John Wayne's *The Alamo* (1960) was easily the most heralded of all the Alamo films. For one thing, it cost more than any previous Alamo film and for a brief time was the most expensive undertaking in motion picture history, with a budget of approximately $11 million. For another, it generated an enormous amount of publicity. The pressbook itself ran to a whopping 183 pages. The makers of *The Alamo* loved to stress its authenticity. Screenwriter James Edward Grant claimed to have done a great deal of research. Experts on Texas lore were consulted, including J. Frank Dobie and Lon Tinkle, author of a popular version of the story, *Thirteen Days to Glory*. Yet the simplest of details of geography were ignored, and several howlers drew the attention of historians. One was the location of the Alamo. The script has the actors referring to the Rio Bravo (the name for the lower part of the Rio Grande, 200 miles away) as the river running near the Alamo. The mission was actually situated, of course, near the San Antonio River. The other piece of errant geography was San Antonio itself. In one scene Colonel Travis draws a picture in the sand and places San Antonio north of the Sabine (the boundary between Texas and Louisiana.) Later, Fannin is said to be marching south to San Antonio from Goliad, but Goliad is nearly a hundred miles southeast of the Alamo City.

Intentional fictionalizing appears in the romance plot devised for John Wayne's Davy Crockett. Wayne pays attention to a beautiful Mexican woman played by Linda Crystal. The reason for such inventions is doubtless generic. On this point, the best evidence for the felt necessity of introducing fictional women characters into the story occurs in the appended remarks of the nineteenth-century dramatist Hiram McLane. McLane said he imported such a figure into his play because of a "general demand for some leading female characters in all works of the kind." Another such made-up character is the innocent youth who either witnesses the Alamo battle from a secret vantage point or is sent away on courier duty to avoid being slaughtered. In Eugene P. Lyle's *The Lone Star* (1907) the narrator hero, a young man, hides under debris on the broken ramparts and witnesses the entire battle. In *The Alamo* the other tack is taken, in a part played by teen heart-throb Frankie Avalon. Avalon is spared death at the Alamo for two reasons: to fit the generic mold and to be able to sing the Oscar-nominated "The Green Leaves of Summer."

Generic conventions aside, *The Alamo* is not as bad as many critics felt at the time, nor is it as good as the Daughters of the Republic of Texas believe. The DRT answered eastern critics of the film both through the press and in private correspondence with magazines. Mrs. Philip Harrell, president of the Alamo Mission Chapter of the DRT, defended against charges of historical inaccuracy by celebrating the film's lofty aim: "It instills into the minds of people today that our wonderful freedom did not come by accident." In a letter to *Time*, Marg-Riette Montgomery, librarian at the Alamo, praised John Wayne's role: "The character of Crockett is the best part of the casting and acting." For them, John Wayne is the definitive Davy Crockett, and a painting on display in the Alamo bears a striking resemblance to Wayne. The Duke, incidentally, was careful to court the approval of the DRT and invited its officers to visit with him on the set.

What is good about *The Alamo*, besides Wayne's performance, is the dramatization of the central myth of democracy that is imbedded in the Alamo story. It is clear from many interview statements that Wayne well understood both the intended form and the meaning of the film. Wayne regarded the story as "real Americana" and film as the appropriate medium for conveying folklore in the modern era: "I think it's the greatest piece of folklore ever brought down through history, and folklore has always been the most successful medium for motion pictures." As for the subject matter itself, Wayne repeatedly drove home the significance that he saw in the material: "If a fiction writer had contrived the story of the Alamo, it might have been believable—because never to my knowledge, have that number of men joined in a suicide pact to remain at their posts rather than to surrender or retreat." In short, Wayne believed that the Alamo embodied a great theme: it dramatized that the men at the fortress were equal in valor and commitment to a great principle and were willing to die for an ideal.

The democratic theme of *The Alamo* is conveyed brilliantly in the pivotal scene. Instead of using the legendary drawing of the line in the sand, *The Alamo* stages this crucial event in a highly original way. Each of the triad—Bowie, Travis, and Crockett—becomes one with the common man in a visually effective manner. All through the film the three are presented as leaders of men. Crockett is the most attractive figure. A man of imposing leadership abilities, he is clearly in charge of the Tennessee detachment. Bowie, also in charge of a band of men loyal to his bidding, is a quarrelsome figure as played by Richard Widmark. Arrogant, cantankerous, and bull-headed, he also carries himself slightly apart from his men, fiercely independent and a stern though sometimes drunken taskmaster. Travis, played by British actor Laurence Harvey, is even more aloof from the common man. He considers many of the men rabble, and is always filmed with low-angle shots, creating an effect of loftiness and isolation. Travis is literally seen above other men, on the ramparts, giving orders, aristocratic and haughty, impatient with those beneath him.

With these reinforced images of isolation, leadership, superiority, the moment of decision gains power, then, from visual symbolism. Travis appears in the Alamo courtyard, on foot, on a level with the anonymous common defenders. Crockett and Bowie are both mounted, ready to take their men out of the Alamo. Fractious encounters between Bowie and Travis have led to Bowie's decision to leave; Crockett's pragmatism has led to his. But there is Travis, and they loom above him, visually superior but on morally tenuous terms. Travis, no longer above the common man, speaks of commitment, of holding the Alamo to buy time for Texas, and the appeal works: Bowie and Crockett dismount, but Crockett last, after the rest of the men have joined Travis. Though *The Alamo* discards the traditional imagery of the line in the dust, it invents a rhetorically effective equivalent. This is the finest moment in the film, though the battle scenes are conducted with considerable élan.

By 1960 it was no longer fashionable to resort to the simple racist contrasts of the early films and novels; by now the emphasis was on evenhandedness. Thus the Mexican army in Wayne's film looks like a marching mass of choir boys. But despite Wayne's care to avoid offending anybody, Mexico banned *The Alamo*, an act that testifies eloquently to the passions that still swirl around the Alamo story. Years before, in 1951, when Wayne first announced plans to make a film about the Alamo, he intended to shoot it in Mexico, to save costs. Two prominent Texans, Jesse H. Jones and Bob O'Donnell, threatened to boycott the film if he did.

The politics of Alamo film making intensified in the next decade. *Viva Max!*, made in volatile 1969, caused a comic-opera uproar among the Daughters of the Republic of Texas. The DRT refused to allow the movie company entrance to the Alamo, as the organization had refused earlier to allow CBS to shoot a documentary inside the Alamo or Ramsey Yelvington to use the Alamo grounds for production of his play, *A Cloud of Witnesses*. *Viva Max!* particularly offended the DRT's sense of proprieties. Mrs. William L. Scarborough, president of the organization, stated her views succinctly: "We feel the movie is a mockery and a desecration of our heroes who died for our liberty here." She also said on another occasion: "Why can't they make a nice movie like John Wayne?" Ever resourceful, the movie company shot the interiors in Rome, Italy.

Viva Max!, based on James Lehrer's light and often very funny novel of the same title, tells the story of a tinpot Mexican general who decides, for the sake of his own self-worth and the greater glory of his native land, to cross the border and retake the Alamo. After all, Mexico won that battle, he reasons. In the ensuing conflict the film is intermittently funny. Some of its best satirical jabs are aimed at Wayne's epic. For example, after Max and his men seize the Alamo, the password for entry is "Richard Widmark." *Viva Max!* poked fun at the Alamo as a sacred cow; it satirized simpleminded Texan chauvinists, fearful of a communist plot behind every statement critical of the establishment; and it sought in a mild way to assert Mexican pride. Because actors such as Peter Ustinov and John Astin played major Mexican roles, however, some of that thrust was obviously diminished.

Seguín (1979) carries forward the revisionism begun in *Viva Max!* This project, originally shot at feature length, was trimmed for public television. It tells the story of the Tejano Juan Nepomuceno Seguín, who played a prominent and complex role in the Texas Revolution and afterward. The director, Jésus S. Treviño, who was acutely aware of making a revisionist film, felt it important to shoot the project as the same Brackettville site where John Wayne had made *The Alamo*. Treviño argued that now "justice was finally being done" and that his film would correct the false impressions, created by Wayne and history texts alike, in ignoring the "Chicano side of American history." Specifically, Treviño said, he objected to the rampant stereotypes present in *The Alamo*: "bandidos, dancing señoritas, sleeping drunks, or fiery temptresses." Treviño must have been thinking of other movies, not of *The Alamo*, because these stereotypes are not present in that film. Indeed, the principal drunks in the film are Crockett's wild Tennesseeans, not Mexicans. In his book, *Images of the Mexican American in Fiction and Film*, Arthur G. Petit could cite only a very few films that avoided negative stereotyping. *The Alamo* was one. Treviño was probably reacting to political perceptions extrinsic to the film. Increasingly it is hard to see the Alamo, in history or in a particular film, with anything like objective lucidity.

Although wrong about Wayne's film, Treviño's general argument is certainly valid, and *Seguín* is an honorable attempt to tell the story of the Alamo and the Republic from a new and historically valid angle. There were a number of Mexican Texans (Tejanos) who died in the Alamo, but in Texas history texts all too often this dimension is underplayed if brought up at all. The historical Juan Seguín, whose father had escorted Stephen F. Austin on his first trip to Texas, was at the Alamo at the start of the siege but was sent on a courier mission and therefore did not die there. He did fight at the battle of San Jacinto, however, and served two terms as senator in the Republic. The film opens with a slow-motion sequence depicting Juan Seguín and his men racing to reach the Alamo. They arrive too late; the Alamo has fallen. "I shall never forget the fall of the Alamo," says Seguín. Then, though a series of flashbacks, the story of Juan Seguín's life before the events of 1836 is related. Much of the film also deals with his life afterwards. In *Seguín*, then, the Alamo provides a smoldering backdrop for racial passions and complex political issues.

Seguín stresses certain themes that are systematically overlooked in Anglo versions of the story. One is the slavery issue. Juan Seguín believes in the American ideal of social and political liberty more than the slave-holding Americans do. Another theme is the rabid hatred of Mexicans by new Anglo settlers who have come to San Antonio to enjoy the fruits of the Texan victory. Thus the freedom that Seguín and the Anglo Texans fought for in 1836 is eroded by ignorance and racism in the years that follow. The original builders of San Antonio, people of Mexican descent, are threatened with displacement by the new conquerors. It is a potent and historically accurate theme that unfortunately is diluted by problems in the script. The drama tries to cover too much time, and certain anachronistic sentiments deflect the film's proper concern with setting the record straight. One example is that Juan Seguín is portrayed as a strong proponent of women's rights, a bit of feminist political correctness by a post-sixties director. For all of Treviño's concern about Anglo distortions, he himself was accused of capitulating to mass media expectations and whitewashing his hero.

Postscript, 1997

The above essay appeared in 1985, commissioned by the *Southwestern Historical Quarterly* to coincide with the buildup for the Texas Sesquicentennial of 1986. Near the end of the essay I mentioned an upcoming made-for-TV movie, *Thirteen Days To Glory*, and predicted that Sesqui-fever might indeed inspire more Alamo films and books. Not a bold prophecy, but an accurate one.

The Alamo: Thirteen Days to Glory aired on NBC in January 1987, but I didn't see it; I was pretty much Alamo-ed out by then. Frank Thompson has a full account of the film in his book *Alamo Movies* (1991). Thompson also includes a rundown of other Alamo treatments in television from 1956 through 1990. My favorite section of Thompson's book, though, is a little chapter on "Alamo Movies That Never Were." These are the ones that never got made, the ones that, blessedly we don't have to see.

The IMAX (for image maximization) film *Alamo . . . The Price of Freedom*, which has been running in a theater across the alley from the Alamo since 1988, has been seen by millions of tourists. It's authentic, violent, and boisterous, an honest effort to tell the story without offending anybody. And best of all, it only lasts a little over forty minutes. For purists and Alamaniacs, however, this very brevity is cause for deep concern, because there's no way the whole story of the thirteen days can be told in such short compass. For the jaded Alamoist like myself, I say hurrah! How much information do pilgrims from the midwest down here for a game at the Alamo-dome need to know about the Alamo anyway?

Of books there has been no lack either. James Michener (*Texas*, 1986), Jeff Long (*Empire of Bones: A Novel of Sam Houston and the Texas Revolution*, 1993), Janice Woods Windle, *True Women* (1993), Elizabeth Crook (*Promised Lands*, 1994), D. Marian Wilkinson (*Not Between Brothers: An Epic Novel of Texas*, 1996), and Will Camp (*Blood of Texas*, 1996) have all had a go at different aspects of the Texas Revolution.

In a Texas novel I read once, I forget which one, it is said of some Texans who are somewhere on horseback, faced with some danger: "Their bowels ran with fear." In the next sentence these same Texans are galloping along the prairie as though nothing had happened. Maybe only metaphor, only cliché, had happened, but my question is, what does it mean that their bowels ran with fear? Does this mean they soiled themselves? And what of their pretty horses? Were they soiled too? The task of bringing the remote past alive is not easy.

Perhaps the best book on the subject is Jeff Long's sometimes tendentious and nearly always gripping history, *Duel of Eagles: The Mexican and U.S. Fight for the Alamo* (1990). Long's grasp of detail brings alive such unrealized historical certainties as the near-starvation conditions of Santa Anna's army in its march through bleak South Texas in the winter of 1836. His book is also winningly iconoclastic. He makes Houston just as much of an opium aficionado as Santa Anna, who was always attacked in the earlier novels and films for his use of the drug.

Fortunately there has been only one epic poem, Michael Lind's *The Alamo*, published in 1997. Lind has said the poem was twelve years in the making. It would seem in all of that time the author would have realized that Travis did not have repeating weapons at the Alamo. If he had, the outcome might have been different. The Colt revolver arrived in Texas in 1837, but here is Travis packing one on the ramparts of the Alamo in March of 1836:

> Two thousand hearts were knelling in the grass
>   around the Alamo when Travis knelt
> beside his rival. Whispering, he pressed
>   one Colt revolver in his hand, and felt
>   a trace of strength that plague alone could melt.
> "Travis?" Sense renewed, and then eluded
> the dying man. A man soon dead saluted.

The poem goes on in this vein for over three hundred pages.

What I wrote in 1985 still stands, I believe: More than anything else, the Alamo story needs the application of critical intelligence to its traditions, legends, and stock images. And that, of course, is what it least often has had. Confronted directly, the Alamo story seems to make the eyes glaze. The heroes take on the smooth patina of public statuary seen from a distance. In fiction or film or poetry such pageant-like figures are deadly, stultifying, lifeless. Houston, we have a problem.

Nowhere Else but Southfork: What Texas Looks Like in the Movies

Muse the contrast between Judge Roy Bean
and Dr. Michael DeBakey. Savor the flavor
of Can Cliburn [sic] and Willie Nelson.
          —Texas! Live the Legend
(Texas Official Highway Travel Map, 1985)

During a trip to the Caribbean in the early nineties, we spent an afternoon at a small cafe in Martinique, eating, drinking, and talking to the locals. On a TV set behind the cash register, reruns of *Dallas* flickered brightly, the owners' small child transfixed by the dubious doings of J.R., Bobby, Sue Ellen, the whole Ewing rabbit warren who were speaking dubbed-in French. As were we at the table with the locals. That is, the four men and Betsy were. Having little French, I was drinking and listening.

They were intellectuals; one was visiting from Paris. They wanted to know if the TV show bore any relation to reality. Betsy said, "I don't know; I've never seen it." Even if I possessed enough French to explain that the show was mostly a lot of Hollywood hokum, there wouldn't have been any point in doing so. This I had learned from other travels. On a plane from Lisbon to London, the woman sitting next to me, an Indian, upon learning I was from Texas, started in on how much she longed to visit Southfork. When I mentioned that she would likely be disappointed at its reduced scale compared to the immensity of the made-up ranch on TV, she said she was certain she wouldn't be surprised at all, she just knew that Southfork would not disappoint.

So it is the world over, I suspect: the image of Texas drilled into generation after generation of myth-seeking moviegoers. A few years ago *Dallas* was still playing in eighty countries round the globe.

The long tracking shot that opens the drama reveals a dreamscape, a vast prairie with God's own sky arching above, then a rambling white mansion with southern overtones—the only hint of a southern orientation, that and the name of this very western ranch. Here's a place where Scarlett could live, in this spacious house well stocked with hot and cold running ethnic servants. The house I was born in was slightly smaller than Southfork and has long since vanished. In those days Collin County was farming country pure and simple. The men wore overalls or khaki work suits, and, usually with their wives and children helping, they raised and harvested (a word they never used) cotton and corn. Blacks picked in the fields alongside the whites, and on any given September day it was possible to imagine that the Old South was alive and well, down Texas way. In fact, the Old South was ailing badly, the small farm system of agricultural production was headed for the last gin, and all the economic currents swirled irresistibly toward Dallas.

Now, going on five decades later, the chief crop in that part of Collin County is real estate development. The southern feel of the place has all but disappeared; "ranchettes" occupy land once used for crops; and down the road a piece, Southfork redefines Texas history, turning the South into the West.

There's plenty of precedent for playing fast and loose with Texas reality. Historically the movies have seen Texas almost exclusively through western lenses, southern California style. The creation of the Southfork image goes back to the beginnings of Texas in the movies, to films and books that trafficked in the western-ness of Texas history. Just as certain prominent sages of Texas culture, chiefly J. Frank Dobie and Walter P. Webb, have created a largely western image of Texas through their writings and public personas, so too have motion pictures traded upon the idea of Texas as a western state, a barren, dry, desert-like land populated by long-legged galoots on horseback. The coefficient of this stereotype has been the neglect or distortion of East and Coastal Texas in movies about the state.

Movies made in the forties, movies made last week, it's all the same. The myth fostered by motion pictures and now, of course, by television, insists upon the western-ness of Texas. At one time everything west of I-35 was West Texas; now everything east of it is, too. Historically, when movies have been set in East Texas, the Texas background has usually blurred into generic southern-ness, thus reinforcing the all-western perception of Texas. Jean Renoir's *The Southerner* (1945) is a case in point. Based on George Sessions Perry's *Hold Autumn in Your Hand*, *The Southerner* seized upon the iconographic similarity between cotton farming in Texas and the deep South and reflected that congruity in its title. Had the movie been titled *The Texan*, it would undoubtedly have raised false audience expectations. They would have bought tickets expecting to see a western. This is precisely what happened when Fred Gipson's farming novel, *The Home Place* (1950), was filmed as *The Return of the Texan* (1952). Audiences expected a shoot-'em-up and were treated instead to a Disney-like family movie. Low box-office returns led studio executive Darryl F. Zanuck to lecture director Delmer Daves about false labeling and genre expectations: "The reason I am writing this note is to again emphasize the necessity of being very careful about the selection of subject material. In other words if you go to Texas— go on a horse with a gun." Truer words. . . .

Zanuck had a half-century of movie history to back him up. From the beginning of films about Texas, the state has been seen as essentially a western landscape. This is true of the first fictional narrative to deal with Texas, called, appropriately, *Texas Tex*, filmed in Denmark in 1908, and of the numerous Tom Mix films in the silent era. Other silent films such as *North of 36* and *The Wind* continued the pattern, and in the scads of B westerns in the 1920s and 1930s, Texas was always the Wild West, never the Old South. In these films, west was west, and east was west, too.

Even in more recent times, the tendency to see Texas through western lenses is a hard habit to break. Horton Foote, Texas-born novelist, playwright, and screenwriter, has told how in 1966, a big, splashy production of his novel *The Chase* falsified his hometown of Wharton, southwest of Houston, by including one scene with a couple of Indians in full tribal regalia inserted to provide a little local color. Foote protested by pointing out that there were no Indians in Wharton during his lifetime, but the Hollywood people, their ideas shaped by previous films about Texas, knew better. The Indians stayed in.

When films were set ostensibly in East Texas, one of two things usually happened. Either the film made East Texas into West Texas, or it blurred East Texas into the Old South, and the sense of Texas was lost or ignored. Examples of the westernization of East Texas are plentiful. In a Sam Houston biopic, *Man of Conquest* (1938) Richard Dix's Houston rides through rugged western terrain said to be East Texas, and in one scene discovers a gooey black liquid that oozes from the ground. He sets it on fire and drives off a band of marauding Indians. In another founding-father film, *The First Texan* (1956), Joel McCrea as Houston leads the Texan army towards San Jacinto, and on all sides stretch the bare, treeless expanses of southern California, with soft, nude hills rising in the distance. In other words, Universal's backlot. San Jacinto is actually marshy, swampy country, located at sea level, its trees festooned with Spanish moss.

In later films, one finds exactly the same misrepresentation of East Texas settings as in the earlier westerns. In *All the Fine Young Cannibals* (1960), for instance, Natalie Wood plays a young girl from East Texas who yearns to escape from her impoverished, fundamentalist, redneck background and live the good life in New York. She boards a train in Dallas headed for the Big Apple and, amazingly, passes through a desert replete with miles of sand, giant cacti, and shimmering vistas of heat. The train must have taken the long route—through Arizona. *A Walk on the Wild Side* (1962) contains an equally laughable instance of skewed geography. Laurence Harvey, completely unbelievable as an East Texas farmer, is on his way to New Orleans when his train stops in the middle of a desert. A sign beside the railroad track says, "Beaumont, One Mile," as a tumbleweed blows past. As a final example of East Texas as Arizona desert, Burt Reynolds' second *Smokey and the Bandit* opus will do. In one of those interminable car chases the bandit passes from cool, lush Louisiana into hot, dusty, barren Texas. The change is instantaneous, taking place the moment Burt crosses the state line.

If East Texas is desert country, it's also very mountainous—in the movies. In *American Empire* (1942) Richard Dix operates a gigantic ranch along the Sabine River, just a few miles from the Louisiana border. Yet his ranch is surrounded by lofty, snow-clad mountains, the high Sierras. In *Four for Texas* (1964), a truly dreadful western starring Frank Sinatra and Dean Martin, Galveston is represented as next door to the high Sierras, a short ride by horseback. In *Uncommon Valor* (1983) a paramilitary unit of ex-Vietnam combat veterans goes into secret training for a POW rescue mission in a training camp situated in a valley surrounded by high mountains, and the legend on the screen says: "North of Galveston." How far north? Colorado?

All of these films parlay an extreme stereotype of Texas landscapes. In most, Texas looks the way it does when Elizabeth Taylor steps down from the train on her first trip to Texas: vast, empty, dusty, flat, and windy. Of course, the part of Texas where *Giant* was filmed—near Marfa in the Big Bend country—looks like that. East Texas does not, but Hollywood has rarely noticed the difference.

"Time-Traveling Through Texas": A Half-century of Lone Star Movies on Video

....

THE SOUTHERNER 1945 *U.A./Producing Artists, Inc.* 1:31
B&W **Director**: *Jean Renoir* **Writer**: *Jean Renoir (on advice from William Faulkner)* **Starring**: *Zachary Scott, Betty Field, Beulah Bondi, Bunny Sunshine, Jay Gilpin, Percy Kilbride, Charles Kemper, J. Carroll Naish, Estelle Taylor*

One of three American films made by famed French director Jean Renoir, who during World War II came to Hollywood to escape the Nazi occupation of his country. A heart-warming, faithful adaptation of George Sessions Perry's novel *Hold Autumn in Your Hand*, this film explores the economic conditions of tenant farming in the late 1930s on a small Texas cotton farm (actually filmed in southern California). Some excellent period photography coupled with some little-house-on-the-prairie sentiments, Renoir's work is best appreciated in the context of an era when few movies about farm life rose above the Ma-and-Pa Kettle comedies. Native Texan Zachary Scott is actually rather miscast, given Scott's urbane persona, and Betty Field is far prettier and sexier than one has any right to expect (she wears designer jeans and smokes cigarettes); still, a film worth seeing provided one approaches it in the right spirit. Awarded "Best of Festival" at the 1946 Venice Film Festival and picked as Number Three of the "Ten Best Films of the Year" by the National Board of Review.

RED RIVER 1948 *MGM-UA* 2:05 *B&W* **Director:** *Howard Hawks* **Writer:** *Borden Chase* **Starring:** *John Wayne, Montgomery Clift, Joanne Dru, Walter Brennan, Coleen Gray, John Ireland, Noah Berry, Jr., Shelley Winters, Harry Carey, Sr., Harry Carey, Jr.*

This film embodies the central myth of the Lone Star State: the seizing of land, miles and miles of Texas, from Mexicans, the building up of a great herd of cattle, and the driving of these bovine bonanzas to the railheads in Kansas. For once the term epic fits in this horseback appropriation of *Mutiny on the Bounty* plot. In one of his best roles, John Wayne plays Tom Dunson, a pioneering rancher who, having consolidated an empire, must survive new dangers and threats to his well-being. The trail north is fraught with dangerous encounters with rivers, rustlers, mutineers, stampeding cattle, and women. The pressure takes its toll on Dunson, turning him into a tyrant who rides roughshod over everybody who gets in his way and some who don't. His foundling son, Matthew Garth, played beautifully by Montgomery Clift, eventually takes the herd away from Dunson in order to save it. The scene where Clift sucks the poison from an arrow wound just above Joanne Dru's breasts had a powerful impact on me when I saw this film as a child. I didn't know what it meant, but I knew I liked it. The "take 'em to Missouri" scene, the start of the long drive, is quoted nicely in Peter Bogdanovich's *The Last Picture Show*.

TO HELL AND BACK 1955 *Universal-International* 1:46
Director: *Jesse Hibbs* **Writer**: *Gil Doud* **Starring**: *Audie Murphy,
Charles Drake, Marshall Thompson, Gregg Palmer, Paul Picerni, Susan
Kohner, Richard Castle, Art Aragon, Denver Pyle*

One of the hits of 1955, this film, based on Murphy's autobiography of the same title, traces the exploits of Texas-born hero
Audie Murphy, the most decorated soldier of World War II. Early
scenes (filmed on Universal's backlot) depict Murphy's impoverished family life in Hunt County, Texas, but the film quickly
moves to recreating his war record in Sicily, Italy, and France.
One memorable moment in the film occurs when Murphy fires at
his reflection in a mirror and another soldier, observing the
action, says, "I never thought I'd see a Texan outdraw himself."
This film, which Murphy considered nothing more than a "western in uniform," presents the hero at his modest best and pretti-
fies the real conditions of combat for a mid-fifties audience with
little knowledge of the real war. Murphy's Medal of Honor
action, which took place on a snowy, frozen afternoon, is presented in the film in a sunny, park-like setting (in Washington
State). A whole generation of young men who would fight in
Vietnam went into the war with visions of Audie Murphy in their
heads. Ron Kovick, for example, says in *Born on the Fourth of July*:
"He was so brave I had chills running up and down my back,
wishing it were me up there. . . . It was the greatest movie I ever
saw in my life." For the rest of the story, see Don Graham's *No
Name on the Bullet: A Biography of Audie Murphy.*

GIANT 1956. *Warner Bros.* 3:21 **Director:** *George Stevens*
Writers: *Fred Gulof, Ivan Moffett* **Starring:** *Elizabeth Taylor, Rock
Hudson, James Dean, Carroll Baker, Jane Withers, Chill Wills,
Mercedes McCambridge, Dennis Hopper, Sal Mineo, Rod Taylor, Earl
Holliman*

Although Edna Ferber thought about calling her novel "Jillion" or "Big Rich" or "No Man is an Island," what she decided on had an air of inevitability: *Giant.* In a review typical of local response to the novel, the Houston *Press* labeled it "the most gargantuan hunk of monstrous, ill informed, hokum-laden hocus-pocus ever turned out about Texas." Yet Texans loved George Stevens' film. And why not: *Giant*, by Gawd, has everything: lusty ranchers, colorful wheeler-dealers, acres of cattle, tacky clothes, plug-ugly mansions, miles of gorgeous emptiness, a thumping rendition of "The Yellow Rose of Texas," and a liberal heart-on-its sleeve subtext about Mexican-Anglo relations. *Giant* gave Texans—long insecure, long self-victimized by a colonial mentality—a consoling secular myth that emphasized everything good about Texas and suggested that everything bad was fixable; it would just take time. Yes, about a hundred years, said Leslie Benedict (Taylor) wife of empire builder Bick Benedict (Hudson). Besides stellar performances by Hudson and Taylor, the rest of the cast is stupendous, too: Dennis Hopper as Bick's wimpy son; Mercedes McCambridge in one of the campier takes on lesbianism in that era; and, in his last and finest role, James Dean as Jett Rink, the dirt-poor redneck oozing with class hatred and itching to get even, who gets stinking rich and tries to put his brand, JR (please note), on everything in Texas. Required viewing for each new generation of natives and snowbirds. New laserdisc release by Warner Bros. has additional plus of "Return to *Giant*," a thoughtful documentary about the making of the film at Marfa in the summer of 1955.

THE SEARCHERS 1956 *Warner Bros. 1:59* **Director:** *John Ford* **Writer:** *Richard Carr* **Starring:** *John Wayne, Natalie Wood, Vera Miles, Jeffrey Hunter, Ward Bond, John Qualen*

One of the most influential movies in recent American cinematic history, according to such directors as Martin Scorcese and Michael Cimino. This film's master plot—a young girl taken captive by the enemy, the racial Other—underlies the dynamics of such celebrated works as *Taxi Driver* and *The Deer Hunter.* Impelled by Shakespeareansized emotions and an epic visual style, it has three flaws: the dreadful score and non-period music imposed on Ford by the studio; the too-broad bumpkin comedy of Ken Curtis' role; and another broad stereotypical comic subplot involving a fat Comanche woman named Look, who tags along after Jeffrey Hunter. Otherwise the film is operatically powerful and compelling. It is also final proof, if any were needed, of John Wayne's consummate presence as a screen actor. Jean-Luc Godard, the French *auteur*, has spoken memorably of the famous moment in the film when Wayne is reunited with his niece: "How can I hate John Wayne upholding Goldwater and yet love him tenderly when abruptly he takes Natalie Wood into his arms in the last reel of *The Searchers?*" The metaphysics of family, race, and destiny have rarely been portrayed as powerfully in American film. Footnote: Wayne's catch-phrase, "That'll be the day," gave Buddy Holly the title for his first hit song.

WRITTEN ON THE WIND 1956 MCA 1:39 **Director:** *Douglas Sirk* **Writer:** *George Zuckerman* **Starring:** *Rock Hudson, Lauren Bacall, Robert Stack, Dorothy Malone, Robert Keith, Grant Williams*

"A splashy sudser," *Variety* might have called this knowing melodrama. Fifties audiences were taken in by the soap opera theatrics of the plot and players, viewers today laugh at the doings of the rich and impotent, and high-brow cineastes continue to celebrate this film as European-born Sirk's masterpiece. Nineteen fifty-six was Rock Hudson's year for playing the virtuous Texan, only this time he's as solemn as a stone. The stand-out performances are those of Robert Stack, a rich playboy scion of an East Texas oil family who falls in love with Lauren Bacall only to have this marriage go south when he proves unable to father a child, and Dorothy Malone as Stack's sister, a spoiled rich girl who sleeps around because her true love, Rock Hudson, won't give her the time of day. Eventually the good but boring couple, Hudson and Bacall, are married, while the bad brother-sister combo end up with Stack dead and Malone inheriting the family oil empire. Both won Oscars. The film is full of phallic symbolism (all those oil derricks), emotional posturing, and canny cinematic riffs.

OLD YELLER 1957 *Walt Disney* 1:23 **Director**: *Robert Stevenson* **Writers**: *Fred Gipson, William Tubberg* **Starring**: *Dorothy McGuire, Tommy Kirk, Kevin Corcoran, Jeff York, Chuck Connors*

One for the kiddos. Based on Texan Fred Gipson's novel, this story of the "best dog-gone dog in the world," as the catchy title song puts it, takes place on a Texas farm in 1859. The film holds up quite well. For adults, it helps if you see the dog-hero as a version of the savior-gunfighter plot. Old Yeller—rather like Shane—protects the family from the threat of a mad dog while the father is away. There is a great temptation scene where Old Yeller has to resist eating a piece of meat dangling just above his head; for his acting here, the dog should have gotten an Oscar. Old Yeller sacrifices his life for the family he loves and, unlike Shane, has to die. Get out the hankies. Fortunately the film ends on a upbeat note, as there's a pup on hand who's the spittin' image of Old Yeller. Classic children's film.

THE UNFORGIVEN 1960 *United Artists* 2:00 **Director**: *John Huston* **Writer**: *Ben Maddow* **Starring**: *Burt Lancaster, Audrey Hepburn, Audie Murphy, Lillian Gish, Doug McClure, John Saxon, Charles Bickford, Albert Salmi, Joseph Wiseman, June Walker, Kipp Hamilton, Arnold Merritt, Carlos Rivas*

Set in nineteenth-century West Texas and filmed in Durango, Mexico, this uneven, sometimes feverishly hysterical, and sometimes compelling film tells the story of a young woman whose racial identity is called into question. Kiowas come to claim her, and there's a gothic, ghostly old man who purports to know the truth. Highly volatile family dynamics result, with fireworks by Lancaster, broad comedy by Doug McClure and others, and the strangely over-wrought style of famed silent actress, Lillian Gish. Audie Murphy, sporting a moustache, looks great in this film and gives perhaps his strongest screen performance, playing a redneck brother in the family who hates "red niggers." Based on a novel by Alan Lemay, this film should be seen as a kind of companion piece to *The Searchers* (also based on a Lemay novel). Both seek to explore issues of racial identity and family structure in a frontier setting, and both resonate powerful emotions.

HUD 1963 *Paramount* 1:52 *B&W* **Director:** *Martin Ritt* **Writers:** *Irving Ravetch, Harriet Frank* **Starring:** *Paul Newman, Patricia Neal, Melvin Douglas, Brandon de Wilde, John Ashley, Whit Bissell*

This adaptation of Larry McMurtry's first novel offers us Paul Newman at his hungry, sad, sexy, studio-method, existential best. He looks great in this film, and, unlike wide-gauged co-star Brandon de Wilde, knows how to wear jeans—and walk. De Wilde's portrayal of the sensitive-young-male-as-proto-English-major looks weaker upon every viewing. Even worse is the treacly Academy Award-winning performance for Best Supporting Actor by Melvyn Douglas, whose sanctimonious interpretation of rancher Homer Bannon makes him seem like somebody on CNN, always talking about ethics this and principles that. Patricia Neal as the earthy housemaid who's driven off by Hud's unbridled lust also won an Academy Award for Best Supporting Actress. Though we're not supposed to, we wind up cheering for Hud instead of the old rancher. The film's smug embrace of soil over oil never went over, and contemporary audience reaction caught director Ritt by surprise: "It shocked me the first time I got a letter and it said that the old man is a pain in the ass and that Hud is right!" Visual power is generated by James Wong Howe's Oscar-winning rendition of Texas landscapes. Shot in art-house black and white, the film, in such scenes as the slaughter of the herd, looks like World War II footage.

BONNIE AND CLYDE 1967 *Warner Bros.* 1:45 **Director:** *Arthur Penn* **Writers:** *David Newman, Robert Benton* **Starring:** *Warren Beatty, Faye Dunaway, Michael J. Pollard, Gene Hackman, Estelle Parsons*

It was all style then, and it's all style now, this artsy look at the live-hard, die-young lives of Texas' most famous outlaw team. Warren Beatty's Clyde is infectiously watchable, with lots of cocky posturing and some nifty "business," such as his love affair with a cigarette. Faye Dunaway's raffish portrayal of Bonnie seems, as the years pass, more and more like a takeoff, before the fact, of that big, horsy, blond model Jerry Hall's rise to fame. Everything in this film is for fun, even the close-up red splatters of exploding faces. The violence is supposed to make us aware that, hey, these young kids are dangerous, but what we really hope is that Bonnie and Clyde will be just like Burt Reynolds' Smokey of the next decade, always escaping from the Rangers and high sheriffs. Wonderful Depression-era compositions: Okies boiling coffee in tin cans, farms foreclosed on, and Bonnie and Clyde, dressed to kill, cavorting in Texas fields. In real life, Clyde once wrote a charming thank-you letter to the Ford Motor Company for building such a fine automobile that allowed him to pull all those bank jobs, and this film captures that exuberance and panache very nicely indeed.

> THE WILD BUNCH 1969 *Warner Bros.* 2:07 **Director**: *Sam Peckinpah* **Writers**: *Sam Peckinpah, Walon Green, Roy N. Sickner, Lee Marvin (uncredited)* **Starring**: *William Holden, Ernest Borgnine, Robert Ryan, Edmond O'Brien, Warren Oates, Ben Johnson, Jaime Sanchez, Strother Martin, L. Q. Jones, Albert Dekker, Bo Hopkins, Emilio Fernandez, Dub Taylor*

The closest the western has come to creating tragic emotions, this ultraviolent film is Peckinpah's masterpiece. The film begins and ends with a massacre. The opening sequence, a slaughter of the innocents in a little South Texas border town, precipitates the outlaw gang's flight into "Mexico linda." The time is revolutionary 1913. Pursued by a despicable set of bounty hunters, the gang finds succor in the village of one of their members, Angel, the purest of the bunch. The scene of departure from Angel's village is one of the most beautiful sequences in American film. As Peckinpah later said of the outlaw gang, "If you can ride with them there and feel it, you can die with them and feel it." Leader Pike Bishop (William Holden in his greatest role) knows that the old days are "closing fast." He wants to make one last score and "back off." He struggles to hold the gang together to complete the last job. At Agua Verde, a town held in the grip of a vicious alliance between General Mapache and some German advisors, Pike and his men contract to steal some weapons from the U.S. Army. In the process he and his men sacrifice Angel (Jaime Sanchez) to the tyrant Mapache. The final Gotterdammerung, when a weary, battered Pike leads his men to rescue Angel, is incredibly powerful. In frame after frame Peckinpah brings out the pathos of the end of an era. It is also a film about honor, one of the old standby themes of the western, but never done with more complexity or beauty than in this film. Editing, composition, music, acting, directing, all are superb. Paul Seydor's documentary about the making of the film, *The Wild Bunch: An Album in Montage*, which was nominated for an Academy Award in 1997, is a must-see also (available in new laserdisc edition accompanying the film).

THE LAST PICTURE SHOW   1971   *RCA/Columbia*   1:58
B&W   **Director**: *Peter Bogdanovich*   **Writers**: *Peter Bogdanovich, Larry McMurtry*   **Starring**: *Timothy Bottoms, Jeff Bridges, Ben Johnson, Cloris Leachman, Ellen Burstyn, Cybill Shepherd, Eileen Brennan, Clu Gulager, Sam Bottoms, Randy Quaid*

A black-and-white tone poem about teenage lust and love in a dusty, desiccated, flyblown Texas town. Among many memorable moments: Sensitive high-school boy (Bottoms) makes love to sad, lonely wife (Leachman) of jock-scratching football coach; beautiful high-school girl (Shepherd) strips on a diving board to prove she's cool enough for a fast, sexually precocious Wichita Falls set; and Ben Johnson as Sam the Lion, the craggy moral center of the film, every time he's on screen. This film scored a flock of Academy Awards, including Best Picture and Best Supporting Roles (Leachman and Johnson). To realize how good it is, see Bogdanovich's sequel, *Texasville* (1990), based on McMurtry's novel by the same title. Except for Jeff Bridges' rather endearing performance as a Duane grown grayish and paunchy, this film about middle-aged love and forgiveness is as punchless as Texas' sesquicentennial celebration.

THE GETAWAY 1972 *Warner Bros.* 2:02 **Director**: *Sam Peckinpah* **Writer**: *Walter Hill* **Starring**: *Steve McQueen, Ali MacGraw, Ben Johnson, Sally Strothers, Al Lettieri, Slim Pickins*

In the 1980s Hollywood discovered down-and-dirty noir novelist Jim Thompson and made *After Dark, My Sweet* and *The Grifters* from his novels, but Peckinpah was there a decade before. His *The Getaway* is a stylish robber-chase film that makes good use of location shooting in San Marcos, San Antonio, and El Paso. Steve McQueen as an ex-con named Doc is great, Ali McGraw as his girlfriend isn't, and Slim Pickens shows up at the end as a drawling Texas angel who presides over the outlaw pair's happy-ending escape into Mexico. Aging character actor Dub Taylor puts in a brilliant appearance as a "juicer" desk clerk at a seedy El Paso hotel. Ben Johnson is his usual reliable self in his role as a crooked law enforcement agent. A highly watchable film, with Peckinpah's signature style of kinetic camera work and dreamlike violence. Don't mistake this one for the more recent I-Can't-Believe-It's-Not-Butter version starring Alec Baldwin and Kim Basinger.

THE SUGARLAND EXPRESS 1974 *MCA* 1:49 **Director**: *Steven Spielberg* **Writers**: *Hal Barwood, Matthew Robbins* **Starring**: *Goldie Hawn, Ben Johnson, Michael Sacks, William Atherton, Gregory Walcott, Louise Latham*

There's a gritty, realistic feel to this chase film, directed by Stephen Spielberg back before he became bigger than DeMille. Drawn from a true story, the movie tells of a young mother who in 1969 helped her husband escape from prison. Their goal: to rescue baby Langston, their two-year-old, who has been placed in a foster home by state authorities. Hawn's Lou Jean is a honey-voiced live wire, an appealing and resourceful survivor; her husband, played by Atherton, has that doomed look about him. The interaction between the couple and the young cop whose car they confiscate is affecting.

The movie's tone keeps the pace light, as though these are just kids on a lark, and by the time they reach Sugarland, where the baby lives, they are celebrities cheered by throngs of admiring small-town citizens. The carnival atmosphere is counterpointed beautifully by Ben Johnson's law-enforcement officer, a sad-faced man who has to make the decision to employ the expertise of two deadly sharp-shooters to end the chase once and for all. This video is not so easy to locate in stores: I found it in the "Best Moms in Movies" section.

DAYS OF HEAVEN 1978 *Paramount 1:32* **Director:** *Terrence Malick* **Writer:** *Terrence Mallick* **Starring:** *Richard Gere, Brooke Adams, Sam Shepard, Linda Manz, Robert Wilkie, Stuart Margolin, Doug Kershaw, King Cole, Jackie Shultis*

The highly regarded *Badlands* was the first film by Malick, a native Texan from Waco, but this one, set in West Texas though filmed in Alberta, Canada, feels a bit too artsy-fartsy to be entirely satisfying. Lots of atmospheric longeurs, moody passages, and some lovely photography in what at times seems almost like a silent movie. The story line follows three immigrants from Chicago who come to Texas seeking a better, healthier life. One of the best things about the film is the tough-guy narration of a young girl; her slangy, ironic tone braces up the long takes between dialogue. There's a send-up of the house in *Giant*, Sam Shepard plays a brooding West Texan, and Richard Gere is about as convincing a penniless immigrant as he would be a derelict on Skid Row. *The New York Times* review was particularly critical of the studied, cinema-as-art direction. Still, it has its fans.

NORTH DALLAS FORTY 1979 *Paramount 1:59* **Director:** *Ted Kotcheff* **Writers:** *Frank Yablans, Ted Kotcheff, and Peter Gent* **Starring:** *Nick Nolte, Mac Davis, Charles Durning, Dayle Haddon, Bo Svenson, Steve Forrest, G. D. Spradlin, Dabney Coleman, Guich Koock*

A fine adaptation of Peter Gent's ahead-of-its-time *roman à clef* novel about the Dallas Cowboys during the Don Meredith-Tom Landry era, this film, wrongly classified under "comedy" in most video stores, examines the darker side of professional football. Like the novel, the film is something of an exposé of the win-at-any-cost mentality of coaches and owners. Players are blue-collar workers in an industrial factory designed to produce league titles. B.A., the Landry-like coach, is a play-it-by-the-computer tyrant who hypocritically over-looks peccadilloes in his stars but ruthlessly discards lesser players. Team members suffer a great deal of physical pain from the violence of the game, and most of them rely on recreational drugs as well as those routinely prescribed by team physicians to get them in shape on game day. Phil Elliot (expertly played by Nolte), a talented but rebellious wide receiver, calls the callous policy "better football through better chemistry." In the end, Elliott proves expendable and is cut from the team. He has something to fall back on, a small ranch where he hopes to live with his girlfriend and raise horses. One of the best football movies ever made.

URBAN COWBOY 1980 *Paramount* 2:15 **Director:** *James Bridges* **Writers:** *James Bridges, Aaron Latham* **Starring:** *John Travolta, Debra Winger, Scott Glenn, Madolyn Smith, Barry Corbin*

Okay, so Gilley's is history, reduced to ashes, and the urban-cowboy phenomenon seems as corny and ancient as "Hootenanny Hoot." Sure, this grits-and-gravy version of Saturday Night Virus has dated and dated badly, and most of the western gear that viewers bought when the movie came out has been recycled in garage sales ever since. There is still one reason to watch this film: Debra Winger as the sexy, soulful Sissy, a working-class Texas girl who drives a tow truck for her daddy and slow dances at Gilley's every night. Sociological ambiance in this film is sometimes perfect, as in a shot of a sink full of unwashed dishes in Bud and Sissy's mobile home. They're young, stupid, and in love. The plot is stupid, too, with a mean-hombre villain imported from the Huntsville penitentiary who dresses like Jack Palance in *Shane* and eats the worm from a tequila bottle. The whole thing feels like a mall western, with most scenes taking place inside the tacky, cavernous confines of an overrated honky-tonk. There is not one good or authentic country and western song in the entire movie. But there's still Debra Winger riding that mechanical bull like it was meant to be rode, and that's enough.

HARD COUNTRY 1981 *Universal 1:44* **Director**: *David Greene* **Writer**: *Michael Kane* **Starring**: *Jan-Michael Vincent, Kim Basinger, Michael Parks, Tanya Tucker*

An addition to the urban-cowboy genre, this film, based on a song by cosmic cowboy Michael Martin Murphey, could have been much, much better if its makers had stuck to the feminist premises underlying the story. Kim Basinger plays a cowgirl named Jody who dreams of something better than life in Midland with Kyle (Jan-Michel Vincent), a shitkicker who works at a chain-link fence factory named Prairie Fence Company. At night they dance at the Stallion, a knock-off of Gilley's, and have spats about stupid macho activities like chug-a-lugging pitchers of beer, etc., ad nauseum. Enter big-time singing star Tanya Tucker, the hometown girl who has made it big on the West Coast. Her manager, a Gucci-wearing swell from L.A., comes in for some serious harassment from Kyle and his loutish cowboy friends. Fed up with the rampant machismo of Midland males, Jody sets out for L.A. to seek her own fame and fortune. The only problem is, she lets her dunderhead boyfriend go with her. This film sometimes rides western motifs a little hard and struggles to find a rhythm, but there are some fine moments along the way.

THE BORDER 1982 *MCA 1:47* **Director**: *Tony Richardson* **Writers**: *Deric Washburn, Walon Green, David Freeman* **Starring**: *Jack Nicholson, Valerie Perrine, Harvey Keitel, Warren Oates, Elpidia Carrillo*

A modern western with Nicholson turning in a stellar performance as a southern California border patrol officer named Charley assigned to duty in El Paso. The drama of his efforts to resist corruption is the center of this film. His tempters include Harvey Keitel, an engaging good 'ol boy on the take, and Valerie Perrine, Charley's sexy, gum-chewing, K-mart-shopping wife, who longs to be a Dallas Cowboys cheerleader and spends every penny he makes on trashy waterbeds and tacky sofas. Reluctantly, Charley accepts the skewed ethics of an everybody-does-it system that preys on the dreams of illegal aliens seeking to come to America, but eventually his redemption comes in the form of another woman, a lovely madonna from Mexico whose baby is stolen by an adoption ring. Though the plot device of the world-weary law officer being softened by a mother and baby is as old as William S. Hart's westerns, there is enough fast-paced action and hard-bitten location shooting along the Texas-Mexico border to disguise the number being done on our emotions. But most of all, there is Nicholson's stubborn, convincing refusal to give up his fundamental decency.

TERMS OF ENDEARMENT   1983   *Paramount*   2:12
Director: *James L. Brooks*   **Writers**: *Larry McMurtry, James L. Brooks*   **Starring**: *Shirley MacLaine, Debra Winger, Jack Nicholson, Jeff Daniels, John Lithgow, Danny DeVito*

Shot in Houston, this film turns the Bayou City into a coastal suburbia, but never mind; the real interest lies in the dynamics of a terrific till-death-do-us-part mother-daughter relationship between MacLaine and Winger, with Jack Nicholson's randy retired-astronaut character thrown in to liven up the neighborhood. Much thinner in Texas ambience than the Larry McMurtry novel on which it was based, *Terms* goes for the heart, creating an authentic tear-jerker that audiences love, whether they've ever heard of Texas or not. Harrowing hospital scenes in the cancer ward would wring tears from a serial killer. A far superior movie to that other mother-daughter favorite, the lampoonish *Steel Magnolias*. Debra Winger gives a wonderful performance, and not far behind is Jeff Daniels' grubby turn as a lying, unfaithful graduate student-English professor.

TENDER MERCIES   1983   *HBO*   1:20   **Director**: *Bruce Beresford*   **Writer**: *Horton Foote*   **Starring**: *Robert Duvall, Tess Harper, Allan Hubbard, Betty Buckley, Ellen Barkin, Wilford Brimley*

The best of Horton Foote's numerous essays in Texas filmmaking, including the overrated *Trip to Bountiful* or the underrated *1918*. This quiet study of a country and western singer on the skids has an authentic and unforced feel to it that you need when you're telling the truth about lives that are as plain as hillbilly ballads. Australian Beresford, director of *Breaker Morant*, brings a sure eye to the characters and the landscape near Waxahachie, Texas. Duvall, who won the Academy Award for Best Actor for this role, is letter perfect as Mac Sledge, both in his Depression-shaped stoic acceptance of life's hard knocks and his twangy accent, the best rendition of East Texas idiom ever recorded in a feature film. Duvall is a flat-out good country singer as well, and does a far better job of impersonating a Texas tunester than real stars such as Dolly Parton, Willie Nelson, and Kris Kristoffersen have been able to in their Texas movies. Tess Harper is also convincing in a stand-by-your-man role typical of the culture being dramatized.

THE BALLAD OF GREGORIO CORTEZ 1983 *Embassy Pictures* 1:39 **Director:** *Robert M. Young* **Writer:** *Victor Villasenor* **Starring:** *Edward James Olmos, Tom Bower, Bruce McGill, James Gammon, Alan Vint, Timothy Scott, Pepe Serna, Brion James, Barry Corbin, Rosana DeSota, Michael McGuire, William Sanderson*

Independent film, a bit amateurish at times, but valuable as a counter-narrative to all those rah-rah Texas Ranger movies. Based on Américo Paredes' *With His Pistol in His Hand: A Border Ballad and Its Hero*, the film tells the story of Mexican-American folk hero, Gregorio Cortez, who in 1901, after shooting a deputy as the result of a misunderstanding over a horse, fled from near Kenedy, Texas, southeast of San Antonio. The chase lasted eleven days, covered 450 miles, and involved a posse of 600 men led by Texas Rangers. Even so, Cortez made his way to the border where he was betrayed by one of his own people and brought back for trial. He served twelve years of a fifty-year sentence before receiving a gubernatorial pardon. Gregorio Cortez became the hero of *corridos*, or border ballads, songs which celebrated his intelligence and courage while mocking the stupidity and cruelty of the hated *rinches* or Rangers. Edward James Olmos lends a convincing dignity to Cortez, though the film never generates imaginative power to match its good intentions. This film enjoyed considerable popularity outside the U.S. I thought at the time that it might lead to more revisionist Mexican-American films about Texas history, but so far filmmakers have not responded.

BLOOD SIMPLE 1984 *MCA 1:36* **Director**: *Joel Coen* **Writers**: *Joel Coen, Ethan Coen* **Starring**: *John Getz, Frances McDormand, Dan Hedaya, Samm-Art Williams, M. Emmet Walsh*

Honky-tonk film noir shot in Austin on a modest budget by Joel and Ethan Coen, the boy wonders who went on to make such talked-about movies as *Raising Arizona, Miller's Crossing*, and *Fargo*. A lean, twisted, devious story of motel love, revenge, double cross, a buried-alive body, and knife-through-the-hand pain. Three terrific characters: a leisure-suited, VW-driving sleazeball of a private detective played by veteran backgrounder M. Emmet Walsh in the role of his life; a snarling, angry, betrayed husband played by Dan Hedaya; and a smart, resourceful, and appealing young woman played by Frances McDormand, the only survivor. She looks absolutely real, the kind of vulnerable beauty you might run into in an all-night laundromat, not one of your big-time Hollywood fake-looking beauties. Great narrative voice by Walsh sets the mood of ultimate bleakness in a trashy, neon Texas.

FLASHPOINT 1984 *Tri-Star 1:33* **Director**: *William Tannen* **Writers**: *Dennis Shryack, Michael Butter* **Starring**: *Kris Kristofferson, Treat Williams, Rip Torn, Tess Harper, Jean Smart, Kurtwood Smith, Roberts Blossom*

Two hardworking border patrol agents (Kristofferson and Williams) in southwest Texas keep finding things in the desert that get them into trouble. They unearth a drug-smuggling operation, two friendly young women asleep in a car, and, most importantly, a buried jeep that contains a sniper's rifle and $800,000.

Kristofferson's worldly character is in favor of splitting the money, but Williams, more idealistic, wants to find out where it came from first. This leads them to investigate clues that the viewer picks up on before they do, and soon they realize that what they have discovered is a rifle used in the Kennedy assassination. They never do find out the identity of the shooter, however. Washington-based bureaucrats in suits are the biggest enemies of all, and the film moves towards a satisfactorily bloody conclusion with one partner dead and one alive on his way to Mexico with the money. Excellent photography and very good performance by Kristofferson. One funny moment occurs when the two agents drive to "San Antonio" and enter what is obviously Tucson standing in for San Antonio: desert-town in a valley with surrounding mountains.

PLACES IN THE HEART 1984 *Tri-Star* 1:50 **Director:** *Robert Benton* **Writer:** *Robert Benton* **Starring:** *Sally Field, Lindsay Crouse, Ed Harris, Amy Madigan, John Malcovich, Danny Glover, Bert Ramses*

Set in a closely observed countryside, Waxahachie and environs, circa 1935, this mortgage melodrama is a family tale with affecting characters and troubles galore. When the husband of Edna Spaulding (Field) dies in an accident, the widow is left with two small children to raise, a farm that is about to be foreclosed on, and a small amount of savings in the bank. Field is her usual plucky self and with the help of a kindly black man (Glover) learns how to plant and harvest cotton. In one scene she seems to be almost dwarfed by huge cotton plants, but any attempt to make a cotton field dramatic is bound to fail. During the cycle of the year a tornado swoops down on the farm, and the KKK poses a menace. Both nature and man's cruelty are overcome. The scenery is beautifully captured in a style that seems to replicate some of the documentary work of the Depression-era photographers.

FANDANGO 1985 *Warner Bros.* 1:31 **Director:** *Kevin Reynolds* **Writer:** *Kevin Reynolds* **Starring:** *Kevin Costner, Sam*

Robards, Judd Nelson, Charles Bush, Brian Cesak, Marvin J.
McIntyre, Suzy Amis

In a place as big as Texas, there has to be a road movie, and this is it.
In May 1971, five University of Texas frat rats leave the wreckage of
their last bash, pile in a car, and head west, their mission to dig up a
bottle of Dom Perignon they buried in the desert. Adventures and
youthful philosophizing ensue. Vietnam, careers, marriage, and
flight from all three are much on their minds. Near Marfa, they pay
homage to the collapsed pile of Bick Benedict's mansion on the
Worth Evans Ranch, where *Giant* was filmed. The movie mixes
moments like this with adolescent pranks, making for an uneven but
energetic film of special interest because of the stars-to-be cast.
Kevin Costner, engaging and likable, is the leader of the pack; Judd
Nelson is so wimpy and unlikable, you wonder why they took him
along. This was the first pairing of the two Kevins (Reynolds and
Costner) whose friendship would later turn sour in wake of
Waterworld, or *Fishtar* as industry wags still love to call that cinematic
disaster.

TALK RADIO 1988 MCA 1:50 **Director**: *Oliver Stone*
Writers: *Eric Bogosian, Oliver Stone* **Starring**: *Eric Bogosian, Ellen
Greene, Leslie Hope, Alec Baldwin, John C. McGinley, John Pankow*

Drawing on a real case in Denver in which talk show host Alan Berg
was murdered, Oliver Stone, following the lead of scriptwriter and
star Eric Bogosian, switches the setting to Dallas, with chilling
atmospherics the result. By means of fluid, searching camera move-
ments and angles, Stone turns the closed-in feeling of a radio broadcast booth into a dynamic site where voices crackle and collide.
Bogosian's talk show host is an abrasive liberal, and all the callers are
either lost, crazed, or paranoid—doubtless fitting Stone's post-assas-
sination view of Dallas as a citadel of conspiracies and political
extremism. The hero is immensely unlikeable, part of the point, and
the disembodied voices that float in the Dallas night are truly scary.
Sometimes the details don't seem right, as when a poorly educated

young woman with a pronounced lower-class accent, calls in from Highland Park. One night the host goes too far and invites one of his more spaced-out callers to visit the studio. The madness that ensues is quite memorable. One of Stone's best films because, narratively, he's not in it and therefore not hammering away in his usual message-heavy manner.

SLACKER 1991 *Orion* 1:37 **Director**: *Richard Linklater* **Writer**: *Richard Linklater* **Starring**: *A large cast of nonprofessional actors*

Slice-of-life cult film about aimless youths and lifers hanging out in Austin, Texas. Said to be based upon notebooks that Linklater kept over a period of several years. The streets of Austin are filled with eccentrics like the stoned soothsayer who announces "We've been on Mars since 1962," a young woman who swears she has Madonna's pap smear, a young man who is an obsessive self-proclaimed expert on the Kennedy assassination, and a University of Texas philosophy professor who gives a manic account of Charles Whitman on the Tower. The film is filled with closely observed data. A passing remark about a young woman who is traveling through Texas photographing Dairy Queens might sound like a throw-away bit of local color, but in fact the young woman in question, a former student of mine named Iris Davis who now lives in Oakland, California, has been making such photographs for years. Walk around the "Drag" (Guadalupe Street at the University of Texas) today, and you may well see someone who appeared in this film. As the years pass, *Slacker* will doubtless acquire documentary authority as a reflection of a particular cultural moment.

FLESH AND BONE 1993 *Paramount* 2:07 **Director**: *Steve Kloves* **Writer**: *Steve Kloves* **Starring**: *Dennis Quaid, Meg Ryan, James Caan, Gwyneth Paltrow, Jerry Swindall, Scott Wilson, Christopher Rydell*

An off-beat, novelistic sort of film about dark doings in West Texas. Dennis Quaid, an underrated actor, is very good as a young man haunted by his early life with a crazed, violent father, played by crazy-eyed James Caan. Quaid travels through the isolated towns of West Texas servicing condom machines, juke boxes, and novelty games with a number of painted chickens named "Brainy Betty." During his perambulations he comes into contact with a sexy young woman (Ryan) whose fate, unbeknownst to either, is entertwined with his own. His father reenters his life, accompanied by a tough-talking young woman con artist (played superbly by Paltrow) whose specialty is robbing corpses lying in state in funeral homes and churches. There is a violent showdown and a highly original denoument, as Quaid's Arliss tells Ryan's Kay: "There's some thing are better left unsaid. Just no good to talk about 'em. No good at all." This refreshing reversal of nineties confessionalism and victimization-pandering is heartening. Excellently photographed Texas landscapes ranging from Austin to Marfa.

A PERFECT WORLD 1994 *Malpaiso* 2:18 **Director**: *Clint Eastwood* **Writer**: *John Lee Hancock* **Starring**: *Kevin Costner, Clint Eastwood, Laura Dern, T. J. Lowther, Keith Szarabajka*

A leisurely paced prison-breakout chase film that makes excellent pictorial use of central Texas rural landscapes. In a completely charming performance Kevin Costner plays Butch Haynes, a philosophical-minded con who bonds with a an equally charming little boy whom he takes hostage. They are "time-traveling through Texas," Costner says at one point. The time, specifically, is 1963, a month or so before the assassination in Dallas. Along the way Costner kills a vicious con and almost kills a black family, in a very unsettling scene. There is also a fine interlude in a little Texas town where everybody tries to out-friendly everybody else, a nice send-up of the state's vaunted friendliness. Despite some plot silliness, including Laura Dern's turn as a "criminologist" commissioned by the governor to assist Texas Ranger Eastwood in the hunt for Costner, the film remains consistently watchable, thanks to the sweet, questioning nature of the finely drawn Costner character.

LONE STAR 1996 *Castle Rock* 2:17 **Director:** *John Sayles*
Writer: *John Sayles* **Starring:** *Chris Cooper, Elizabeth Peña, Kris
Kristofferson, Miriam Colon, Joe Morton, Matthew McConaughey,
Clifton James, Ron Canada, Frances McDormand*

An ambitious auteur effort by John Sayles to "do" modern multicu-
lural Texas. Understanding "the complexity of our situation down
here" in Frontere, an imaginary border town, is not easy, as plot lines
involving Tejanos, Anglos, African Americans, and even Black
Seminoles are entertwined. The main story line follows the efforts of
Sheriff Sam Deeds (Cooper) to uncover who murdered a former
racist sheriff (played brilliantly by Kris Kristofferson in flashback
scenes). His chief suspect is his own legendary father, Buddy Deeds,
against whose shadow Sam has a hard time measuring up. History
has a way of blindsiding those who probe its secrets, and Sam finds
out not that his father was a murderer, but that he fathered another
child, a half-sister, a Chicana woman (Peña) with whom Sam has
been in love his whole life. In an abandoned, dilapidated drive-in
movie, the site of Texas mythology, the woman, a history teacher,
says, "Forget the Alamo," and the two of them resolve to live their
lives together, forging a sharply ironic commentary on the old racial
enmities and divisions wrought by real and imaginary borders.

Acknowledgments

Grateful acknowledgment is made to the following for permission to reprint portions of material which appeared, in an earlier form, on their pages under the titles indicated:

"Riding the Range in Philadelphia," *Pennsylvania Gazette,* 82 (November 1983) 32-35.

"A Proper Ceremony," *Texas Humanist* (May-June 1984) 32-33.

"Introduction," *WPA Guide to Texas.* Austin: Texas Monthly Press, 1986. Pp. 1-7.

"Doing England," *Southwest Review,* 74, No. 3 (Summer 1989) 340-356.

"American Narratives," *Texas Observer* (May 10, 1995) 22-24.

"Giant Country," *New Texas '95: Poetry and Fiction.* Kathryn S. McGuire and James Ward Lee, eds. Denton: Center for Texas Studies, 1995. Pp. 101-112.

"George Sessions Perry: Cotton and Classicism," *Texas Studies Annual* I (1994) 88-94.

"Katherine the Great," *Texas Monthly,* 24 (May 1997) 76, 81-82, 84-86.

"Pen Pals," *Texas Monthly,* 24 (March 1996) 100-103; 120-132.

"J. Frank Dobie: A Reappraisal," *Southwestern Historical Quarterly,* vol. 92 (July 1988) 1-15. Reprinted with permission from the Texas State Historical Association.

"Last of the Southern Belle-Lettrists." *Texas Observer* (September 12, 1997) 30-33.

"John Graves, *Goodbye to a River*, and Texas Letters," *Texas Studies Annual*, 2 (1995) 205-213.

"The Two John Graves: Reconsidering a Writer and a Texan," *Texas Observer* (November 8, 1996) 21-25.

"Bill Brammer's *The Gay Place*," *Southwestern American Literature*, vol.20 (Fall 1994) 7-27.

"*Lonesome Dove*: Butch and Sundance Go on a Cattle Drive," *Southwestern American Literature*, vol.12 (Fall 1986) 7-12.

"Take My Sequel from the Wall: McMurtry Revisits McMurtry," *Austin Chronicle* (August 13, 1993) 20, 22.

"Dead Man's Curve: Gus and Call Pay a Revisionist Visit to Texas History," *Texas Observer* (September 29, 1995) 17-18.

"Palefaces vs. Redskins: A Literary Skirmish," *Texas Humanist*, vol. 6 (November/December 1984) 10-11.

"Land without Myth; or, Texas and the Mystique of Nostalgia," *Open Spaces, City Places: Contemporary Writers on the Changing Southwest.* Judy Nolte Temple, ed. Tucson: The University of Arizona Press, 1994. 87-94

"Anything for Larry," *Texas Observer*, (September 15, 1995) 12-13.

"What Have They Done to My Town?" *Southwest Airlines Spirit* (August 1985) 34, 36.

"Puerto Vallarta Squeezed," *Dallas Morning News* (November 24, 1995) C1, 4.

"What the World Wants to Know," *El Paso Herald-Post* (November 13, 1996) D5.

"Moo-vie Cows: The Trail to Hollywood," *Southwestern American Literature*, vol.18 (Fall 1992), 1-11.

"The Big Show," *Southwest Media Review*, vol.3 (Spring 1985), 27-29. Reprinted by permission of Southwest Alternate Media Project, Celia Lightfoot, Executive Director.

"Remembering the Alamo: The Story of the Texas Revolution in Popular Culture," *Southwestern Historical Quarterly*, vol.89 (July 1985)

35-67. Reprinted with permission from the Texas State Historical Association.

"Nowhere Else but Southfork," *Texas Humanist,* vol. 6 (November/December 1983) 10-12.

"The Displacement of East Texas in Movies about Texas," *East Texas Historical Journal,* vol. 25 (1987) 18-22.

"Time-Traveling Through Texas," *Texas Books in Review,* vol. 14 (Fall 1995) 5.

"When Myths Collide," *Texas Monthly,* vol.14 (January 1986) 42, 98.

"Texas Videos," *Texas Monthly,* vol 19 (July 1991) 94-101.